CN

PHILIP JODIDIO

ARCHITECTURE IN CHINA

TASCHEN

HONG KONG KÖLN LONDON LOS ANGELES MADRID PARIS TOKYO

#18

#2/4/5/6/11/14/
15/18/18
#12
#3/13
#1/1/9/12/19
#8
#2
#5/17
#10
#7/16/16

INTRODUCTION

RED STAR RISING

It is difficult to read a paper or see a televised news program today without hearing about China, the great economic success story of the past ten years. There can be no doubt that the world's largest country in terms of population (1 313 973 000 people according to a July 2006 CIA estimate) has awakened from its long somnolence. While more developed countries go through cyclical periods of expansion and reduction of their economic activity, China has felt the need to build anew on a historically unprecedented scale. New spending on construction and factory equipment in the five months ending May 30, 2006, was up 30% over the same period in 2005, and such investments are likely to exceed $1.3 trillion in 2006, or almost half the country's gross domestic product (GDP). Development on this scale obviously does not often pay attention to quality, though the exceptions to that sweeping statement are frequent enough and match or exceed what is being done in any Western country. The same intelligence and hard work that is evidenced in other areas of economic activity is also becoming more obvious in architecture, in large part because of recent changes in Chinese laws governing the profession itself. It is this change, the unchaining of the architect, as it were, that is the most important event in the midst of an unprecedented outpouring of construction.

ARCHITECTURE IS EVERYTHING

There has been no shortage of analysis of the consequences of China's ferocious development, ranging from catastrophic pollution warnings to dire predictions about the price of raw materials. Architecture and the lack of coherent planning and quality control have also been amply commented upon. One of the most interesting studies of the subject was compiled by Rem Koolhaas and the Harvard Design School Project on the City (*Great Leap Forward*, Taschen, 2001). Taking as their basis the extraordinary development of the Pearl River Delta, near the China-Hong Kong border, where the Special Economic Zone (SEZ) of Shenzhen was created in 1980, Koolhaas and his team go so far as to say that the very definition of architecture (which they call "Architecture©" in this context) must be changed. In a piece entitled "Architecture Shenzhen," Nancy Lin wrote, "Architecture© has become a channel for investment. Building construction has become such a profit-making tool that a building's primary function is no longer to serve human needs. The traditional concepts associated with architecture such as aesthetics, comfortable environment, advanced building technology, and human occupancy have been suppressed to emphasize quantitative measures like construction volume, capital investment, construction time, cost and profit return." Lin goes on to conclude that "in these various states, architecture is no longer only present in physical form: architecture is everything, appearing as a topic of daily conversation, as well as an abstraction of numbers, published like stock quotes in newspapers." The cynical reader might observe that such niceties as aesthetics and a comfortable environment have long since been sacrificed by Western architects as well, but Koolhaas et al. are keen on making another point: the "Chinese Architect© is the most important, influential and powerful architect on earth. The average lifetime construction volume of the Chinese Architect© in housing alone is approximately three dozen thirty-story high rise buildings... There is one-tenth the number of architects in China than in the United States, designing five times the project volume in one-fifth the time, earning one-tenth the design fee. This implies an efficiency of 2500 times that of an American architect." Simply put, for Koolhaas, in China, architecture is everything, but architects are not what they used to be either.

GREAT LEAP FORWARD

When *Great Leap Forward* was published in 2001, the fabulous building boom in China was entirely in the hands of "design institutes," state-run enterprises with very large staffs and little interest in architectural creativity. Even very well-known foreign architects were obliged to hand their plans over to these institutes with little or no control over what was actually built. At about that time, the law was changed in order to allow individuals to practice as architects. Although the demand for construction is such and the ingrained order so firmly established that this legal change cannot immediately alter the order of things observed by the Harvard team, the past five years have seen another revolution of sorts in Chinese architecture—the emergence of rising stars of architecture, and above all new and interesting buildings that are not the product of Western designers. Though many of the new leaders of this movement are Western-educated, at least in part, they have already laid the groundwork for an indigenous modernity that differentiates itself from pure occidental taste as well as eschewing the temptation to put a "Chinese-style" roof on an ordinary office block. The fact that Beijing has been chosen to host the 2008 Summer Olympic Games has been more than a catalyst for the development of high-quality contemporary architecture in China as well. Though major foreign firms like Rem Koolhaas/OMA or Herzog & de Meuron are participating in the design of buildings that will have a function during the Games, Chinese architect, too, have been mobilized in this massive effort to bring the country up to international levels.

SHINING RED STARS

Though the list of influential Chinese architects is growing by the day, a certain number of key figures can be cited. The first independent Chinese architectural firm created in Beijing, in 1993, even before the modifications in the law, was Atelier Feichang Jianzhu, or FCJZ, headed by Yung Ho Chang. Born in Beijing in 1956 and educated at the University of California at Berkeley, Chang founded the Graduate Center of Architecture at Beijing University and became head of MIT's Department of Architecture in 2005. His unusual situation, at the heart of contemporary architecture in China, but also in the United States, is symbolic of the emergence of Chinese architects on the world scene.

Another significant contributor to the rapid-fire developments in the country is the artist-architect Ai Wei Wei. Born in 1957 in Beijing, the son of the well-known poet Ai Qing, he studied film in Beijing before going to the Parson's School of Design in New York. He returned to Shanghai in 1999 and opened his own office, FAKE Design, there in 1999. Artistic advisor for Herzog & de Meuron on their National Stadium for the 2008 Olympic Games, Ai is also the driving force behind the Jinhua Architecture Park that is bringing together cutting-edge Chinese architects as well as such American designers as Michael Maltzan and Toshiko Mori. Here, as in Beijing, he has collaborated with Herzog & de Meuron. The austerity and pragmatism with which Ai Wei Wei approached a project like his Courtyard 105 (Beijing, 2004–05) speaks volumes about the emergence of Chinese contemporary architecture, daring to use simple materials and even to renovate old industrial buildings in the face of the waves of look-alike towers sweeping the past from the urban centers.

A third major player in the emerging architecture scene is surely Ma Qingyun, who obtained his degree in architecture from the Graduate School of Fine Art at the University of Pennsylvania in 1991. As the coordinator of the Harvard *Great Leap Forward* book, Ma certainly had grounding in the difficulties facing his country's architecture. He created his own office, MADA s.p.a.m., in a 1980s Modernist school building in Shanghai (2003–04). It is significant that rather than trying to mask the past of the Red Star School, Ma made a virtue of reusing an otherwise undistinguished relic of an era when architects were not yet free to comment on society. He says that he is "fascinated by the opportunity to engage in the discourse of urban mutation caused by systematic obsolescence." He might also have spoken of systemic obsolescence given the continuing tendency to see architecture as something to be done quickly and without much attention to quality.

FROM SHENZHEN TO TIBET AND BACK AGAIN

Liu Xiaodu, Meng Yan, and Wang Hui all studied in the late 1990s at Miami University, Oxford, Ohio, before founding URBANUS Architecture & Design in Shenzhen and Beijing together with Pei Zhu. With projects such as their "Proposal for the Dynamic Rehabilitation of Gangsha Village" (Shenzhen, 2005), these young architects are seeking to attack the very real problems of explosive urbanization highlighted by the Harvard group in *Great Leap Forward*. Made sensitive to foreign theories of urban development during their stay in the United States, the architects bring their own culture and intelligence to bear on a particularly Chinese problem. It is doubtful that foreigners, no matter what their experience, could provide such innovative solutions to local difficulties, and the rise of indigenous talents brought about by the laws easing the grip of design institutes on architecture promises many more such positive surprises.

Another architect of consequence cited in this volume, though he has not yet attained the notoriety of the others, is Wang Hui (not of URBANUS). Born in Xi'an in 1969, he attended the Northwest Polytechnic University there before working in the office of FCJZ in Beijing, on projects such as Villa Shizilin published here. Three relatively modest projects by Wang, his Mima Café (Beijing, 2003), the Neno Corridor (Beijing, 2004), and perhaps most all the Apple Elementary School (A Li, Tibet, 2004–05), show a willingness to take on both the weight of tradition in a location like the Summer Palace near Beijing (Mima Café) or one of the most rugged and difficult landscapes on the periphery of the country (Apple Elementary School). A graduate of Chinese institutions with no foreign experience as yet, but with the nerve to shake things up, Wang Hui will surely be one of the major architects of his generation.

Even younger than Wang Hui, Zhu Xiaofeng was born in Shanghai in 1972 and received his B.Arch degree from the Shenzhen University School of Architecture before obtaining his M.Arch diploma from the Harvard Graduate School of Design (1997). He created his own firm, Scenic Architecture, in Shanghai in 2004. Although he has already worked on a number of projects that do not concern renovations, his Green Pine Garden (Qingpu, Shanghai, 2004–05) brings to light a number of the characteristics that seem to be emerging from the younger generation of Chinese architects. Converting existing factory buildings along a highway outside Shanghai into a bar and restaurant, he created a large green area and designed an innovative folding screen made of local pine battens for one building and used typical gray bricks for the other. Though this project does not have the massive aspect of many current works of Chinese architecture, it does make subtle reference to tradition of various sorts, even that of the factory. Nor does it look like anything seen recently in the West. With light screens made of pine contrasting with the solidity of gray brick, Zhu conjures up a distant past while affirming the present. With his solid academic background and foreign experience, Zhu is representative of the new generation that is beginning to leave its mark despite the onward march of the economy.

MASTERS OF THE UNIVERSE

A large number of talented foreign architects have worked in China recently, surely with more freedom and control of their work than they were afforded before 2000. Despite the historic tensions that mark Sino-Japanese relations, architects like Arata Isozaki and Kengo Kuma have completed some very interesting buildings in China. With his Shenzhen Cultural Center (1997–2005), Isozaki certainly breaks out of the cookie-cutter mold derided by Koolhaas in his description of the fabulous productivity of the architects of the SEZ. So, too, Kuma demonstrates his inventive, heterogenous style with the Zhongtai Box (Shanghai, 2003–06). The real stars of the moment here, as in the United States, for example, are the Dutch architects OMA and the Swiss firm Herzog & de Meuron. The former has imagined a tower for the CCTV companies that seeks to become a "new icon" of the capital city, and will be used as the media center for the upcoming Olympic Games. The latter are deeply engaged in the construction of the Main Stadium for the Games, a "bird's nest of interwoven twigs" that are made of structural steel. Here too, the goal is to create an iconic building, a symbol not only of a moment but of the emergence of China on the world scene, in sports, the economy, or, at last, architecture. As Jacques Herzog says, "To realize that project there is amazing, such a structure you couldn't do anywhere else."

PROMETHEUS UNBOUND

One reason that such large-scale projects become feasible is the extraordinary rapidity and capacity of the Chinese construction industry, capable, as Rem Koolhaas suggested in an ironic way, of churning out Architecture©, but also able to deliver huge projects far faster than they could advance in The Netherlands, for example. These buildings, like the even more controversial Beijing Opera by the French architect Paul Andreu, have been the subject of criticism, but they do mark an exceptional level of desire, and, indeed, a capacity to attain world standards, and perhaps to set new standards tomorrow. Significantly, neither Koolhaas nor his Swiss counterparts have been naive enough to try to create a new "Chinese" style of architecture, despite the high-profile nature of their projects. Nor are they building for Rotterdam or Basel. Rooting their projects in their specific circumstances and without ignoring deep local feelings and culture, they are bringing forth "icons" for a new age, one in which China is taking its rightful place on the world stage. Jacques Herzog's words about the current attitude of the Chinese may offer one key to understanding just how and why the dreadful juggernaut of architecture without "aesthetics, comfortable environment, advanced building technology, and human occupancy" can advance even as a remarkably inventive and intelligent new generation of architects comes to the fore. He says, "They are so fresh in their mind, they have the most radical things in their tradition, the most amazing faience and perforated jades and scholar's rocks... They don't have as much of a barrier between good taste and bad taste, between the minimal and expressive."[1] This may be a somewhat rapid overview of one of the greatest and most ancient civilizations on earth, but in the age of Architecture©, it is an informed one. The pace and scope of economic development in contemporary China surely encourages the best and the worst expressions of architecture. What is new and highly encouraging is the emergence of individual architects, freed by legal reforms that have somewhat reduced the stranglehold of the design institutes. Given the scale of the events in China, this means that new buildings of quality will be designed and built there in greater numbers than almost anywhere else on earth. In short, the new architecture of China is a force to be reckoned with.[2]

Philip Jodidio

[1] Jacques Herzog, quoted in the article "The China Syndrome," by Arthur Lubow, *The New York Times*, May 21, 2006.

[2] People's Architecture was founded on October 1, 2005, in Beijing. A non-profit organization headquartered in New York City with a regional office in Beijing, People's Architecture "is a multidisciplinary forum for the exchange of ideas, with the goal of facilitating a better global understanding of China's architectural, cultural and economic development." Wei Wei Shannon, a co-founder of People's Architecture, was kind enough to help with a number of the contacts in China required for this book. See http://www.peoplesarchitecture.org/.

EINLEITUNG

AUFGEHENDER ROTER STERN

Es ist heutzutage kaum möglich, eine Zeitung aufzuschlagen oder ein Nachrichtenprogramm im Fernsehen zu sehen, ohne von China zu lesen oder zu hören – und von seiner großen wirtschaftlichen Erfolgsgeschichte der letzten Dekade. Ohne Zweifel ist das im Hinblick auf die Bevölkerung größte Land der Erde (1 313 973 000 Einwohner laut einer CIA-Schätzung vom Juli 2006) aus seiner langen Schläfrigkeit erwacht. Während die meisten westlichen Länder zyklische Phasen des Auf- und Abschwungs ihrer Wirtschaftstätigkeit durchlaufen, begann China in einem historisch beispiellosen Umfang mit einem Neuanfang. Die Ausgaben für Bauten und Betriebsanlagen lagen in den ersten fünf Monaten 2006 über 30 % über denen im gleichen Zeitraum des Vorjahres. Investitionen dieser Art werden 2006 aller Wahrscheinlichkeit nach die Summe von 984,8 Millionen Euro übersteigen und damit nahezu die Hälfte des Bruttoinlandsproduktes ausmachen. Bei einer Bautätigkeit in diesem Umfang spielt Qualität im Normalfall eine untergeordnete Rolle, wenngleich die Ausnahmen von dieser pauschalen Aussage zahlreich genug sind, um jedem westlichen Land Paroli zu bieten oder ihm sogar überlegen zu sein. Die Klugheit und harte Arbeit, die in anderen Wirtschaftsbereichen anzutreffen sind, werden jetzt auch in der Architektur sichtbar, vor allem aufgrund der kürzlichen Änderung der gesetzlichen Regelungen der Architektentätigkeit. Die regelrechte Befreiung dieses Berufsstandes ist das bedeutendste Ereignis inmitten eines enormen Baubooms.

ARCHITEKTUR IST ALLES

Es herrscht kein Mangel an Vorhersagen über die Folgen von Chinas Wachstum, angefangen bei Warnungen vor katastrophaler Umweltverschmutzung bis hin zur unheilvollen Steigerung der Rohstoffpreise. Auch wurde im Zusammenhang mit Architektur das Fehlen kohärenter Planung und Qualitätskontrolle umfassend kommentiert. Eine der interessantesten Studien zum Thema wurde von Rem Koolhaas und dem Harvard Design School Project on the City vorgelegt (*Great Leap Forward*, Taschen 2001). Koolhaas und sein Team, denen als Grundlage die außerordentliche Entwicklung des Perlflussdeltas nahe der Grenze zwischen China und Hongkong diente, wo 1980 die Sonderwirtschaftszone von Shenzhen eingerichtet wurde, gehen so weit zu sagen, die eigentliche Definition von Architektur (die sie in diesem Zusammenhang als »Architektur©« bezeichnen) müsse geändert werden. In einem Text mit dem Titel »Architecture Shenzhen« schreibt Nancy Lin: »Architektur© wurde zu einer Investition und der Wohnungsbau zu einer solch profitablen Sache, dass die Primärfunktion eines Gebäudes nicht mehr in seinem Nutzen für den Menschen gesehen wird. Die traditionellerweise mit Architektur in Zusammenhang gebrachten Begriffe wie Ästhetik, angenehmes Umfeld, fortschrittliche Bautechnik und Besitzergreifung durch Menschen wurden verdrängt, um das Gewicht auf quantitative Maßeinheiten wie Bauvolumen, Kapitalanlage, Bauzeit, Kosten und Gewinn zu legen.« Lin schließt mit der Feststellung, dass »Architektur in diesen verschiedenen Stadien nicht mehr länger nur in greifbarer Form präsent ist: Architektur ist alles, sie dient als alltägliches Gesprächsthema ebenso wie als Abstraktion von Zahlen, die wie Börsenkurse in der Zeitung publiziert werden«. Ein zynischer Leser könnte anmerken, dass Annehmlichkeiten wie Ästhetik und ein angenehmes Umfeld schon vor Langem auch von westlichen Architekten geopfert wurden, aber Koolhaas und seine Kollegen sind darauf aus, ein anderes Argument anzubringen: »Der chinesische Architekt© ist der wichtigste, einflussreichste und mächtigste Architekt der Welt. Das durchschnittliche Bauvolumen, das ein chinesischer Architekt© im Lauf seines Lebens allein im Wohnungsbau errichtet, umfasst etwa drei Dutzend 30-geschossige Hochhäuser ... Es gibt in China etwa ein Zehntel der Architektenschaft der USA, das in einem Fünftel der Zeit das fünffache Projektvolumen erbaut und dafür ein Zehntel des Honorars kassiert. Verglichen mit einem amerikanischen Kollegen impliziert das eine 2500-fache Effizienz.« Schlicht gesagt bedeutet nach Ansicht von Koolhaas in China die Architektur alles, aber Architekten sind nicht mehr das, was sie früher einmal waren.

GROẞER SPRUNG VORWÄRTS

Als 2001 *Great Leap Forward* erschien, lag Chinas sagenhafter Bauboom zur Gänze in den Händen von »Planungsinstituten«, staatlichen Unternehmen mit sehr großer Belegschaft und sehr wenig Interesse an architektonischer Kreativität. Selbst prominente ausländische Architekten waren verpflichtet, ihre Pläne diesen Instituten auszuhändigen und damit weitgehend die Kontrolle über die tatsächliche Bauausführung aus der Hand zu geben. Etwa zu dieser Zeit wurde die Gesetzgebung geändert, und fortan war es Einzelpersonen möglich, als Architekten tätig zu werden. Obwohl der Bedarf an Neubauten anhält und die eingefahrene Ordnung so fest etabliert ist, dass diese gesetzliche Änderung den von dem Harvard-Team bemerkten Ablauf der Dinge nicht unmittelbar ändert, hat sich in den letzten fünf Jahren in der chinesischen Architektur eine weitere revolutionäre Wandlung vollzogen – es tauchten kommende Stararchitekten auf, und es entstanden neue, interessante Bauten, die nicht das Werk westlicher Planer sind. Obgleich viele der führenden Köpfe der neuen Bewegung zumindest einen Teil ihrer Ausbildung im westlichen Ausland absolvierten, schufen sie die Grundlagen für eine heimische Moderne, die sich einerseits von einem rein fernöstlichen Geschmack abgrenzt und andererseits der Versuchung widersteht, einen gewöhnlichen Büroblock mit einem Pagodendach zu bekrönen. Darüber hinaus erwies sich die Tatsache, dass Peking die Olympischen Sommerspiele 2008 zugesprochen bekam, als treibende Kraft bei der Entstehung qualitätvoller zeitgenössischer Architektur in China. Zwar sind auch bedeutende ausländische Büros wie Rem Koolhaas/OMA und Herzog & de Meuron an der Planung von Bauten im Zusammenhang mit den Spielen beteiligt, doch auch chinesische Architekten sind in die gewaltige Anstrengung involviert, das Land auf internationales Niveau zu bringen.

LEUCHTENDE ROTE STERNE

Obwohl die Liste der maßgeblichen chinesischen Architekten täglich länger wird, kann man doch eine Reihe von Schlüsselfiguren nennen. Das erste unabhängige Architekturbüro Chinas, das 1993 und damit noch vor der Gesetzesänderung in Peking gegründet wurde, war das von Yung Ho Chang geleitete FCJZ. Der 1956 in Peking geborene und an der University of California in Berkeley ausgebildete Chang gründete an der Universität Peking das Graduiertenkolleg für Architektur und wurde 2005 zum Ordinarius des Fachbereichs Architektur am Massachusetts

Institute of Technology (MIT) berufen. Chang, der zugleich im Zentrum der zeitgenössischen Architektur Chinas und der Vereinigten Staaten wirkt, verkörpert das Erscheinen chinesischer Architekten auf der internationalen Szene.

Einen weiteren bedeutenden Beitrag zu den rasanten Entwicklungen im Land leistet der Künstler und Architekt Ai Wei Wei. 1957 als Sohn des bekannten Dichters Ai Qing in Peking geboren, studierte er in seiner Heimatstadt Filmwissenschaft, ehe er sich an der Parson's School of Design in New York einschrieb. 1999 kehrte er nach China zurück und eröffnete in Shanghai sein eigenes Büro namens FAKE Design. Herzog & de Meuron stand er beim Bau des Olympiastadions für 2008 als künstlerischer Berater zur Seite. Er wirkt ebenfalls als treibende Kraft bei dem Projekt des Architekturparks in Jinhua, bei dem führende chinesische Architekten mit ausländischen Kollegen wie den Amerikanern Michael Maltzan und Toshiko Mori zusammenarbeiten. Wie beim Olympiastadion in Peking kooperiert er hier mit Herzog & de Meuron. Die Strenge und Pragmatik, mit denen Ai Wei Wei ein Projekt wie Hof 105 (Peking, 2004–05) in Angriff nimmt, spricht Bände über das Erscheinen der zeitgenössischen chinesischen Architektur, die es riskiert, einfache Materialien zu verwenden und alte Industriebauten zu renovieren und dies angesichts einer Flut von geklonten Hochhäusern, die die Vergangenheit aus den Stadtzentren fegen.

Eine dritte zentrale Figur in der aufkommenden Architekturszene ist sicherlich Ma Qing Yun, der 1991 seinen Abschluss in Architektur an der Graduate School of Fine Arts an der University of Pennsylvania erhielt. Als Koordinator des in Harvard erschienen Buches *Great Leap Foward* verfügt Ma mit Sicherheit über Vorkenntnisse im Hinblick auf die Schwierigkeiten, denen sich die Architektur seines Landes gegenübersah und -sieht. Sein eigenes Büro MADA s.p.a.m. gründete er 2003/04 in Shanghai in einem modernistischen Schulgebäude von 1980. Es ist bezeichnend, dass Ma nicht den Versuch unternahm, die Vergangenheit der Schule »Roter Stern« zu verschleiern, sondern das Beste aus der Umnutzung eines gesichtslosen Relikts einer Ära zu machen, als es Architekten noch nicht freistand, ihren Kommentar zu gesellschaftlichen Fragen abzugeben. Er sagt, er sei »fasziniert von der Möglichkeit, sich an dem Diskurs über den urbanen Wandel zu beteiligen, der durch die systematische Vernachlässigung verursacht wurde.« Auch die anhaltende Tendenz, Architektur als etwas zu betrachten, das schnell und ohne viel Rücksicht auf Qualität zu erledigen ist, könnte er als systematische Vernachlässigung bezeichnen.

VON SHENZHEN NACH TIBET UND WIEDER ZURÜCK

Liu Xiaodu, Meng Yan und Wang Hui studierten alle Ende der 1990er-Jahre an der Miami University in Oxford, Ohio, ehe sie zusammen mit Pei Zhu in Shenzhen und Peking Urbanus Architecture and Design gründeten. Mit Projekten wie ihrem »Vorschlag für eine dynamische Sanierung von Gangsha« (Shenzhen, 2005) versuchen diese jungen Architekten, den äußerst realen Problemen einer explosiven Verstädterung beizukommen, die von der Harvard-Gruppe in *Great Leap Forward* dargestellt wurden. Die während ihres Aufenthalts in den Vereinigten Staaten für fremde Theorien zur Stadtentwicklung empfänglich gewordenen Architekten setzen ihre eigene Kultur und Intelligenz auf ein spezifisch chinesisches Problem um. Es ist fraglich, ob noch so erfahrene Ausländer derartig innovative Lösungen für Schwierigkeiten in Wohnvierteln vorlegen könnten, und der Aufstieg heimischer Talente, möglich geworden durch die Gesetzgebung, die den Zugriff der staatlichen »Planungsinstitute« auf die Architektur lockerte, verspricht noch zahlreiche solch positiver Überraschungen.

Ein weiterer, in diesem Band erwähnter, wichtiger Architekt, der allerdings noch nicht die Bekanntheit der anderen erreicht hat, ist Wang Hui (nicht von Urbanus). 1969 in Xi'an geboren, besuchte er die dortige Nordwestliche Polytechnische Universität, ehe er im Büro von FCJZ in Peking an Projekten wie der hier publizierten Villa Shizilin mitarbeitete. Drei relativ bescheidene Projekte Wangs, sein Mima Café (Peking, 2003), der Neno Korridor (Peking, 2004) und vielleicht am meisten die Apfel-Grundschule (A Li, Tibet, 2004–05) zeugen von seiner Bereitschaft, sich sowohl auf die gewichtige Tradition einzulassen (Mima Café beim Sommerpalast nahe Peking) als auch auf eine der kargsten, zerklüftetsten Landschaften an der Peripherie des Landes (Apfel-Grundschule). Wang Hui, der als Absolvent einer chinesischen Einrichtung bisher über keine Erfahrung im Ausland verfügt, hat den Mut, die Dinge umzukrempeln und wird sich gewiss als einer der bedeutendsten Architekten seiner Generation erweisen.

Noch jünger als Wang Hui wurde Zhu Xiaofeng 1972 in Shanghai geboren und erwarb zuerst den Grad eines Bachelor am Fachbereich der Universität Shenzhen, um 1997 die Prüfung zum Master of Architecture an der Harvard Graduate School of Design abzulegen. 2004 gründete er in Shanghai sein eigenes Büro namens Scenic Architecture. Obgleich er schon an einer Reihe von Projekten beteiligt war, bei denen es nicht um Renovierungen ging, offenbart sein Grüne Kiefer-Garten (Qingpu, Shanghai, 2004–05) einige der für die jüngere Generation chinesischer Architekten typischen Merkmale. Als er ein vorhandenes Fabrikgebäude an einer Fernstraße außerhalb von Shanghai zu einer Kombination von Bar und Restaurant umbaute, schuf er eine große Grünfläche und entwarf für das eine Gebäude eine innovative Faltwand aus heimischen Kiefernleisten, für das andere verwendete er den ortstypischen grauen Backstein. Obgleich dieses Projekt sich nicht durch die für so viele aktuelle chinesische Bauten typische Wuchtigkeit auszeichnet, gibt es doch subtile Verweise auf unterschiedliche Traditionen, sogar die der Fabrik. Es ähnelt allerdings auch keinem in jüngerer Zeit im Westen entstandenen Gebäude. Mit leichten Gittern aus Kiefernholz im Kontrast zur Solidität des grauen Backsteins beschwört Zhu eine fernere Vergangenheit, während er die Gegenwart anerkennt. Mit seiner soliden akademischen Ausbildung und der Erfahrung im Ausland verkörpert Zhu die neue Generation, die ungeachtet des rasanten Wirtschaftswachstums beginnt, ihre Spuren zu hinterlassen.

MASTERS OF THE UNIVERSE

Eine große Zahl auswärtiger Architekten ist in jüngster Zeit in China tätig, gewiss mit größerer Freiheit und stärkerem Einfluss auf die eigene Arbeit, als man ihnen vor dem Jahr 2000 zugestanden hätte. Ungeachtet der historischen Spannungen, die die chinesisch-japanischen Beziehungen belasten, konnten Architekten wie Arata Isozaki und Kengo Kuma in China einige höchst interessante Bauten errichten. Mit seinem Kulturzentrum in Shenzhen gelang es Isozaki zweifellos, das schablonenhafte Bauen zu durchbrechen, das Rem Koolhaas in seiner Schilderung der sagenhaften Produktivität der in der Sonderwirtschaftszone tätigen Architekten verspottet. Ebenso demonstriert Kuma mit der Zhongtai Box (Shanghai, 2003–06) seinen einfallsreichen, vielgestaltigen Stil. Im Augenblick allerdings gelten, ebenso wie in den Vereinigten Staaten, die niederländischen Architekten von OMA und das Schweizer Büro von Herzog & de Meuron als die wahren Stars. Erstere planen ein Hochhaus für die CCTV-Gesellschaften, das eine »neue Ikone« der Hauptstadt werden möchte und als Medienzentrum der kommenden Olympischen Spiele dienen soll. Die beiden Schweizer sind in den Bau des Hauptstadions der Spiele vertieft, »einem Vogelnest aus miteinander verflochtenen Zweigen«, die aus Profilstahl bestehen. Auch in diesem Fall soll ein zeichenhaftes Gebäude geschaffen werden, ein Symbol nicht nur für den Moment, sondern für Chinas Auftritt auf der Weltbühne des Sports, der Wirtschaft und endlich auch der Architektur. Jacques Herzog äußert: »Es ist erstaunlich, das Projekt dort zu realisieren, solch einen Bau könnte man nirgendwo sonst errichten.«

ENTFESSELTER PROMETHEUS

Derart gigantische Projekte sind nur realisierbar wegen der außerordentlichen Schnelligkeit und Kapazität der chinesischen Bauindustrie, die – wie Rem Koolhaas ironisch bemerkt – in der Lage ist, Architektur© am laufenden Band zu produzieren, andererseits aber auch riesige Projekte weit schneller als beispielsweise in den Niederlanden fertigzustellen. Diese Bauten, wie die noch umstrittenere Pekinger Oper des französischen Architekten Paul Andreu, stießen auf Kritik, wenngleich sie Ausdruck des außergewöhnlich starken Wunsches, ja der Fähigkeit sind, Weltniveau zu erreichen und vielleicht morgen neue Maßstäbe zu setzen. Ungeachtet der großen öffentlichen Beachtung ihrer Projekte waren bezeichnenderweise weder Koolhaas noch seine Schweizer Kollegen naiv genug, um sich an der Kreation eines neuen »chinesischen« Architekturstils zu versuchen. Ebensowenig bauen sie für Rotterdam oder Basel. Indem sie ihre Projekte in den jeweiligen spezifischen Gegebenheiten verankern und die vor Ort herrschende Gefühlslage und Kultur nicht ignorieren, schaffen sie »Ikonen« für ein neues Zeitalter, in dem China seinen rechtmäßigen Platz auf der Weltbühne einnimmt. Jacques Herzogs Worte über die derzeit herrschende Einstellung der Chinesen mögen einen Ansatz zum Verständnis dafür bieten, wie und warum der schreckliche Moloch Architektur ohne »Ästhetik, angenehmes Umfeld, fortschrittliche Bautechnik und Besitzergreifung durch Menschen«Fortschritte machen kann, selbst wenn eine auffallend einfallsreiche und kluge, neue Architektengeneration sich hervortut. Er sagt: »In ihren Köpfen herrscht eine solche Frische und in ihrer Tradition gibt es äußerst radikale Dinge, die erstaunlichsten Fayencen, durchbrochene Jade und sogenannte Gongshi oder auch Gelehrtensteine ... Es gibt bei ihnen keine so hohe Schwelle zwischen gutem und schlechtem Geschmack, zwischen dem Minimalen und Expressiven.«[1] Dies mag ein etwas rasanter Überblick über eine der großartigsten und ältesten Zivilisationen dieser Welt sein, aber im Zeitalter von Architektur© kann er als sachkundig gelten. Geschwindigkeit und Umfang der wirtschaftlichen Entwicklung im heutigen China leisten zweifellos den besten und schlechtesten Formen von Architektur Vorschub. Neu und höchst ermutigend ist das Auftreten selbstständiger Architekten, nachdem sie durch Reformen der Gesetzgebung befreit und der Würgegriff der »Planungsinstitute« etwas gelockert wurde. Angesichts des Ausmaßes dieser neuen Entwicklung in China kann man davon ausgehen, dass dort qualitätvolle Neubauten in größerer Zahl entworfen und realisiert werden, als irgendwo sonst auf der Welt. Kurz, die neue Architektur in China ist eine Macht, mit der zu rechnen ist.[2]

Philip Jodidio

[1] Jacques Herzog, zitiert in dem Aufsatz »The China Syndrom« von Arthur Lubow, *The New York Times*, 21. Mai 2006.

[2] People's Architecture (www.peoplesarchitecture.org) wurde am 1. Oktober 2005 in Peking gegründet. Diese gemeinnützige Organisation mit Sitz in New York und einem Regionalbüro in Peking »ist ein multidisziplinäres Forum zum Austausch von Ideen, mit dem Ziel, ein besseres globales Verständnis der architektonischen, kulturellen und ökonomischen Entwicklung Chinas zu ermöglichen«. Wei Wei Shannon, ein Mitbegründer von People's Architecture, war freundlicherweise bei der Vermittlung einer Reihe von für dieses Buch unverzichtbaren Kontakten in China behilflich.

INTRODUCTION

UNE ÉTOILE ROUGE SE LÈVE

Difficile aujourd'hui de lire un journal ou de regarder un programme de télévision sans tomber sur un article ou une émission sur la Chine, la grande réussite économique de ces dix dernières années. Il est maintenant certain que le pays le plus peuplé du monde (1 313 973 000 habitants, estimation CIA juillet 2006) s'est réveillé de sa longue somnolence. Alors que des pays plus développés traversaient des périodes cycliques d'expansion et de récession, la Chine s'est reconstruite à neuf à une échelle sans précédent. Les nouveaux investissements dans le bâtiment et les équipements d'usine des cinq premiers mois de 2006 étaient de 30 % supérieurs à ceux de la même période de l'année précédente et ils auront dépassé 984,8 millions d'euros en 2006, soit près de la moitié du produit national brut du pays. Un développement à cette échelle ne se préoccupe généralement guère de qualité, bien que les exceptions à cette règle banale soient suffisamment nombreuses pour égaler ou dépasser ce qui se fait actuellement dans beaucoup de pays occidentaux. L'intelligence et le travail acharné que l'on constate à l'œuvre dans d'autres secteurs de l'économie sont de plus en plus évidents en architecture, en grande partie grâce aux modifications intervenues dans la réglementation de la profession. C'est ce changement – la libération de l'architecte – qui constitue l'événement le plus important au milieu d'une explosion sans précédent du nombre de chantiers.

L'ARCHITECTURE AU PREMIER PLAN

On ne manque certes pas d'analyses sur les conséquences de ce développement féroce qui vont d'avertissements concernant l'état de pollution catastrophique enregistré aux prédictions désastreuses faites sur le prix des matières premières. L'architecture et l'absence de planification cohérente et de contrôle de qualité ont déjà été amplement commentées. L'une des plus intéressantes études sur ce sujet a été compilée par Rem Koolhaas et l'Harvard Design School Project on the City (*Great Leap Forward*, Taschen, 2001). S'appuyant sur l'extraordinaire développement du bassin de la Rivière des Perles, près de la frontière avec Hongkong, où a été créée la zone économique spéciale de Shenzen en 1980, Koolhaas et son équipe vont jusqu'à dire que la définition même de l'architecture (qu'ils appellent dans ce contexte Architecture©) doit être modifiée. Dans un article intitulé « Architecture Shenzen », Nancy Lin écrit : « L'Architecture© est devenue un outil d'investissement. Le secteur de la construction offre de tels profits que la première fonction d'un bâtiment n'est plus de répondre aux besoins humains. Les concepts traditionnels associés à l'architecture tels l'esthétique, un environnement confortable, une technologie de construction avancée et l'usage qui en est fait par l'homme ont été supprimés pour faire venir au premier plan des valeurs quantitatives comme le volume de construction, l'investissement en capital, la durée de chantier, les coûts et la rentabilité. » Lin conclut que « dans ces divers états, l'architecture n'est plus seulement présente sous forme physique : elle est partout, devient le sujet de conversations quotidiennes et une abstraction de chiffres publiés comme les cours de la bourse dans un journal ». Le lecteur cynique pourrait faire observer que des joliesses du type de l'esthétique et d'un environnement confortable ont également été sacrifiées depuis longtemps par les architectes occidentaux, mais Koolhaas et al insistent sur un autre point : « L'architecte© chinois est l'architecte le plus important, le plus influent et le plus puissant de cette planète. Le volume moyen de projets réalisés dans le seul domaine du logement au cours de la vie d'un architecte© chinois est approximativement de trois douzaines d'immeubles de trente niveaux… On trouve en Chine un dixième du nombre d'architectes américains, mais ils conçoivent cinq fois plus de projets en un cinquième du temps, tout en gagnant un dixième de leurs honoraires. Ceci signifie une productivité 2 500 fois supérieure à celle d'un praticien américain. » En bref, pour Koolhaas, si l'architecture en Chine est tout, les architectes ne sont plus ce qu'ils étaient.

LE GRAND BOND EN AVANT

Lorsque *Great Leap Forward* fut publié en 2001, le « boom » fantastique de la construction en Chine reposait entièrement entre les mains de « design institutes », entreprises d'État au personnel innombrable et peu intéressées par la créativité architecturale. Même les architectes étrangers célèbres étaient obligés de remettre leurs plans à ces instituts sans guère conserver de contrôle sur ce qui allait être réellement bâti. À peu près à la même époque, la loi fut modifiée afin de permettre à des architectes « indépendants » de pratiquer. Bien que la demande de construction soit telle et l'ordre enraciné si établi que ce changement légal ne puisse immédiatement modifier l'ordre des choses observé par l'équipe d'Harvard, ces cinq dernières années ont été témoins d'une autre révolution, l'émergence de stars montantes et surtout de constructions nouvelles et intéressantes non signées par des Occidentaux. Bien que beaucoup des nouveaux chefs de ce mouvement soient de formation occidentale, du moins en partie, ils ont déjà jeté les bases d'une modernité pleine d'invention, qui se différencie du goût purement occidental tout en échappant à la tentation de coiffer d'un toit « à la chinoise » une tour de bureaux ordinaire. L'organisation par Pékin des Jeux olympiques d'été 2008 a également joué un rôle de catalyseur majeur dans le développement d'une architecture contemporaine de qualité. De très grandes agences étrangères, comme celles de Rem Koolhaas/OMA ou d'Herzog & de Meuron participent à la conception des installations pour ces Jeux, mais les architectes chinois ont été mobilisés eux aussi dans cet effort massif accompli pour élever le pays au niveau international.

ASTRES ROUGES

Si la liste des architectes chinois influents s'accroît de jour en jour, un certain nombre de figures-clés peuvent déjà être citées. La première agence indépendante créée à Pékin en 1993, avant même la modification de la loi, est FCJZ dirigée par Yung Ho Chang. Né à Pékin en 1956 et formé à l'Université de Californie à Berkeley, Chang a fondé le Centre d'études supérieures d'architecture à l'Université de Pékin, puis a été nommé responsable du Département d'architecture du MIT en 2005. Sa situation inhabituelle au cœur de l'architecture contemporaine de son pays, mais également aux États-Unis, est symbolique de l'émergence des Chinois sur la scène architecturale mondiale.

Un autre contributeur important aux développements accélérés que connaît ce pays est l'artiste-architecte Ai Wei Wei. Né en 1957 à Pékin, fils du poète très connu Ai Qing, il a étudié le cinéma à Pékin avant de suivre les cours de la Parson's

School of Design à New York. Il est revenu à Shanghai en 1999 où il a ouvert son agence, Fake Design, la même année. Conseiller artistique auprès d'Herzog & de Meuron pour le Stade national destiné aux J. O., Ai est également l'animateur du projet du parc d'architecture Jinhua qui réunit des architectes d'avant-garde chinois et des praticiens étrangers dont les Américains Michael Maltzan et Toshiko Mori. Ici, comme à Pékin, il a collaboré avec Herzog & de Meuron. L'austérité et le pragmatisme avec lesquels il a abordé un projet comme celui de Courtyard 105 (Pékin, 2004–05) en dit beaucoup sur l'émergence de l'architecture contemporaine chinoise qui n'hésite pas, face à la vague de tours toutes semblables qui peuplent les centres urbains récents, à utiliser des matériaux simples et même à rénover des bâtiments industriels.

Un troisième acteur majeur de cette émergence est certainement Ma Qing Yun, diplômé en architecture de la Graduate School of Fine Art de l'Université de Pennsylvanie en 1991. Coordinateur du livre *Great Leap Forward*, Ma Qing Yun est plus qu'informé sur les difficultés que rencontre l'architecture dans son pays. Il a installé sa propre agence MADA s.p.a.m. dans un bâtiment scolaire moderniste de Shanghai des années 1980 (2003–04). Il est intéressant de voir que, plutôt que de tenter de masquer le passé de cette école de l'Étoile rouge, il a réussi à réutiliser cette relique sans grand intérêt d'une période où les architectes ne possédaient pas la liberté de s'exprimer sur la société. Il se dit « fasciné par l'opportunité de s'impliquer dans le discours sur les mutations urbaines provoquées par une obsolescence systématique ».Il aurait pu aussi parler d'obsolescence systémique étant donnée la tendance persistante à voir dans l'architecture une activité qui se pratique rapidement et sans grand souci de qualité.

DE SHENZEN AU TIBET ET RETOUR

Liu Xiadu, Meng Yan et Wang Hui ont tous étudié à la fin des années 1990 à la Miami University (Oxford, OH) avant de fonder l'agence Urbanus Architecture and Design à Shenzen et Pékin, en association avec Pei Zhu. À travers des projets comme leur « Proposition de réhabilitation dynamique du village de Gansha » (Shenzen, 2005), ces jeunes architectes cherchent à s'attaquer aux problèmes très concrets de l'urbanisation explosive soulevés par le groupe de Harvard. Sensibilisés aux théories étrangères du développement urbain au cours de leur séjour aux États-Unis, ils ont enrichi cette réflexion de leur culture et de leur intelligence personnelles pour affronter un problème spécifique à la Chine. Il serait étonnant que des étrangers, quelle que soit leur expérience, puissent offrir des solutions aussi novatrices aux difficultés de voisinage. Cette montée de talents nationaux qui s'émancipent des lois et de la puissance des instituts officiels d'architecture promet de nombreuses autres surprises positives.

Un autre architecte important cité dans cet ouvrage, bien qu'il n'ait pas encore atteint la notoriété des autres, est Wang Hui (sans lien avec Urbanus). Né à Xian en 1969, il a étudié à l'Université polytechnique du Nord-Ouest avant de travailler pour l'agence FCJZ à Pékin, sur des projets tels que la Villa Shizilin publié ici. Trois de ses réalisations relativement modestes, à savoir son Café Mima (Pékin, 2003), le Neno Corridor (Pékin, 2004) et peut-être surtout son école élémentaire de La Pomme (A Li, Tibet, 2004–05) illustrent sa volonté de prendre en compte le poids de la tradition dans un site proche du Palais d'été près de Pékin (Café Mima) ou l'un des paysages les plus rudes aux frontières du pays (École élémentaire de La Pomme). Diplômé de l'enseignement supérieur chinois, sans expérience à l'étranger pour l'instant, mais avec l'envie de bousculer les choses, Wang Hui sera certainement l'un des grands architectes de sa génération.

Plus jeune encore que Wang Hui, Zhu Xiafeng est né à Shanghai en 1972. Il est diplômé de l'École d'architecture de l'Université de Shenzhen et M.Arch. d'Harvard Graduate School of Design (1997). Il a créé sa propre agence, Scenic Architecture, à Shanghai en 2004. Bien qu'il soit déjà intervenu sur un certain nombre de projets qui ne concernent pas la rénovation urbaine, son Jardin du Pin Vert (Qingpu, Shanghai, 2004–05) met en lumière un certain nombre des caractéristiques qui paraissent liées à la nouvelle génération d'architectes chinois. En convertissant des bâtiments d'usine le long d'une autoroute de la banlieue de Shanghai en bars-restaurants, il a créé un vaste espace vert et conçu un nouveau type d'écran repliable en lattes de pin local pour un bâtiment et en brique grise habituelle pour l'autre. Ce projet, qui ne présente aucun des aspects massifs de beaucoup de réalisations chinoises actuelles, fait de subtiles références à la tradition, y compris à celle de l'usine. Il ne ressemble à rien à ce que l'on a pu voir récemment en Occident. À travers ses légers écrans de pin contrastant avec la solidité de la brique grise, il fait appel à un passé plus lointain tout en affirmant sa contemporanéité. Doté d'une base universitaire solide, Zhu Xiafeng représente une nouvelle génération qui commence à poser ses marques malgré la marche en avant précipitée de l'économie.

MAÎTRES DE L'UNIVERS

Un grand nombre d'architectes étrangers de talent ont récemment travaillé en Chine. Ils disposent aujourd'hui de davantage de liberté et de pouvoir de contrôle sur leurs projets qu'avant 2000. Malgré les tensions qui marquent périodiquement les relations sino-japonaises, des architectes comme Arata Isozaki et Kengo Kuma ont pu achever quelques réalisations très intéressantes. Le Centre culturel de Shenzhen d'Isozaki rompt certainement avec les réalisations faites au moule et découpées au couteau dont se moquait Koolhaas dans sa description de la fabuleuse productivité des architectes de la Zone économique spéciale. Kuma, lui aussi, a illustré son style inventif et hétérogène dans la Zhongtai Box (Shanghai, 2003–06). Les vraies stars du moment ici, comme aux États-Unis d'ailleurs, sont l'agence néerlandaise OMA et l'agence suisse Herzog & de Meuron. La première a imaginé une tour pour le groupe CCTV qui devrait devenir une nouvelle « icône » de la capitale et sera le centre des médias pour les J. O. La seconde se consacre à la construction du principal stade des Jeux, un « nid de brindilles entrelacées » en acier structurel. Ici aussi, l'objectif est de créer un bâtiment iconique symbole non seulement d'un moment fort, mais de l'émergence de la Chine sur la scène mondiale dans les sports, l'économie et finalement, l'architecture. Comme le dit Jacques Herzog : « Réaliser ici ce projet est étonnant, on n'aurait pu construire une telle structure ailleurs. »

PROMÉTHÉE DÉCHAÎNÉ

Une des raisons de la faisabilité de projets à si vaste échelle tient à l'extraordinaire rapidité et capacité de l'industrie du bâtiment chinoise, en mesure, comme le suggérait ironiquement Rem Koolhaas, de débiter de l'architecture©, mais aussi de livrer des projets gigantesques bien plus vite qu'aux Pays-Bas par exemple. Ces bâtiments, comme l'Opéra encore plus controversé de l'architecte français Paul Andreu, ont été l'objet de critiques, mais signalent néanmoins un niveau exceptionnel de désir et certainement de talent pour accéder aux standards mondiaux avant, demain peut-être, d'en définir de nouveaux. Il est significatif que ni Koolhaas ni ses homologues suisses n'ont été assez naïfs pour essayer de créer un nouveau style d'architecture « chinois » malgré la nature très remarquée de leurs réalisations. Mais ils ne construisent pas pour autant la même chose qu'à Rotterdam ou Bâle. Enracinant leurs projets dans la spécificité du contexte et sans ignorer la profondeur de la culture et des réactions locales, ils conçoivent les « icônes » d'une ère nouvelle qui verra la Chine prendre la place qu'elle mérite sur la scène mondiale. Les mots de Jacques Herzog sur l'attitude actuelle des Chinois offrent peut-être une clé à une meilleure compréhension du poids écrasant d'une architecture ne se préoccupant pas « d'esthétique, d'environnement confortable, de technologies de construction avancées et de l'occupation des habitants ». Ils nous aide à mieux appréhender la façon dont elle peut progresser, voire même ils nous éclairent sur le comment une nouvelle génération d'architectes remarquablement inventifs et intelligents peut apparaître déjà au premier plan. Herzog poursuit : « Ils ont l'esprit si libre, ils possèdent dans leur tradition les choses les plus radicales, les faïences, les jades percés et les suiseki les plus étonnants... Ils ne sont pas limités par autant de barrières entre le bon et le mauvais goût, entre le minimal et l'expressif. »[1] Ce survol de l'une des plus grandes et des plus anciennes civilisations existantes est peut-être un peu rapide, mais, à l'âge d'Architecture©, il est cependant représentatif. Le rythme et l'ampleur du développement économique actuel encouragent certainement l'émergence des pires et des meilleures expressions architecturales. Ce qui est nouveau et hautement encourageant, c'est l'apparition d'architectes libérés par les réformes législatives qui ont quelque peu réduit le bâillon des instituts officiels. Étant donné l'échelle de ce qui se passe en Chine, ceci signifie également que de nouvelles constructions de qualité vont être édifiées en plus grand nombre que presque partout ailleurs. En bref, la nouvelle architecture chinoise est une force avec laquelle il va falloir compter.[2]

Philip Jodidio

[1] Jacques Herzog, cité dans l'article « The China Syndrome » par Arthur Lubow.

[2] People's Architecture a été fondé le 1er octobre 2005 à Pékin. Organisme à but non-lucratif dont le siège est à New York et qui dispose d'un bureau régional à Pékin, People's Architecture « est un forum multidisciplinaire pour l'échange d'idées dans le but de faciliter une compréhension internationale meilleure du développement architectural, culturel et économique de la Chine ». Wei Wei Shannon, co-fondateur de cet organisme a aimablement fourni un certain nombre de contacts en Chine pour la réalisation de cet ouvrage. http ://www.peoplesarchitecture.org

#1

ATELIER DESHAUS

ATELIER DESHAUS
C3-202 Red Town
No. 570,West Huaihai Road
Shanghai 200052

Tel: +86 21 6124 8118
Fax: +86 21 6124 8119
e-mail: info@deshaus.com
Web: www.deshaus.com

LIU YICHUN was born in Haiyang, Shandong, in 1969. He received a B.Arch. degree from Tongji University, Shanghai (1991), continued his architecture studies at the Guangzhou Design Institute (1991–94), and received his M.Arch degree from Tongji University in 1997. From 1997 to 2000, he was the Chief Architect of the Architectural Design and Research Institute of Tongji University, Shanghai. He has been a partner and principal of Atelier Deshaus since 2001. ZHUANG SHEN was born in Wujiang, Jiangsu, in 1971. He received his B.Arch (1994) and his M.Arch (1997) degrees from Tongji University and was a Senior Architect at the Architectural Design and Research Institute of Tongji University, from 1997 to 2000, before becoming a partner and principal of Atelier Deshaus in 2001. CHEN YIFENG was born in Kunshan, Jiangsu, in 1972 and also received his B.Arch (1995) and his M.Arch (1998) degrees from Tongji University. Like Zhuang, he was a Senior Architect at the Architectural Design and Research Institute of Tongji University (1998–2000) before also becoming a partner and principal of Atelier Deshaus. The architects plead for "an attitude of 'realness' toward the changes of the world that occur everyday, and to understand and evaluate them as promptly as possible." The work of the firm, which has 10 employees, includes the Dongguan Institute of Technology Dongguan, the office building for the Qingpu Private Enterprise Association, both published here, and the Kindergarten, Hanlinfudi, Jiaxing, Zhejiang (2003).

QINGPU PRIVATE ENTERPRISE ASSOCIATION
SHANGHAI 2003-05

FLOOR AREA: 6745 m^2
CLIENT: Qingpu Private Enterprise Association, Shanghai
COST: $ 834 000

Located on Qinglong Road, on the east side of Xiayang Lake in Qingpu New Town, Shanghai, this office was designed with views both from the interior and the exterior in mind, according to the architects. With its basic 60 x 60 meter, square floor plan, the three-story building has printed glass curtain walls and encloses a green courtyard. The pattern chosen for the glass is described as resembling "broken ice," and is adapted from traditional Chinese interior décor. As the architects write, "The patterns are designed so that they affirm the unity of the building even when different parts come together. The dominant white color of the interior also adds to the purity of the building." Containing only the reception and a restaurant, the ground floor allows open views through the building to the central garden. Despite its strict square form and perfect north-south alignment, the building's interior spaces and transparency make it more varied and unusual than might be expected.

Das an der Qinglong-Straße am Ostufer des Xiayang-Sees in Qingpu New Town, Shanghai, gelegene Gebäude der Qingpu Private Enterprise Association wurde den Architekten zufolge sowohl für Blicke von Innen wie von Außen entworfen. Der Grundriss des dreigeschossigen Gebäudes, das eine Fassade aus bedrucktem Glas hat und einen begrünten Innenhof umgibt, basiert auf einem Quadrat von 60 x 60 m. Das für das Glas gewählte Muster wird als »gesplittertes Eis« beschrieben und geht auf ein traditionelles chinesisches Innendekor zurück. Dazu führen die Architekten aus: »Die Muster wurden in der Absicht gestaltet, die Einheit des Gebäudes zu stärken, auch wenn unterschiedliche Teile zusammentreffen. Die den Innenraum beherrschende weiße Farbe trägt darüber hinaus zur Strenge des Gebäudes bei.« Vom Erdgeschoss aus, in dem sich lediglich der Empfang und ein Restaurant befinden, bieten sich freie Ausblicke durch das Gebäude auf die zentrale Gartenanlage. Unbeschadet der streng quadratischen Form und der strikten Nord-Süd-Ausrichtung, lassen Interieurs und Transparenz das Gebäude unerwartet abwechslungsreich und ungewöhnlich erscheinen.

En bordure de la route de Qinlong, sur la rive occidentale du lac d'Xiayang dans la ville nouvelle de Qingpu, près de Shanghai, ce projet a été conçu en pensant à la fois aux vues de l'intérieur et de l'extérieur. De 60 x 60 m de surface au sol, cet immeuble de trois niveaux est doté de murs-rideaux en verre imprimé et possède en partie centrale une cour plantée. Le motif choisi pour le verre qui évoque selon le descriptif « de la glace brisée » est adapté d'un motif traditionnel de décoration intérieure chinoise. Comme l'écrit l'architecte : « Les motifs sont dessinés de façon à affirmer l'unité du bâtiment, même lorsque les différentes parties viennent en contact. La couleur blanche dominante de l'aménagement intérieur ajoute à l'impression de pureté donnée par ce projet. » Du rez-de-chaussée qui ne contient que le hall d'accueil et un restaurant, la vue traverse l'immeuble jusqu'au jardin central. Malgré sa forme strictement carrée et son alignement impeccable Nord-Sud, ses aménagements intérieurs et sa transparence lui confèrent un aspect plus varié et original que l'on ne pouvait s'y attendre.

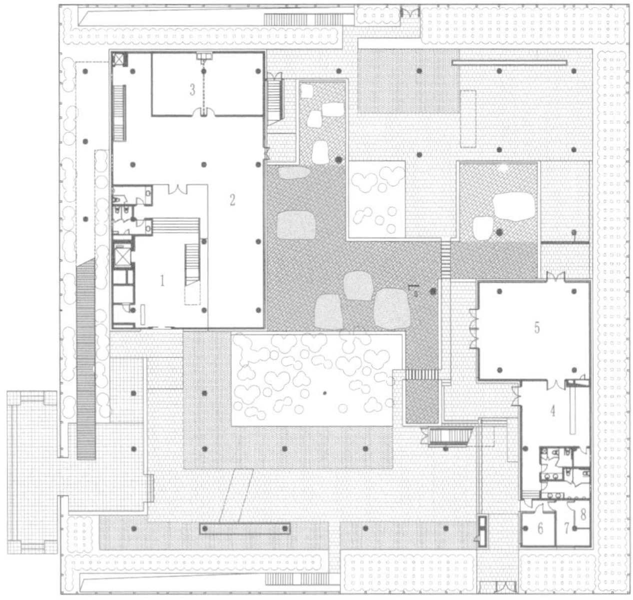

The basic square floor plan of the building is enlivened by numerous openings and internal, angled surfaces. Lifted up in part on pilotis, the structure has an almost ethereal quality in these images.

Der quadratische Grundriss des Gebäudes wird durch zahlreiche Öffnungen und winkelförmige Innenwände aufgelockert. Der zum Teil auf Pfeiler gestellte Bau bildet eine Struktur mit einer nahezu ätherischen Anmutung.

Le plan au sol de forme carrée est animé par de multiples ouvertures et des partitions internes en biais. Reposant en partie sur pilotis, la structure revêt ici un aspect presque éthéré.

QINGPU XIAYU KINDERGARTEN
SHANGHAI 2003-05

FLOOR AREA: 6328 m^2
CLIENT: Qingpu Xiayu Kindergarten
COST: $ 770 000

This kindergarten facility, located on Qinglong Road in Qingpu New Town, contains 15 classes, each of which has living, dining, and sleeping areas as well as an outdoor playground. After initially planning the structure in a linear pattern on the narrow site, the architects selected a curved plan with two clusters containing the classrooms and teachers' offices. The "living" areas and outdoor playgrounds are at ground level with brightly colored bedroom spaces above. As the architects explain, "In order to emphasize the floating and uncertain feeling we sought, we detached the floors of the colored boxes from the roof of the ground floor." The effect is to encourage "random convergence" and spatial tension. Every third bedroom unit is linked by raised wooden walkways, "to create a friendly and kind atmosphere like a bedroom village." Tall trees are integrated into courtyards on the riverside site.

Dieser Kindergarten an der Qinglong-Straße in Qingpu New Town verfügt über 15 Räume, von denen jeder über Aufenthalts-, Ess- und Schlafbereiche sowie über einen Spielplatz im Freien verfügt. Nachdem sie den Bau auf dem schmalen Grundstück ursprünglich als lineare Anlage geplant hatten, entschieden sich die Architekten für eine leicht gebogene Grundform mit zwei Gebäudegruppen, in denen die Klassenzimmer und Büros der Lehrer untergebracht sind. Aufenthaltsbereiche und Spielplätze liegen im Parterre, die farbig verputzten Schlafräume darüber. Seitens der Architekten heißt es dazu: »Um das von uns angestrebte vage Gefühl des Schwebens zu unterstreichen, hoben wir die Grundflächen der farbigen Kästen vom Dach des Erdgeschosses ab.« Damit werden »zufällige Konvergenz und räumliche Spannung unterstützt. Jede dritte Schlafbox ist durch erhöhte hölzerne Laufstege verbunden, »um eine freundliche Atmosphäre, wie in einem Schlafdorf zu erzeugen«. Hohe Bäume sind in die Gestaltung der Innenhöfe der am Flussufer gelegenen Anlage einbezogen.

Ce jardin d'enfants au bord de la route de Qinglong dans la ville nouvelle de Qingpu compte quinze classes, chacune équipée de zones d'activités, de repas et de repos ainsi que d'un terrain de jeu en plein air. Après avoir travaillé à l'origine sur un plan linéaire imposé par l'étroitesse du terrain, les architectes ont opté pour un plan incurvé en deux ensembles contenant les salles d'une part et les bureaux des enseignants d'autre part. Les zones « de séjour » et les terrains de jeux sont au rez-de-chaussée surmonté d'espaces de repos de couleurs vives. L'architecte explique son choix : « Pour renforcer l'effet de flottement et d'incertitude que nous recherchions, nous avons détaché les planchers des boîtes colorées du toit des salles du rez-de-chaussée. » L'effet encourage « une convergence aléatoire » et une tension spatiale. Une salle de repos sur trois est réunie par un passage surélevé en bois destiné « à créer une atmosphère sympathique, celle d'un village de chambres ». De grands arbres poussent dans les cours du côté du fleuve.

The gently curving, almost amoeboid, form of the plan encloses the living and teaching areas for the children—with bright colors indicating function as much as if not more than any specific detail of the architecture.

Der sanft geschwungene, ja fast amöbenförmige Grundriss umfasst die Aufenthalts- und Unterrichtsbereiche für die Kinder; hier zeigen eher die leuchtenden Farben als architektonische Details die jeweilige Funktion an.

Le plan aux courbes douces, presque amibiennes, regroupe les zones de vie et d'enseignement pour les enfants. Les couleurs vives en signalent les fonctions tout autant ou même plus que certains détails architecturaux spécifiques.

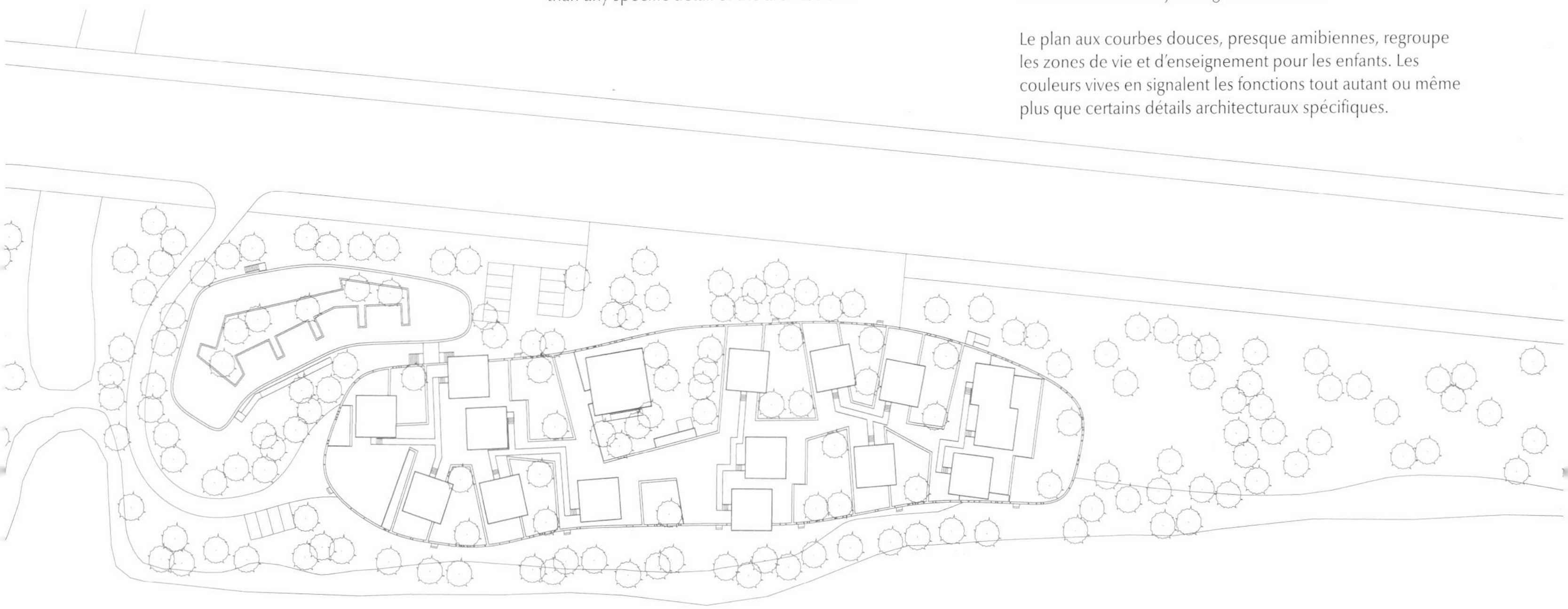

#2

ATELIER FEICHANG JIANZHU

ATELIER FEICHANG JIANZHU (FCJZ)
Yuan Ming Yuan East Gate
Nei Yard No.1, northside,
Hai Dian District,
Beijing 100084

Tel: +86 10 8262 6123
Fax: +86 10 8262 2712
e-mail: fcjz@fcjz.com
Web: www.fcjz.com

YUNG HO CHANG was born in Beijing in 1956, received his M.Arch from the University of California at Berkeley in 1984, and became a licensed architect in the United States in 1989. He has been practicing in China since 1992 and established Atelier Feichang Jianzhu (FCJZ) in 1993 with his wife, Lijia Lu. Translated as "unusual architecture," FCJZ was the Chinese capital's first independent architectural firm. He is currently the principal architect of Atelier FCJZ as well as the Head of the Architecture Department at Massachusetts Institute of Technology (MIT). He has won a number of prizes, including First Place in the Shinkenchiku Residential Design Competition (1987), a Progressive Architecture Citation Award (1996), and the 2000 UNESCO Prize for the Promotion of the Arts. In 2006, he received an Academy Award in Architecture from the American Academy of Arts and Letters. He has taught at various architecture schools in the United States, including Ball State, Michigan, U. C. Berkeley, Rice, and Harvard, where he was the Kenzo Tange Chair Professor (2002). In 1999, he founded the Beijing University Graduate Center of Architecture and remains its director. The work of FCJZ includes the Split House, Yanqing, Beijing (2002), the Commune at the Great Wall, Beijing (2002); Hebei Education Publishing House, Hebei (2004); the Tourist Orientation Center, Dalinor National Natural Reserve, Inner Mongolia (2005).

VILLA SHIZILIN BEIJING 2003-04

FLOOR AREA: 4800 m^2 SITE AREA: 200 100 m^2
CLIENT: Antaeus Group COST: not disclosed
PROJECT DESIGNERS: Yung Ho Chang, Wang Hui

Built for a couple of promoters, this house is located in a persimmon orchard near the Ming Tombs outside Beijing, and willfully combines traditional ideas, forms, and materials in a thoroughly modern context. In particular, nine tapered spaces are conceived like camera rangefinders, oriented toward different views and echoing the landscape. The rolling artificial landscape of the rooftops is inspired by neighboring hills. The very large residence is also intended to function as a club, including a cinema and indoor pool. Local granite is used as exterior cladding on the concrete walls. Corten steel is also used for some outside surfaces. Dark cement tiles are employed on the roof and a number of the existing persimmon trees have been integrated into the design. Through the choice of materials, the topographic nature of the design and the specific attention paid to views from the site, Villa Shizilin represents a strong effort to develop an indigenous modernity in residential architecture.

Das für zwei Promoter erbaute Haus liegt in einer Dattelpflaumenplantage außerhalb von Peking in der Nähe der Ming-Gräber und kombiniert bewusst traditionelle Auffassungen, Formen und Materialien mit einem gänzlich modernen Kontext. Neun sich verjüngende Räume sind wie Entfernungsmesser von Kameras auf verschiedene Blickpunkte ausgerichtet und geben gleichsam ein Echo der Landschaft. Die geschwungene künstliche Dachlandschaft wurde von den benachbarten Hügelketten inspiriert. Das äußerst geräumige Wohnhaus ist auch als Club gedacht und verfügt über ein Kino und eine Schwimmhalle. Abgesehen von einigen mit Cortenstahl plattierten Flächen sind die äußeren Betonwände zum größten Teil mit heimischem Granit verkleidet. Auf den Dachflächen kommen dunkelfarbige Zementfliesen zum Einsatz, außerdem wurde eine Reihe der vorhandenen Dattelpflaumenbäume in den Entwurf integriert. Durch die Materialwahl, den topografischen Charakter der Ausführung und den besonderen Wert, den man auf die Ausblicke vom Gelände legte, verkörpert die Villa Shizilin das Bemühen um Entfaltung einer ortsgebundenen Modernität in der Wohnarchitektur.

Construite pour un couple de promoteurs, cette maison est située dans un verger de plaqueminiers, non loin des Tombeaux Ming, dans la banlieue de Pékin. Dans son approche extrêmement moderne, elle combine habilement des idées, des formes et des matériaux traditionnels. En particulier, neuf volumes coniques, rappelant des objectifs d'appareils photo, visent différentes vues choisies dans le paysage. Le paysage artificiel créé par l'ondulation de la couverture s'inspire de celui des collines voisines. Cette grande résidence est également un club, comprenant un cinéma et une piscine. Les murs en béton sont habillés de granit local, ainsi que de panneaux en acier Corten. Le toit est recouvert de tuiles en ciment de couleur sombre et un certain nombre de plaqueminiers ont été intégrés dans le projet. Par le choix des matériaux, la nature topographique du projet et l'attention particulière portée aux vues, la Villa Shizilin représente un important effort de recherche d'une modernité locale dans l'architecture résidentielle chinoise.

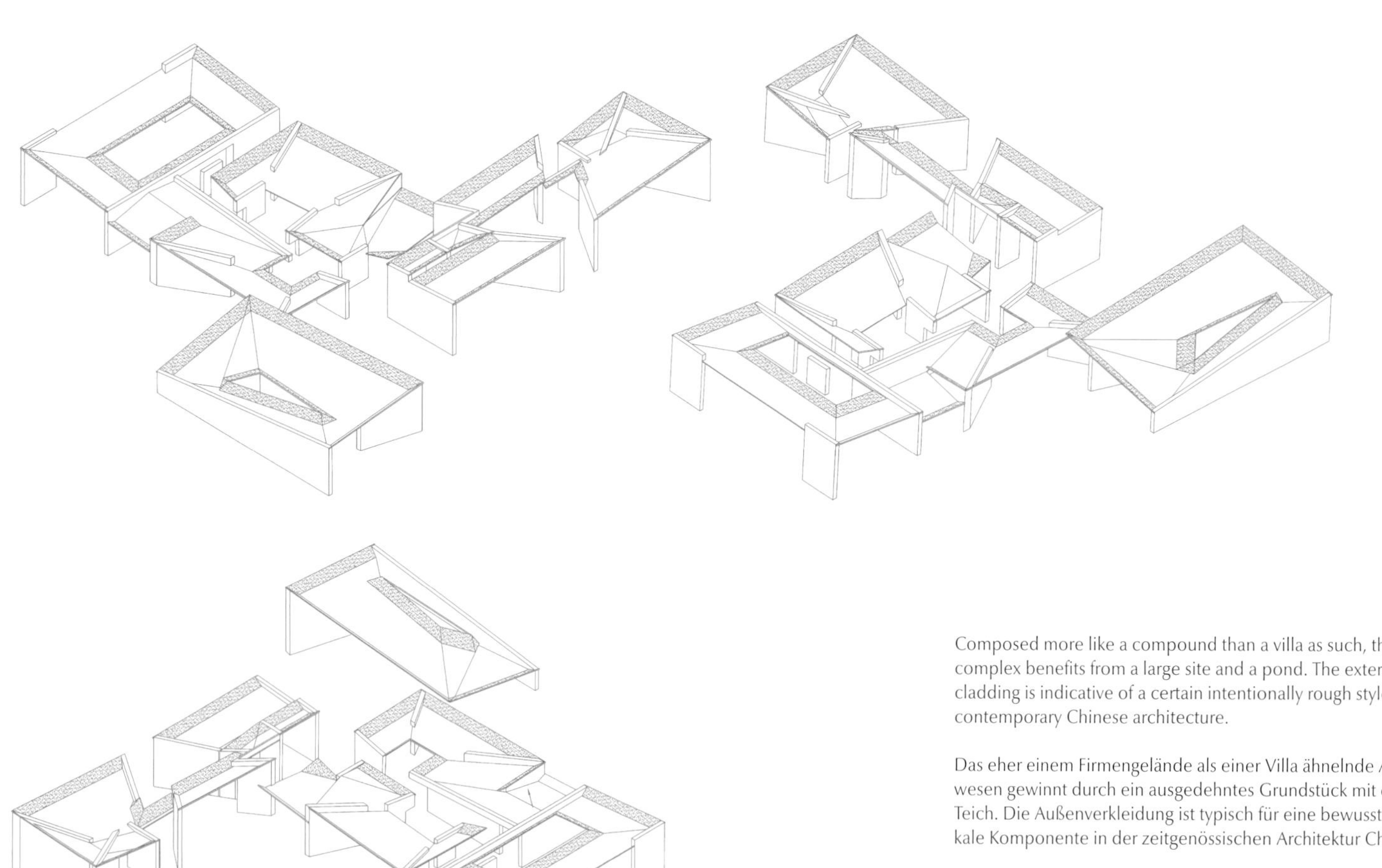

Composed more like a compound than a villa as such, the complex benefits from a large site and a pond. The exterior cladding is indicative of a certain intentionally rough style in contemporary Chinese architecture.

Das eher einem Firmengelände als einer Villa ähnelnde Anwesen gewinnt durch ein ausgedehntes Grundstück mit einem Teich. Die Außenverkleidung ist typisch für eine bewusst rustikale Komponente in der zeitgenössischen Architektur Chinas.

Plus composée à la manière d'un complexe que d'une villa, la résidence bénéficie d'un vaste terrain et d'un étang. L'habillage extérieur, témoigne de la présence d'un style volontairement rêche dans l'architecture chinoise contemporaine.

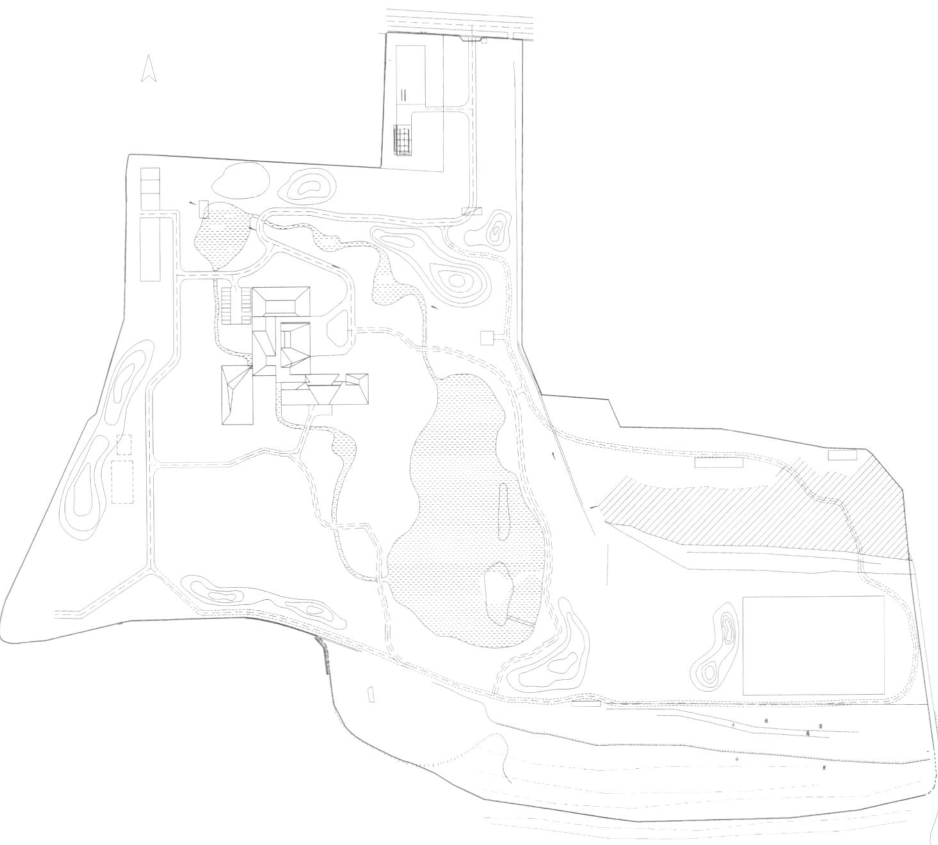

A site plan to the left gives a clear idea of the entire compound. Above, the varying roof angles, glazing patterns and use of cladding materials create what might be termed a dissonant harmony in the architecture.

Ein Lageplan links gibt eine klare Vorstellung des gesamten Geländes. In der Abbildung oben erwecken die verschiedenen Winkel der Dächer, die verglasten Flächen und der Einsatz von Verkleidungsmaterialien einen Eindruck, den man mit dissonanter Harmonie beschreiben könnte.

Le plan du site, à gauche, donne une idée claire du complexe dans son entier. Ci-dessus, les différentes pentes des toitures, les formes de découpes du verre et les matériaux d'habillage entrent en une sorte d'harmonie dissonante avec l'architecture.

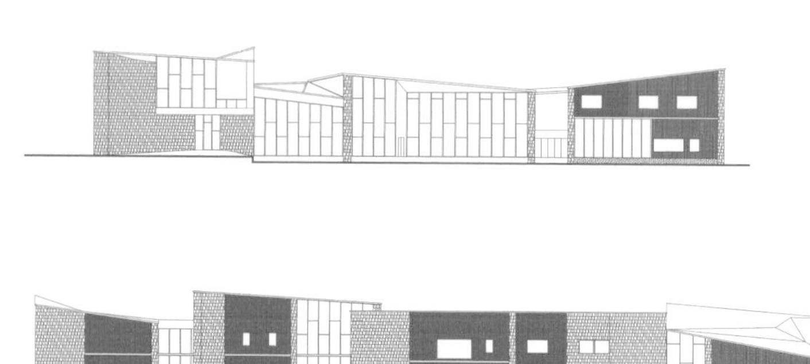

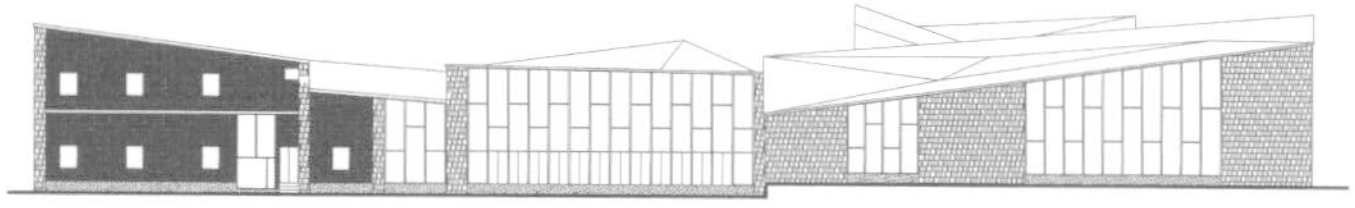

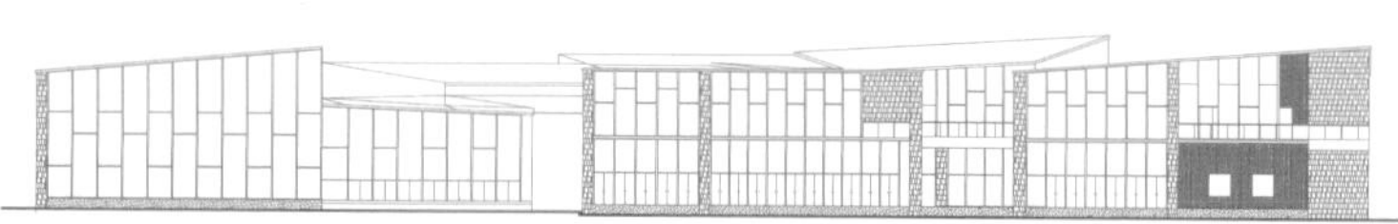

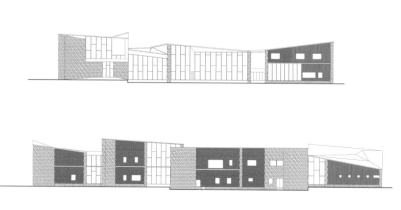

Sloping and angled roofs, or large glazed surfaces alternating with stone blocks and wood, create an unexpected rhythm and characteristics that might in some sense be termed typically Chinese.

Abfallende und gewinkelte Dächer sowie große Glasflächen im Wechsel mit Natursteinen und Holz schaffen eine überraschende Rhythmik und Charakteristik, die man in gewissem Sinn als typisch chinesisch bezeichnen könnte.

Les toits en pente ou les vastes surfaces vitrées, alternant avec les moellons de pierre et de bois, créent un rythme surprenant et génèrent un caractère qui pourrait être d'une certaine façon qualifié de « chinois ».

The irregular articulation of surfaces, varying not only in their materials but also in their setting within the partly stone frame, makes for unusual features in this project. A terrace image above voluntarily frames a view of neighboring hills.

Die unregelmäßige Beschaffenheit von Oberflächen, die sich sowohl im Material als auch formal in der Anordnung innerhalb der teilweise steinernen Umrandung unterscheiden, sorgt bei diesem Projekt für eine ungewöhnliche Erscheinung. Ein Blick über die Terrasse (oben) rahmt die Aussicht auf die nahe gelegenen Hügel.

L'articulation irrégulière des surfaces, qui varient à la fois dans leurs matériaux et leur intégration dans l'ossature partiellement en pierre, est une des caractéristiques inhabituelles de ce projet. L'image de terrasse, en haut, encadre volontairement une vue sur les collines avoisinantes.

The complexity and alternation in the use of materials seen on the exterior of the building carry through in these interior views, in particular in the glass box enclosing a tree (above left).

Die am Außenbau zu erkennende Komplexität und die Abwechslung beim Gebrauch der Materialien setzen sich auch auf den Innenansichten fort, insbesondere bei dem Glaskubus, der einen Baum umgibt (oben links).

La complexité et l'alternance dans l'utilisation des matériaux notée à l'extérieur se retrouvent dans ces vues intérieures, en particulier dans la boîte de verre contenant un arbre (en haut à gauche).

Elevations to the right and another interior view show the great variety introduced by the architect in the use of types of openings and cladding.

Die Aufrisse rechts und eine weitere Innenansicht belegen die vom Architekten durch unterschiedliche Öffnungen und Verkleidungen hervorgerufene große Vielfalt.

Les élévations de droite et une vue d'intérieur témoignent de la grande variété d'ouvertures et d'habillages introduite par l'architecte.

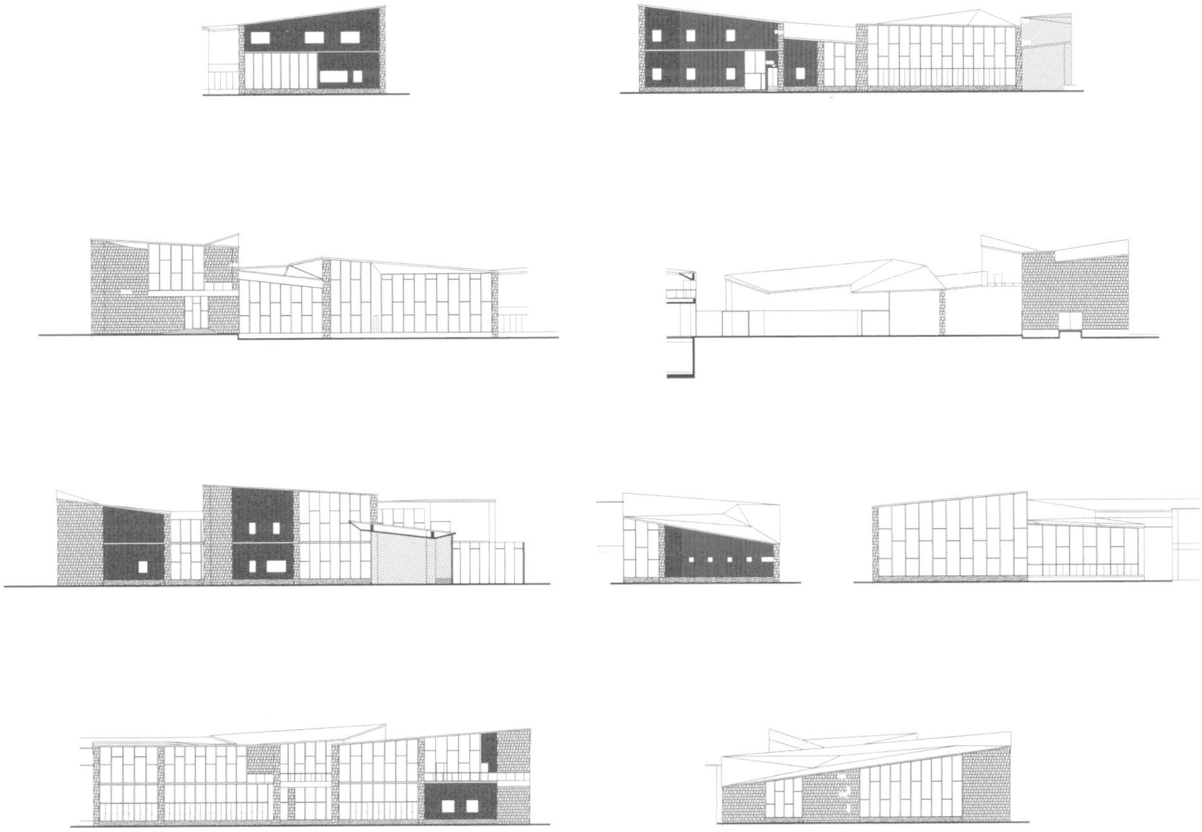

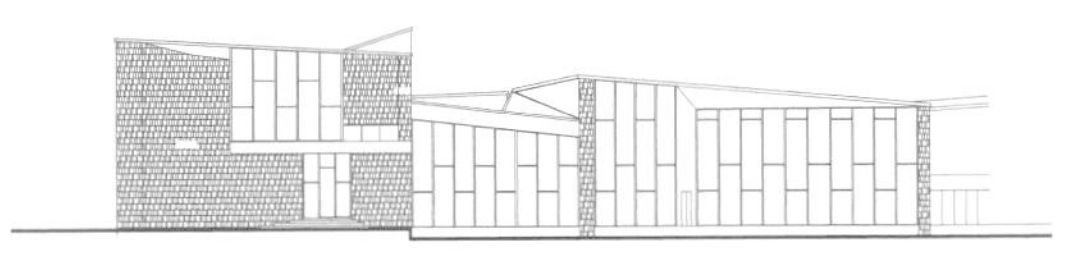
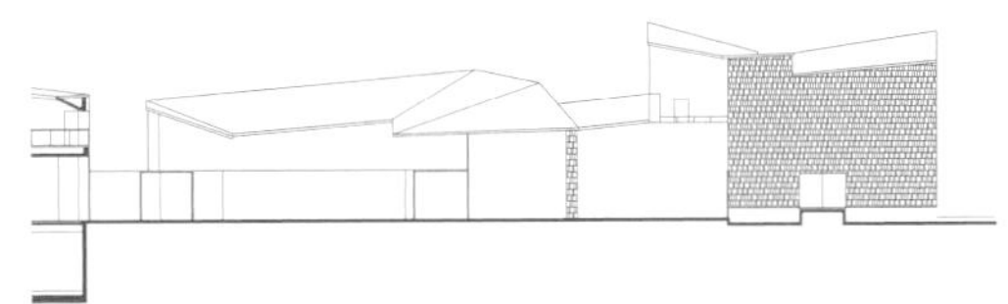
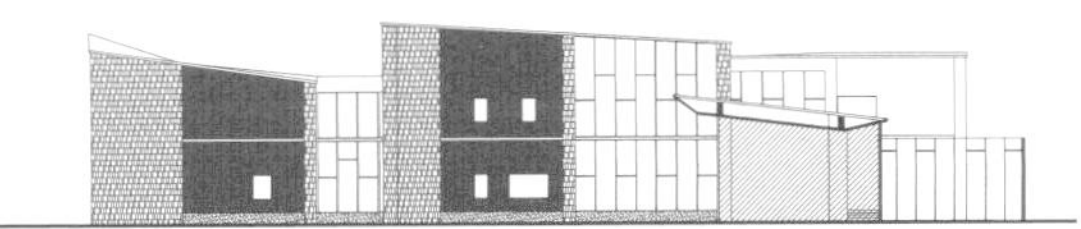
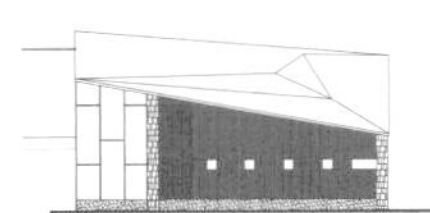
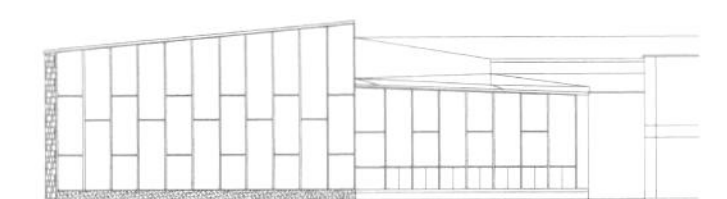

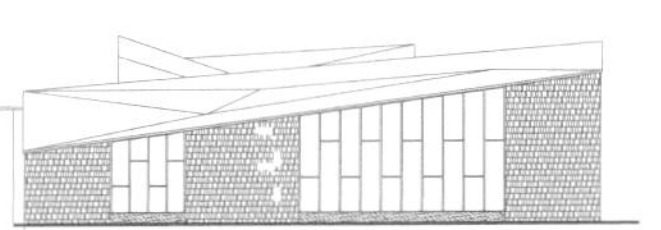

Within essentially geometric floor plans made up of an accumulation of rectangles, the structure is fragmented and enlivened from within, producing a most unexpected variety of spaces, lighting effects, and framed views of the natural surroundings.

Die geometrischen Grundrisse, die aus einer Ansammlung von Rechtecken bestehen, gliedern die Struktur des Gebäudes und beleben es von innen, was zu einer höchst überraschenden Vielfalt von Räumen, Beleuchtungseffekten und gerahmten Ansichten der umgebenden Landschaft führt.

Le plan, essentiellement géométrique, composé d'une multiplicité de rectangles, fragmente la structure et l'anime de l'intérieur pour offrir la diversité la plus inattendue d'espaces, d'effets d'éclairage et de vues cadrées sur l'environnement naturel.

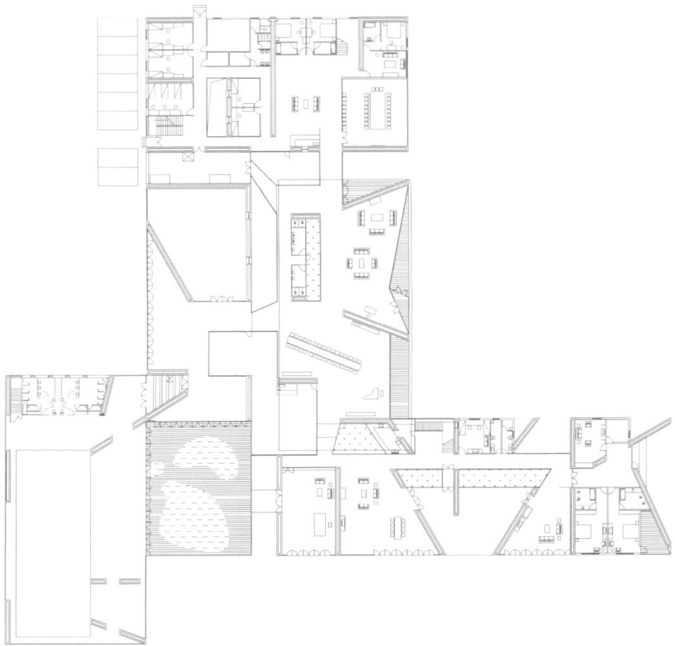

BRIDGE MUSEUM FOR POSTERS FROM THE CULTURAL REVOLUTION

ANREN, SICHUAN 2003–

FLOOR AREA: 1645 m^2
CLIENT: Chengdu Jianchuan Industrial Group
COST: not disclosed
PROJECT ARCHITECT: Lu Xiang

The architects explain that "as one of the master planners for the Jianchuan Museum Town in Anren, Sichuan, our office has been asked to develop a component of the town's infrastructure: a bridge, which also serves as the Museum for Posters from the Cultural Revolution period. Because of the juxtaposition of the bridge and the museum, this poster collection, more than 20 000 pieces and growing, inclines to be more of a public urban space and less of a private cultural institution." The intention of the project is to provide three different experiences of the river—a ground level connecting the natural and landscape elements of both riverbanks, a bridge level that combines street and museum, and a rooftop garden with skylights for the museum. 35-centimeter-diameter concrete columns "vary morphologically in response to different geological conditions." The museum structure is made essentially with concrete blocks and wood panels "to echo the accent of the vernacular architecture." The levels of the structure itself undulate "according to either natural or artificially adapted topographical conditions." Here, as in the Villa Shizilin, the architects seek to combine a vision of modernity in tune with local conditions.

Die Architekten erläutern, dass ihr Büro »als einer der leitenden Planer der Museumsstadt Jianchuan in Anren, Sichuan, aufgefordert wurde, ein Element der städtischen Infrastruktur zu gestalten: eine Brücke, die darüber hinaus als Museum für Plakate aus der Zeit der Kulturrevolution dient. Bedingt durch das Nebeneinander von Brücke und Museum hat die 20 000 Stücke umfassende und immer noch wachsende Plakatsammlung eher den Charakter eines Stadtraumes als den einer privaten Kultureinrichtung.« Das Projekt soll dem Besucher drei verschiedene Begegnungen mit dem Fluss verschaffen – ebenerdig werden die natürlichen, landschaftlichen Elemente beider Flussufer verbunden, auf Brückenhöhe treffen Straße und Museum zusammen, und der Dachgarten weist Oberlichter für das Museum auf. Die Betonpfeiler mit einem Durchmesser von 35 cm »sind aufgrund unterschiedlicher geologischer Bedingungen verschieden geformt«. Der Museumsbau besteht im Wesentlichen aus Betonblöcken und Holzplatten, »um den Charakter der hier heimischen Architektur aufzugreifen«. Die Ebenen des Bauwerks selbst verlaufen wellenförmig »entsprechend den natürlichen oder künstlich nachempfundenen topografischen Verhältnissen«. Wie im Fall der Villa Shizilin waren die Architekten auch hier bestrebt, ihre Vorstellung von Modernität mit den lokalen Bedingungen zu verbinden.

Selon l'architecte : « Comme nous étions l'une des agences d'urbanisme de la ville-musée de Jianchuan à Anren, dans le Sichuan, nous avons été chargés de l'étude de l'une des composantes des infrastructures de la ville, un pont qui devait également faire fonction de Musée d'affiches de la révolution culturelle. Du fait de cette juxtaposition, cette collection de plus de 20 000 affiches en accroissement constant devait être traitée davantage comme un espace urbain public que comme une institution culturelle privée. » Une des intentions de ce projet est d'offrir trois approches différentes du fleuve : un rez-de-chaussée qui connecte les éléments naturels du paysage des deux rives, le niveau du pont lui-même qui combine le franchissement et le musée, et celui du jardin en terrasse percée de verrières pour assurer l'éclairage naturel du musée. Les colonnes de 35 cm de diamètre « empruntent des formes variées en fonction des conditions géologiques ». La structure du musée est essentiellement en parpaings de béton et panneaux de bois, « en écho à l'architecture vernaculaire locale ». Les niveaux ondulent « en fonction des contraintes topographiques naturelles ou artificielles ». Comme dans la Villa Shizilin, les architectes ont essayé ici de combiner une vision de la modernité au contexte local.

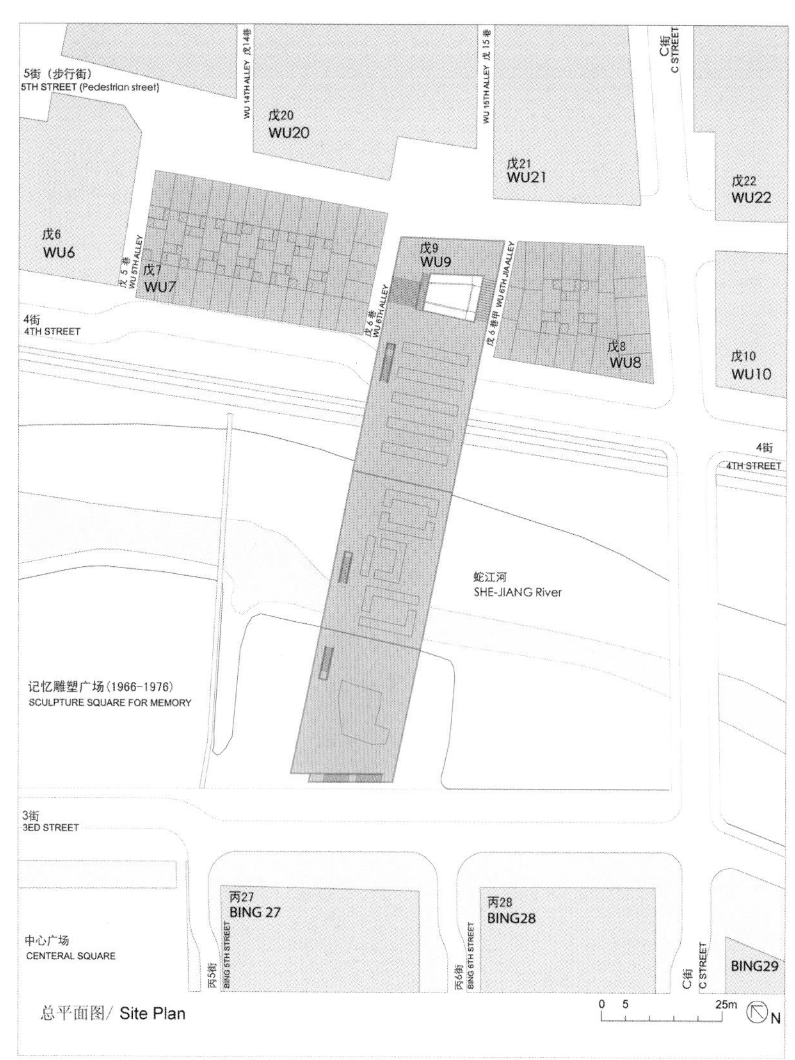

总平面图/ Site Plan

Although the idea of inhabited bridges is very old, that of creating a museum that becomes a real public space because of its assimilation with the idea of movement and passage is more original. Irregular forms and varying support columns contribute to creating a dynamic image.

Im Vergleich zu dem sehr alten Typus bewohnter Brücken wirkt der Plan, hier ein Museum zu schaffen, das aufgrund seiner Assoziation mit der Idee von Bewegung und Durchgang zu einem wirklich öffentlichen Raum wird, sehr viel origineller. Unregelmäßige Formen und unterschiedliche Stützpfeiler tragen zur dynamischen Anmutung bei.

Si l'idée d'un pont habité est très ancienne, celle d'en faire un musée qui se transforme en espace public par assimilation au mouvement et au passage est plus originale. L'irrégularité des formes et la diversité des colonnes de soutien contribuent à créer une image dynamique.

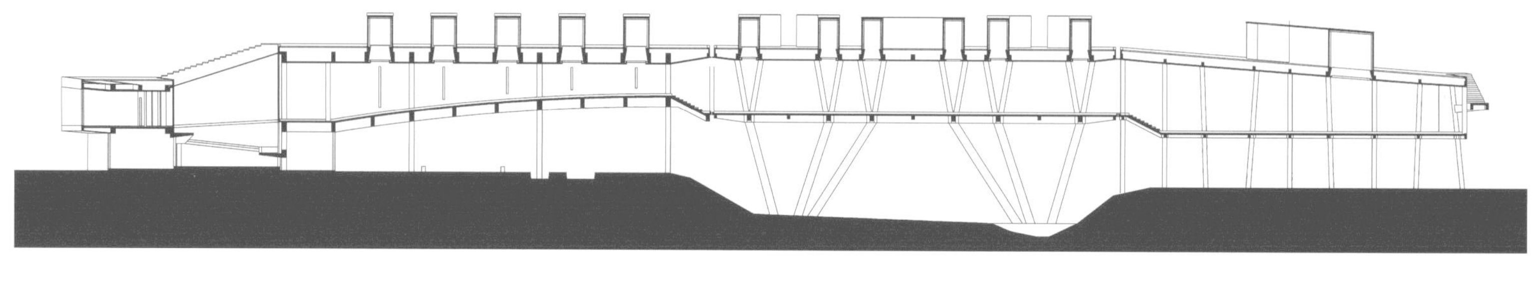

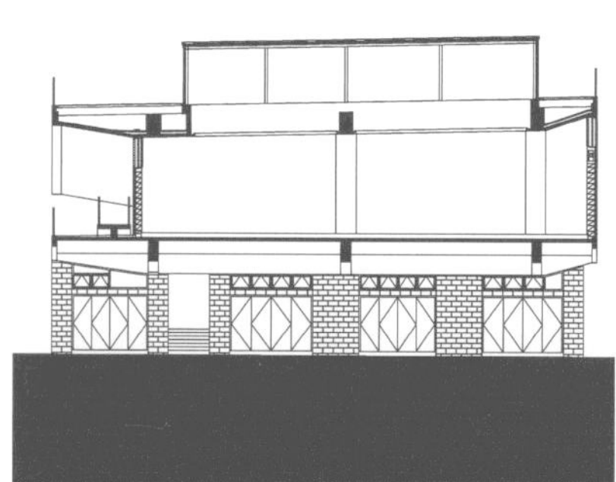

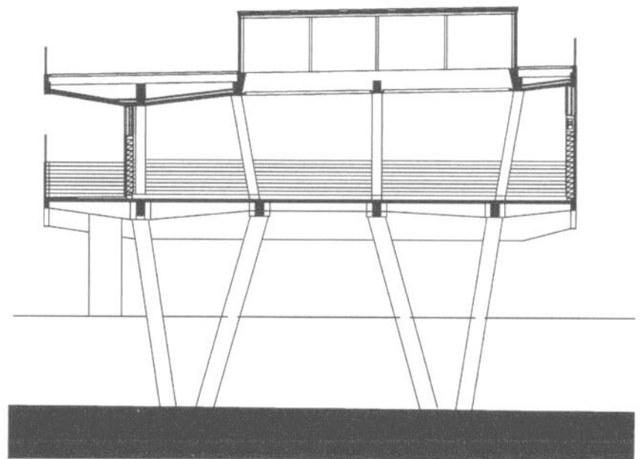

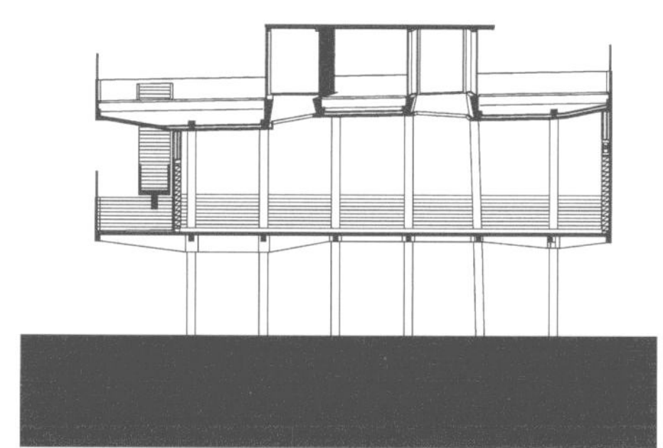

The sections above show the way the support columns of the structure vary or lean in accordance with their precise location.

Die Schnitte oben lassen erkennen, wie die Stützpfeiler des Bauwerks variieren oder sich der Neigung ihrer Umgebung anpassen.

La coupe ci-dessus montre la façon dont les colonnes de soutien varient leur inclinaison selon leur implantation.

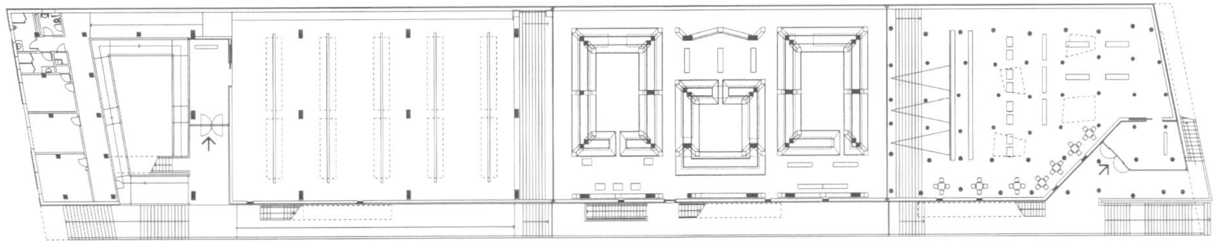

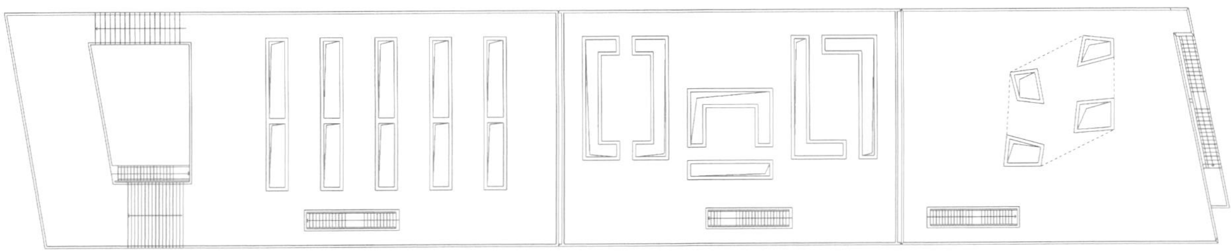

The dynamic aspects of the design are somewhat less evident in the plans, which show the form of a fairly standard parallelogram. Color and movement will surely be introduced into the exhibition spaces by the Cultural Revolution posters to be exhibited in the museum.

Die dynamischen Aspekte des Entwurfs kommen in den Grundrissen, die die Form eines Parallelogramms aufweisen, weniger zur Geltung. Mit den künftig hier gezeigten Plakaten der Kulturrevolution werden Farbe und Bewegung in die Ausstellungsräume Einzug halten.

Les aspects dynamiques de la conception sont parfois moins évidents dans les plans qui ne montrent qu'un parallélogramme assez classique. La couleur et le mouvement seront certainement introduits par les expositions d'affiches de la révolution culturelle prévues dans cet espace.

#3

AZL ATELIER ZHANGLEI

AZL
Atelier Zhanglei
Architecture Design Institute, NJU
Hankou Road 22
Nanjing, Jiangsu 210093

Tel: +86 25 8368 6146
Fax: +86 25 8359 5673
e-mail: atelierzhanglei@163.com

ZHANG LEI was born in 1964 in Jiangsu Province, whose major city is Nanjing. From 1981 to 1985, he studied architecture at the Nanjing Institute of Technology, which then went on to complete postgraduate studies at the ETH in Zurich (1992–93). He created his own office, Atelier Zhanglei, in 2000, and presently has 14 employees. He has been a Professor of Architectural Design at Nanjing University since 2000, and has also taught at the ETH and the University of Hong Kong. His major projects include: Student Dormitory, Nantong Foreign Language School, Nantong (1998–99); Pottery Studio of Nanjing Normal University (2001); Taoyuan 02 Graduate Student Dormitory, Nanjing University, Nanjing (2001–03); office building for the Xinhua Construction Company, Xinhua (2002–03); the Office and Lab Building of the Model Animal Research Center, Nanjing, published here; Staff Residence of Dongguan Institute of Technology, Dongguan (2002–04); Jianye Sport Mansion, Nanjing (2004–05); Cross Show Room, Qingpu, Shanghai (2005); No. 4 House, CIPEA, Nanjing (2005–06); and the Split House, Nanjing (2006). Current work includes the N-Park, Jiangsu Software Park, Nanjing (2006–07), and the Memorial Hall for the N4A Army, Liyang (2006–07).

MODEL ANIMAL RESEARCH CENTER

NANJING, JIANGSU 2002–03

FLOOR AREA: 7700 m²
CLIENT: Model Animal Research Center, Nanjing University
COST: € 2,5 million

Located in the Pukou High-Tech Park in Nanjing, this is a reinforced concrete and brick structure. The architect explains that the relationship between the courtyards and the other parts of this building is "somewhat similar to the spatial organization of traditional Chinese gardens." Six staircases located in a two-story-high corridor connect the different parts of the complex. "Sky windows" are located in such a way as to allow the "researchers to meet and communicate with one another in the public spaces." In describing his design philosophy, Zhang Lei writes, "Architecture is a process associated with almost all aspects in our social life today. Meanwhile, it can be as abstract as the most fundamental spatial enclosure, confronting all the basic problems it must solve in terms of adaptability and helping us to establish specific visual order in this chaotic world. The basic principle that the design should be concerned about is solving problems with the most reasonable and direct way of construction, responding to requirements of adaptability with ordinary materials and construction methods, as well as trying to find out the potential visual expressiveness from among ordinary materials. This should further become a work-strategy applicable to the large-scale construction in the rapid development of Chinese urbanization today, as well as benefiting the control of consumption of limited human resources."

Dieses aus Stahlbeton und Backstein errichtete Gebäude befindet sich im Hightechpark Pukou in Nanking. Der Architekt erläutert, dass die Beziehung zwischen den Innenhöfen und den übrigen Teilen des Gebäudes »etwas der räumlichen Gliederung traditioneller chinesischer Gärten ähnelt«. Sechs Treppen, die in einem zweistöckigen Korridor untergebracht sind, verbinden die verschiedenen Teile des Komplexes. Sogenannte Himmelsfenster gestatten es den Forschern, »sich in öffentlichen Bereichen zu treffen und miteinander zu kommunizieren«. Zhang Lei beschreibt seine Entwurfsphilosophie mit den folgenden Worten: »Architektur ist eine mit nahezu sämtlichen Aspekten unseres heutigen sozialen Lebens verbundener Prozess. Mittlerweile kann sie so abstrakt sein wie die elementarste räumliche Einfassung; konfrontiert mit den fundamentalen Problemen muss sie anwendbare Lösungen finden und uns helfen, in dieser chaotischen Welt eine spezifische visuelle Ordnung zu schaffen. Das Grundprinzip eines Entwurfs sollte es sein, Probleme mit dem vernünftigsten und direktesten Bauverfahren zu lösen. Dabei soll den Vorgaben des Einsatzes von gewöhnlichen Materialien und Bauverfahren entsprochen werden, ebenso wie es auch darum geht, die potenzielle visuelle Ausdruckskraft gewöhnlicher Materialien auszuloten. Dies soll darüber hinaus zu einer Arbeitsstrategie führen, die sich auf die großen Bauvorhaben im Zuge der rasanten Urbanisierung Chinas anwenden lässt und auch der Kontrolle in der Begrenzung menschlicher Ressourcen zugute kommen.«

Ce bâtiment en béton armé et brique est situé dans le Parc High-Tech de Pukou à Nankin. Pour l'architecte, la relation entre les cours et les autres parties est « un peu similaire à l'organisation spatiale des jardins chinois traditionnels ». Six escaliers partant d'un corridor de deux niveaux de haut réunissent les différentes composantes de l'ensemble. Des « verrières » sont implantées de façon à permettre aux « chercheurs de se rencontrer et de communiquer dans les espaces publics ». Selon la philosophie de conception de Zhang Lei, « l'architecture est un processus lié à pratiquement tous les aspects de la vie sociale d'aujourd'hui. Mais, en même temps, dans sa confrontation à tous les problèmes de base qu'elle est censée résoudre en terme d'adaptabilité, elle peut être aussi abstraite que l'enclos spatial le plus primitif et nous aider à établir un ordre visuel spécifique dans un monde chaotique. Le principe de base dont doit se préoccuper le projet est de résoudre les problèmes par le mode de construction le plus raisonnable et le plus direct, répondant aux attentes d'adaptabilité au moyen de matériaux et de méthodes de construction ordinaires en essayant d'en exploiter le potentiel visuel d'expressivité. Ce devrait être une stratégie de travail applicable aux projets de construction à grande échelle que connaît le développement rapide de l'urbanisation chinoise, et faciliter une consommation plus sensée de ressources humaines limitées. »

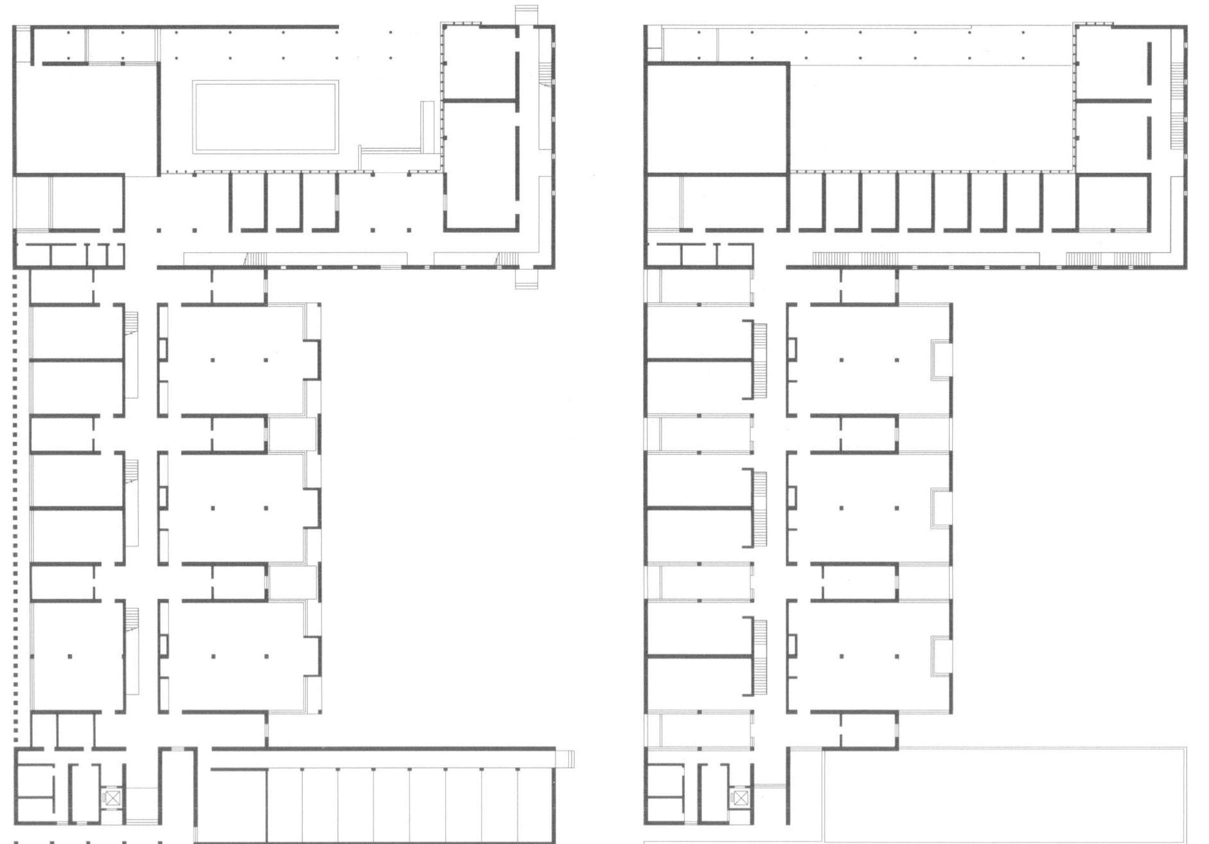

A strict, almost minimalist design nonetheless leaves room for a good number of spatial surprises and unexpected, big openings. Thin columns contribute to an impression of lightness, contrasting with large, blank walls.

Das strenge, fast minimalistische Design ermöglicht dennoch eine erfreuliche Vielzahl räumlicher Überraschungen und unerwartet großer Öffnungen. Schlanke Pfeiler, die mit großflächigen, leeren Wänden kontrastieren, tragen zu dem Eindruck von Leichtigkeit bei.

La conception stricte, presque minimaliste, laisse néanmoins la place à un certain nombre de surprises spatiales et à de grandes ouvertures que l'on n'attendait pas. De fines colonnes, contrastant avec de grands murs aveugles, contribuent à donner une impression de légèreté

#4

EDGE DESIGN INSTITUTE

EDGE DESIGN INSTITUTE LTD.
Suite 1604, Eastern Harbour Center
28 Hoi Chak Street, Quarry Bay
Hong Kong 510170

Tel: +852 2802 6212
Fax: +852 2802 6213
e-mail: edgeltd@netvigator.com
Web: www.edge.hk.com

GARY CHANG was born in Hong Kong in 1962 and obtained his B.A. in Architectural Studies (1985) and B.Arch (1987) from Hong Kong University. He founded EDGE in 1994 and renamed the firm EDGE Design Institute in 2003. Since 1995, he has taught at the University of Hong Kong and a number of other institutions. Over the years, his involvement has increased to giving lectures at conferences and various institutions around the world, such as in China, Taiwan, Singapore, Malaysia, India, Japan, Italy, Holland, Slovenia, France, Austria, the UK, and the United States. In the past decade, his cultural and educational commissions have included such varied works as the Suitcase House, published here; Domestic Express (a holiday home in the suburbs of Moscow); his own 32-square meter apartment; the Kung Fu Tea Set Alessi; a Workstation for Ogilvy & Mather Asia Pacific; the Broadway Cinematheque in Hong Kong; a recalibration of the Hong Kong Arts Centre; the Mega-iAdvantage Data Centre Building in Hong Kong; and numerous other projects, including apartment and house designs for private clients. His commercial commissions include clubhouses, retail outlets, hotels, restaurants, offices, as well as yacht and aircraft interiors.

SUITCASE HOUSE
BADALING-SHUIGUAN, BEIJING 2000-01

CLIENT: SOHO China Ltd.
LENGTH x WIDTH: 43.2 m x 4.8 m (ratio 9:1)
TOTAL FLOOR AREA: 260 m^2
COST: not disclosed
DESIGN DIRECTOR: Gary Chang
DESIGN TEAM: Andrew Holt, Howard Chang, Popeye Tsang, Yee Lee

The Suitcase House is part of the Commune by the Great Wall development in which 12 young Asian architects, including such figures as Kengo Kuma, participated. The architect explains that "casting a question mark on the proverbial image of the house, the Suitcase House Hotel attempts to rethink the nature of intimacy, privacy, spontaneity and flexibility. It is a simple demonstration of the desire for ultimate adaptability, in pursuit of a proscenium for infinite scenarios, a plane of sensual (p)leisure." A series of compartments are concealed by a "landscape of pneumatically assisted floor panels," allowing only required elements to have a spatial presence in the visible house. Aside from the bedroom, bathroom, kitchen, or storage areas, there is a meditation chamber with a glazed floor offering views of the valley below, a music chamber, library, study, and sauna. According to the needs of the occupants, when all of the sliding partitions are open, the indoor space measures 43.2 x 4.8 meters. The outer layer of the house is made of full-height double-glazed folding doors, with a series of screens inside. The actual appearance of the house is thus altered according to the way its inhabitants wish to use it. A concrete base houses a pantry, maid's quarters, boiler room, and sauna. The Great Wall of China is visible from the major spaces of the house.

Das »Kofferhaus« ist Teil des Bauvorhabens »Commune by the Great Wall«, an dem zwölf junge asiatische Architekten, darunter Kengo Kuma, beteiligt sind. Dem Architekten zufolge »versucht das Kofferhaushotel, den Charakter von Intimität, Privatheit, Spontaneität und Flexibilität neu zu überdenken, indem es das sprichwörtliche Bild des Hauses mit einem Fragezeichen versieht. Es geht um eine einfache Demonstration des Wunsches nach höchster Anpassungsfähigkeit, auf der Suche nach einer Bühne für unendliche Szenarien, einer Ebene sinnlichen Wohlbefindens.« Eine Reihe von Zellen wird durch »eine Landschaft aus pneumatisch gesteuerten Bodenplatten verdeckt«, die es nur notwendigen Elementen gestattet, im Haus eine räumliche Präsenz einzunehmen. Neben Schlafzimmer, Bad, Küche und Abstellflächen, gibt es einen Meditationsraum mit Glasboden, der Ausblicke auf das unten liegende Tal erlaubt, Musikraum, Bibliothek, Arbeitszimmer und Sauna. Entsprechend der Bedürfnisse der Bewohner misst der Innenraum, wenn sämtliche verschiebbaren Raumteiler geöffnet sind, 43.2 x 4.8 m. Die äußere Wandschale des Hauses besteht aus deckenhohen, doppelt verglasten Flügeltüren mit einer Reihe von Trennwänden auf der Innenseite. Somit ändert sich das tatsächliche Erscheinungsbild des Hauses entsprechend der jeweiligen Nutzung durch seine Bewohner. In dem Betonsockel sind ein Vorratsraum, Dienstbotenzimmer, Heizungsraum und Sauna untergebracht. Von den Haupträumen des Hauses aus ist die Chinesische Mauer zu sehen.

La « maison-valise » fait partie du projet de la « Commune près de la Grande Muraille » auquel douze architectes asiatiques, dont des célébrités comme Kengo Kuma, ont participé. Pour son architecte : « En plaçant un point d'interrogation sur l'image traditionnelle de la maison, le Suitcase House Hotel tente de repenser la nature même de l'intimité, de la spontanéité et de la flexibilité. C'est une simple démonstration du désir d'une adaptabilité ultime, à la recherche d'une mise en scène de scénari infiniment variés, un plan ouvert aux loisirs/plaisirs sensuels. » Une série de compartiments se dissimule dans une composition de panneaux de sol « à vérins pneumatiques » qui font que seuls les éléments dont on a besoin prennent une présence spatiale visible. En dehors de la chambre, de la salle de bains, de la cuisine et de rangements, on trouve une pièce de méditation à sol vitré d'où l'on a une vue sur la vallée en contrebas, un salon de musique, une bibliothèque, un bureau et un sauna. Selon les besoins des occupants, lorsque toutes les cloisons coulissantes sont ouvertes, l'espace intérieur peut mesurer jusqu'à 43.2 x 4.8 m. L'enveloppe extérieure de la maison se compose de portes pliables toute hauteur à double vitrage dans lesquelles sont insérés des écrans. Concrètement, l'aspect de la maison peut ainsi être modifié selon l'utilisation qu'en font ses habitants. Le socle en béton accueille un office, un studio pour domestique, une chaufferie et le sauna. La Grande Muraille de Chine est visible des principales pièces de la maison.

Lifted off the ground on a concrete base, the long rectangular volume is cantilevered over the site on one side. All of its surfaces, including the roof, are intended to be flexible, allowing for multiple uses.

Der auf einer Betonplatte vom Boden abgehobene, lang gestreckte, rechteckige Baukörper kragt auf einer Seite über die Grundstücksgrenze aus. Sämtliche Flächen, einschließlich des Dachs, sind flexibel, um Mehrfachnutzungen zu erlauben.

Suspendu au-dessus du sol sur son socle en béton, le long volume rectangulaire se retrouve d'un côté en porte-à-faux au-dessus du terrain. Tous les plans, y compris celui du toit, sont mobiles pour s'adapter à de multiples fonctions.

Seen from the angle below, the house has an ephemeral or temporary feeling about it, as though it could be placed on the back of a truck and driven away.

Aus dem unten abgebildeten Blickwinkel gesehen, mutet das Haus wie ein Provisorium an – so als könne man es auf einen Lastwagen laden und mit ihm davonfahren.

Vue en contre-plongée, la maison donne une impression d'éphémère ou de temporaire, comme si elle allait être chargée sur une remorque et transportée ailleurs.

Movable floor panels allow for numerous configurations of the internal space, ranging from a blank surface to a series of varied, more private indentations that can be closed at will.

Bewegliche Bodenplatten erlauben zahlreiche Variationen der inneren Aufteilung – von einer leeren Fläche bis zu einer Abfolge von eher privaten Räumen, die sich beliebig verschließen lassen.

Des panneaux de sol mobiles permettent de multiples configurations du volume intérieur, du plan totalement vide à une série d'espaces plus privés qui peuvent se fermer à volonté.

Although non-load-bearing walls are actually rather temporary affairs in any case, the architect here transgresses the idea of the wall altogether. Walls (and floors) become interchangeable and movable, and few spaces have fixed functions.

Nicht tragende Wände sind in jedem Fall eher temporäre Elemente, hier aber kommt der Architekt gänzlich von der traditionellen Vorstellung von Wand ab. Wände (und Böden) sind austauschbar und beweglich, und nur wenige Räume haben festgelegte Funktionen.

Si les murs, non porteurs, sont par nature temporaires, l'architecte transgresse ici l'idée même de mur. Ceux-ci – et les sols également – deviennent interchangeables et mobiles. Quelques rares espaces sont affectés à une fonction déterminée.

Privacy for the bathroom space is provided by panels that lift up, while curtains and a number of pieces of pastel-colored furniture give further variety to the interior.

Hochgestellte Platten gewährleisten Sichtschutz für das Badezimmer, während Vorhänge und eine Reihe pastellfarbener Möbelstücke im Inneren für Abwechslung sorgen.

L'intimité des salles de bains est assurée par des panneaux soulevés par des vérins. Des rideaux et un certain nombre d'éléments de mobilier de couleur pastel participent à la diversité spatiale.

FAKE DESIGN

AI WEI WEI / FAKE DESIGN
258 Caochangdi
Chaoyang District
Beijing 100015

Tel/Fax: +86 10 8456 4194
e-mail: aiweiwei.fake@gmail.com
Web: www.aiweiwei.com

The artist-architect AI WEI WEI was born in 1957 in Beijing, the son of the well-known poet Ai Qing. In 1978, after a 20-year period during which his family was banished from the capital for political reasons, Ai Wei Wei returned to Beijing to study at the Film Institute. He went to New York in 1981 and studied at the Parson's School of Design. He returned to China in 1994 and opened his studio in Shanghai in 1999. His 400-square-meter home-studio, with a 1300-square-meter courtyard made of brick, was his first widely published work. It was built with the help of local workers. In 2000, he organized the city's first independent art biennial, under the evocative title "Fuck Off." His firm, FAKE Design, currently has nine employees and works on landscape and interior-design as well as architecture. Their design philosophy is "Make it simple." They participated with Herzog & de Meuron in the 2002 competition for the Beijing Stadium intended for the 2008 Olympic Games. Ai Wei Wei is the coordinator and a participant in the Jinhua Architecture Park. Other recent work includes the Gowhere Restaurant, a renovation and construction project located in Beijing (2004), and the 9 Boxes-Taihe Complex, Beijing (2004). Current work includes the Shulang Factory, Yantai, and the Treehouse, Waterville, Yunnan (in collaboration with HHF Architects).

YIWU RIVER BANK
JINDONG DISTRICT, JINHUA, ZHEJIANG 2002-04

SITE AREA: 1 595 000 m² LENGTH: 5.8 km
WIDTH: 200–350 m
CLIENT: Construction Authority, Jindong District, Jinhua
COST: not disclosed TEAM: Lu Jing, Sun Zhipeng, Ma Yandong

Jinhua, located southwest of Shanghai, is the birthplace of Ai Wei Wei's father, and, in 2002, the city asked the artist-architect to design a monument to Ai Qing on the south bank of the Yiwu River. The success of this project led the city to offer Ai Wei Wei the possibility to design the Architecture Park on the north bank of the river together with the Ai Qing culture park. The landscape design of the south riverbank started in February 2002, and lasted for one and a half years. By early 2004, the construction work using local granite and covering 5.8 kilometers of the south bank of the river was completed. As Ai Wei Wei explains, "The purpose of this comprehensive project is to resume the traditional relationship between man and water neglected in the past; to make the river an active part of the city; to revive the use of economical traditional local materials and to bring a better environment to urban life." In practical terms, the structure is intended to prevent potential flood damage at higher standards than those afforded by the previous riverbank installations.

Im südwestlich von Shanghai gelegenen Jinhua wurde Ai Wei Weis Vater, Ai Qing, geboren. 2002 bat die Stadt den Künstlerarchitekten, seinem Vater zu Ehren am Südufer des Flusses Yiwu ein Denkmal zu errichten. Nach erfolgreichem Abschluss dieses Projekts bot die Stadt Ai Wei Wei die Möglichkeit, am Nordufer des Flusses einen Architekturpark gemeinsam mit dem Ai-Qing-Kulturpark zu entwerfen. Im Februar 2002 wurde die landschaftliche Gestaltung des südlichen Flussufers in Angriff genommen und nach anderthalb Jahren abgeschlossen. Anfang 2004 waren die Bauarbeiten, die sich über 5,8 km des Südufers erstrecken, mit heimischem Granit beendet. Ai Wei Wei erläutert dazu: »Der Zweck dieses umfassenden Projekts bestand darin, die in der Vergangenheit vernachlässigte traditionelle Beziehung zwischen Mensch und Fluss wieder aufzunehmen, den Fluss zu einem aktiven Teil der Stadt zu machen, die Verwendung traditioneller heimischer Materialien wiederzubeleben und für das Stadtleben ein besseres Umfeld zu schaffen.« In praktischer Hinsicht soll das Bauwerk bei möglichen Überflutungen einen besseren Schutz vor Schäden gewährleisten als die früheren Uferanlagen.

Jinhua, ville située au sud-ouest de Shanghai et lieu de naissance du poète Ai Qing, père d'Ai Wei Wei, a demandé en 2002 à l'artiste-architecte de concevoir un monument à celui-ci sur la rive sud du fleuve Yiwù. La réussite de cette réalisation incita la municipalité à lui confier la conception d'un Parc d'architecture sur la rive nord ainsi que du Parc culturel Ai Qing. La réalisation du projet de la rive sud a débuté en février 2002 et a duré un an et demi. Les travaux qui concernent 5,8 km de rives ont été achevés début 2004 et ont fait appel à du granit local. Pour l'architecte : « L'objectif de ce projet d'ensemble est de faire revivre la relation traditionnelle entre l'homme et l'eau négligée dans le passé, redonner un rôle actif au fleuve dans la ville, refaire une place aux matériaux traditionnels économiques locaux et créer un meilleur environnement pour la vie urbaine. » Concrètement, cette structure devrait permettre de mieux limiter l'effet des inondations que les précédentes installations.

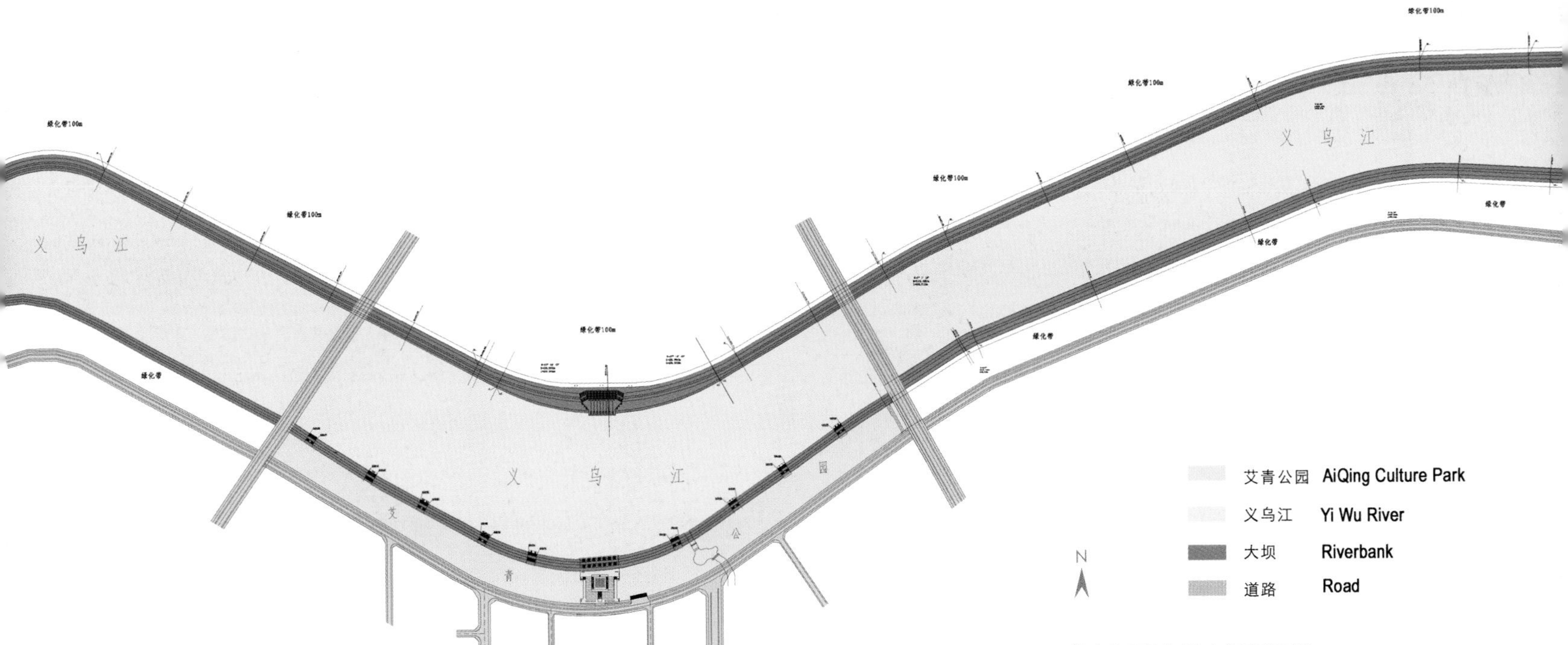

	艾青公园	AiQing Culture Park
	义乌江	Yi Wu River
	大坝	Riverbank
	道路	Road

义乌江南北岸大坝平面图

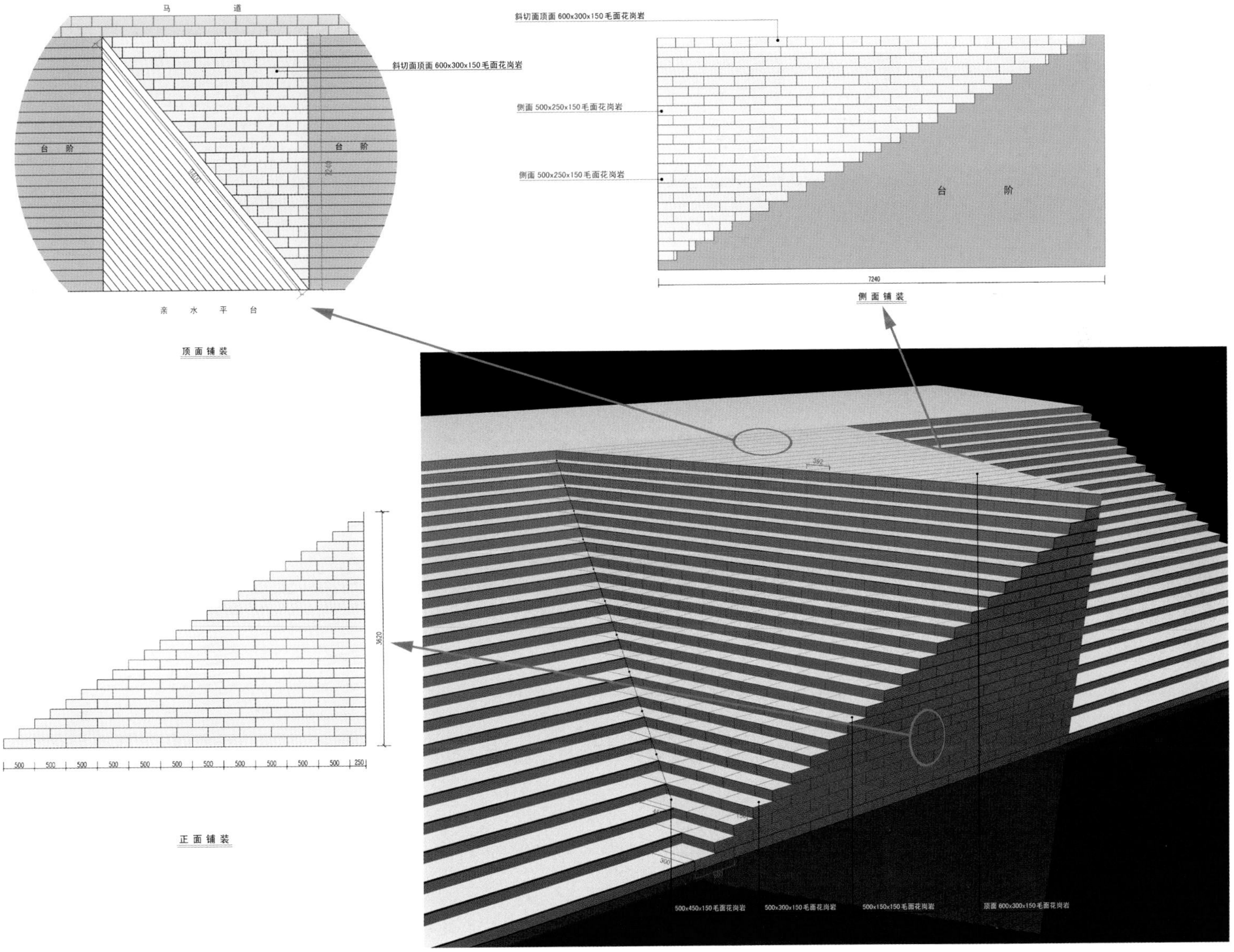

顶面铺装

侧面铺装

正面铺装

COURTYARD 105
CAOCHANGDI, BEIJING 2004–05

SITE AREA: 3044 m^2
EXISTING BUILDING AREA: 1322 m^2
NEW BUILDING AREA: 281 m^2
CLIENT: Mao Ran COST: not disclosed

Located in Caochangdi, an eastern suburb of Beijing, where Ai Wei Wei has his studio, Courtyard 105 is a former company office and warehouse converted into a studio with living areas, offices, and rehearsal space. As Ai Wei Wei says, "We kept most of the existing construction. The renovation of the northern part was carried out mainly by adding a gray brick wall to the old façades and adjusting the windows, so as to keep them consistent with the new extension. The former condition of the courtyard," he concludes, "reflected its surroundings, temporary, cheap and ready to be either rebuilt or torn down at any moment. The design simply follows these economical and practical principles of reality. The new order divides the courtyard according to function; a clear relationship is established for the different parts of the buildings, so they can show respect for each other." Simple wooden fences and austere brick façades mark the project and immediately impart Ai Wei Wei's sense of architecture without any decorative elements. A second project, Courtyard 104, adjacent to the north side of Courtyard 105, was completed in 2006. Made with brick and exposed construction materials, the second project retains the pragmatic spirit of the earlier intervention on this site.

Bei dem in Caochangdi, einem östlichen Vorort von Peking, gelegenen Hof 105, in dem sich Ai Wei Weis Studio befindet, handelt es sich um früher als Büro und Lagerhaus genutzte Liegenschaften, die in ein Studio mit Wohnfläche, Büros und Probenräumen umgewandelt wurden. Ai Wei Wei erläutert: »Wir behielten einen Großteil der vorhandenen Anlage bei. Bei der Renovierung des Nordteils ging es in erster Linie um das Verblenden der alten Fassaden mit einer grauen Backsteinwand und die Anpassung der Fenster an den neuen Anbau. Der frühere Zustand des Hofs spiegelte die Umgebung wider – provisorisch, billig und bereit, entweder neu gebaut oder abgerissen zu werden. Der Entwurf folgt einfach diesen von der Realität diktierten wirtschaftlichen und praktischen Prinzipien. Die neue Ordnung unterteilt den Hof nach Funktionen; die verschiedenen Teile des Gebäudes wurden in eine klare Beziehung zueinander gesetzt, so dass sie sich respektieren können.« Einfache Holzzäune und nüchterne Backsteinfassaden kennzeichnen das Projekt und künden unmittelbar von Ai Wei Weis Gespür für eine Architektur ohne schmückende Elemente. Hof 104, ein an die Nordseite von Hof 105 angrenzendes zweites Projekt, wurde 2006 fertiggestellt. Das mit Backstein und freiliegenden Baumaterialien errichtete zweite Projekt bewahrt den pragmatischen Geist seines Vorgängers.

Situé à Caochangli, une banlieue de l'est de Pékin où Ai Wei Wei possède son agence, Courtyard 105 est un ensemble entrepôt-bureaux transformé en studio, bureaux et espace de répétition. Comme l'explique Wei Wei : « Nous avons conservé la plus grande partie des constructions existantes. La rénovation de la partie nord consiste essentiellement en l'adjonction d'un mur de brique grise sur les anciennes façades et à l'ajustement du fenêtrage pour l'accorder à l'extension nouvelle. L'état initial de la cour était celui de l'environnement local, pauvre, temporaire, sur le point d'être démoli et reconstruit à tout moment. Le projet s'adapte simplement à cette réalité économique et pratique. La nouvelle organisation divise la cour selon les fonctions. Une relation claire est établie entre les différentes parties du bâtiment de telle façon qu'elles se respectent mutuellement. » De simples clôtures en bois et d'austères façades en brique caractérisent ce projet et expriment le penchant d'Ai Wei Wei pour une architecture sans ornement décoratif. Un second projet, Courtyard 104, adjacent au côté nord de la Courtyard 105 a été achevé en 2006. En brique et matériaux de construction laissés apparents, il conserve l'esprit pragmatique de la première intervention.

HERZOG & DE MEURON

HERZOG & DE MEURON
Rheinschanze 6
4056 Basel
Switzerland

Tel: +41 61 385 5757
Fax: +41 61 385 5758
e-mail: info@herzogdemeuron.com

JACQUES HERZOG and PIERRE DE MEURON, were both born in Basel in 1950. They received degrees in architecture at the ETH in Zurich in 1975, after studying with Aldo Rossi, and founded their firm Herzog & de Meuron in Basel in 1978. Harry Gugger and Christine Binswanger joined the practice as partners in 1991 and 1994 respectively, followed by Robert Hösl and Ascan Mergenthaler in 2004 and Stefan Marbach in 2006. Their built work includes the Ricola Storage Building in Laufen (1987), the Antipodes I Student Housing at the Université de Bourgogne, Dijon (1991–92); the Goetz Collection, a gallery for a private collection of contemporary art in Munich (1991–92); and the Ricola Europe Factory in Mulhouse (1993). Most notably they were chosen early in 1995 to design the new Tate Gallery extension for contemporary art, situated in the Bankside Power Station, on the Thames opposite St Paul's Cathedral, which opened in May 2000. They were also short-listed in the competition for the new design of the Museum of Modern Art in New York (1997). More recently, they have built the Prada Aoyama Epicenter, Tokyo (2001–03); the Forum 2004 Building and Plaza, Barcelona (2002–04); Allianz Arena, Munich (2002–05); the De Young Museum, San Francisco, California (2002–05); and the Walker Art Center, Expansion of the Museum and Cultural Center, Minneapolis, Minnesota (2003–05). They are presently working on the CaixaForum-Madrid; the Elbphilharmonie, Philharmonic Hall in Hamburg; and the National Stadium, the Main Stadium for the 2008 Olympic Games in Beijing, published here. Herzog & de Meuron have been awarded the Royal Gold Medal 2007 by the Royal Institute of British Architects (RIBA) in London.

BEIJING NATIONAL STADIUM

BEIJING 2003–07

SITE AREA: 20.29 hectares
FLOOR AREA: 258 000 m²
DIMENSIONS: 320 m (N-S) x 300 m (E-W) x 69 m (maximum height)
CLIENT: National Stadium Co. Ltd. COST: $ 422 million
ARCHITECTURAL DESIGN: Herzog & de Meuron, Basel, Switzerland
PROJECT TEAM PARTNERS: Jacques Herzog, Pierre de Meuron, Stefan Marbach
PROJECT ARCHITECTS: Mia Hägg (associate), Tobias Winkelmann, Thomas Polster
ENGINEERING AND SPORTS ARCHITECTURE: China Architectural Design & Research Group, Beijing, China; Ove Arup & Partners Hong Kong Ltd., Kowloon, Hong Kong; Arup Sports, London, United Kingdom
COLLABORATION: Ai Wei Wei (artistic advisor)

Herzog & de Meuron were selected for this project subsequent to a 2002 competition organized by the Beijing Municipal Planning Commission. The almost circular design optimizes viewing for the 91 000 seats planned for the Olympic Games. The architects describe the structure as follows: "The bowl superstructure consists of *in situ* concrete. The primary structure of the roof is independent of the bowl structure and is conceived as a series of steel space frames wrapped around the bowl. The overall depth of the structure is 12 meters. The spaces between the members will be filled with ETFE foil." Façade and structure are identical in this instance, in a form likened by the architects to a bird's nest of interwoven twigs. As the architects write, "The spatial effect of the stadium is novel and radical and yet simple and of an almost archaic immediacy. Its appearance is pure structure." Soccer games and athletic events will be held in the stadium, which will be the venue for the opening and closing ceremonies of the 2008 Olympic Games. Set on the Olympic Green designed by Sasaki Associates, the stadium is also not far from Pei Zhu's Digital Beijing control and data center for the Games.

Herzog & de Meuron wurden nach einem 2002 vom kommunalen Pekinger Planungsausschuss ausgeschriebenen Wettbewerb für dieses Projekt ausgewählt. Ihr nahezu kreisförmiger Entwurf gewährleistet für die geplanten 91 000 Sitzplätze optimale Sichtverhältnisse. Die Architekten beschreiben den Bau wie folgt: »Die Aufbauten des Stadions bestehen aus Ortbeton. Die Primärkonstruktion des Daches ist unabhängig von der Konstruktion des Stadionrunds und als stählernes Rahmentragwerk konzipiert, das die Schüssel umgibt. Die Gesamthöhe des Bauwerks beträgt 12 m. Die Zwischenräume zwischen den Bauteilen werden mit ETFE-Folie [Ethylentetrafluorethylen] gefüllt.« In diesem Fall sind Fassade und Baukörper identisch in einer Form, die von den Architekten mit einem Vogelnest aus miteinander verflochtenen Zweigen verglichen wird. Dazu die Architekten: »Die Raumwirkung des Stadions ist neuartig und radikal und doch einfach und von einer fast archaischen Unmittelbarkeit. Die Erscheinungsform ist pure Konstruktion.« In dem Stadion, dem Austragungsort der Eröffnungs- und Schlusszeremonie der Olympischen Spiele 2008, werden Fußballspiele und andere Sportereignisse stattfinden. Inmitten der von Sasaki Associates gestalteten olympischen Grünanlage gelegen, befindet sich das Stadion überdies in der Nähe von Pei Zhus Kontroll- und Datenzentrum der Spiele.

Herzog & de Meuron ont été sélectionnés pour ce projet à l'issue d'un concours organisé en 2002 par la Commission municipale de l'urbanisme de Pékin. Le plan presque circulaire optimise la vue des 91 000 sièges de ce stade construit pour les Jeux olympiques. Les architectes décrivent ainsi leur projet : « La superstructure en forme de coupe est en béton coulé in situ. La structure primaire de la couverture, indépendante de la coupe, est constituée d'une série d'ossatures tridimensionnelles en acier enveloppées autour de celle-ci. La profondeur d'ensemble de la structure est de 12 m. Les espaces vides entre les poutres seront fermés par un film ETFE. » La façade et la structure forment donc un seul et même objet d'une forme que les architectes comparent à un nid d'oiseaux en brindilles entrelacées. « L'effet spatial du stade est novateur, radical mais simple cependant et d'une immédiateté presque archaïque. Son aspect est celui d'une structure pure. » Des matches de football et des compétitions d'athlétisme se dérouleront dans ce stade qui sera le site des cérémonies d'ouverture et de clôture des Jeux de 2008. Dressé sur la Pelouse olympique dessinée par Sasaki & Associates, il est à proximité du Centre de contrôle et d'informatique des Jeux de Pékin conçu par Pei Zhu.

SUPERIOR CLUB
东方资通
online

Although it is very much an urban structure, the stadium appears in these images almost to be part of a natural setting – pleading no doubt for the architects' vision of an "archaic immediacy." Plans show an almost circular configuration despite the more pronounced oval of the field.

Obgleich es sich bei dem Stadion um einen urbanen Baukörper handelt, wirkt es auf diesen Bildern fast wie ein Teil der Landschaft, offenkundig in der Absicht, die Vision des Architekten von einer »archaischen Unmittelbarkeit« deutlich zu machen. Ungeachtet des ovalen Spielfelds ist auf den Plänen eine fast kreisrunde Form zu erkennen.

Bien qu'il s'agisse d'une construction urbaine, le stade semble ici faire presque partie de l'environnement naturel, sans doute pour défendre la vision des architectes de l'e « immédiateté archaïque ». Si le terrain de jeu est nettement ovale, la configuration d'ensemble est presque circulaire.

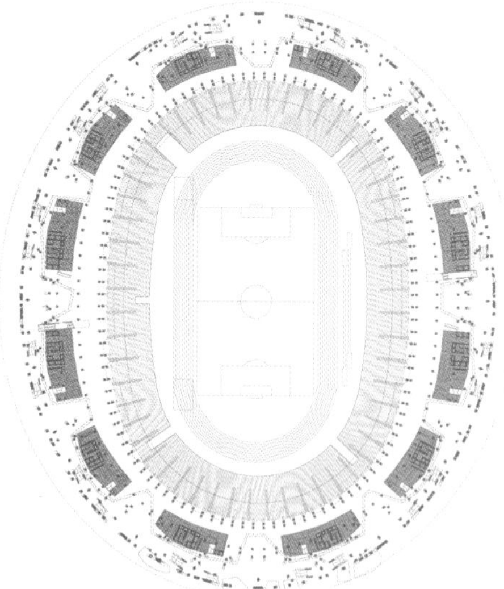

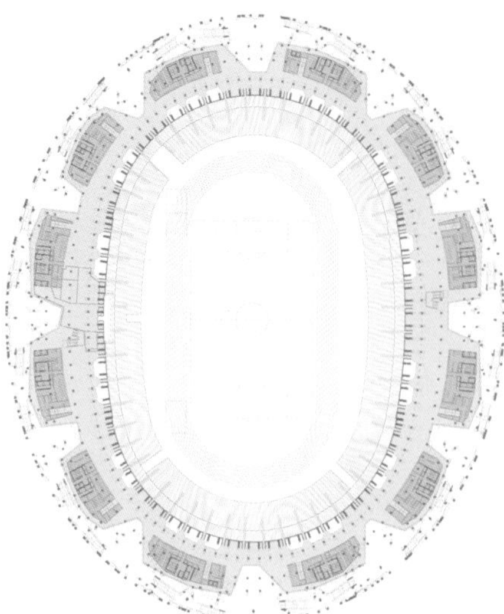

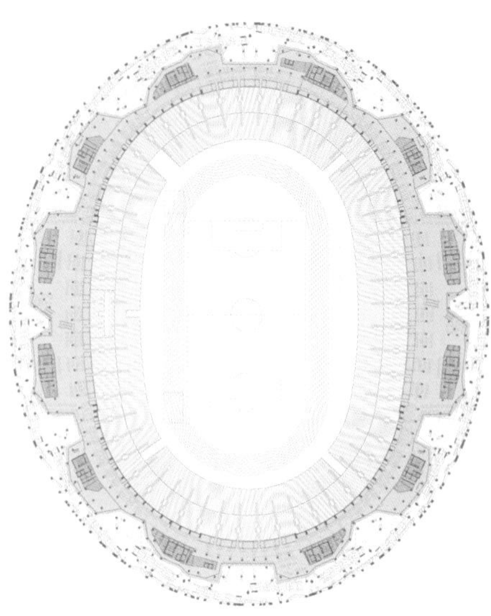

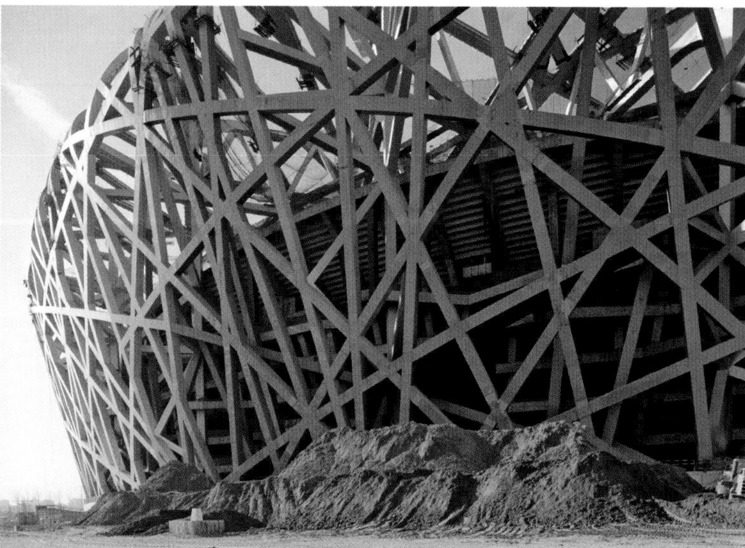

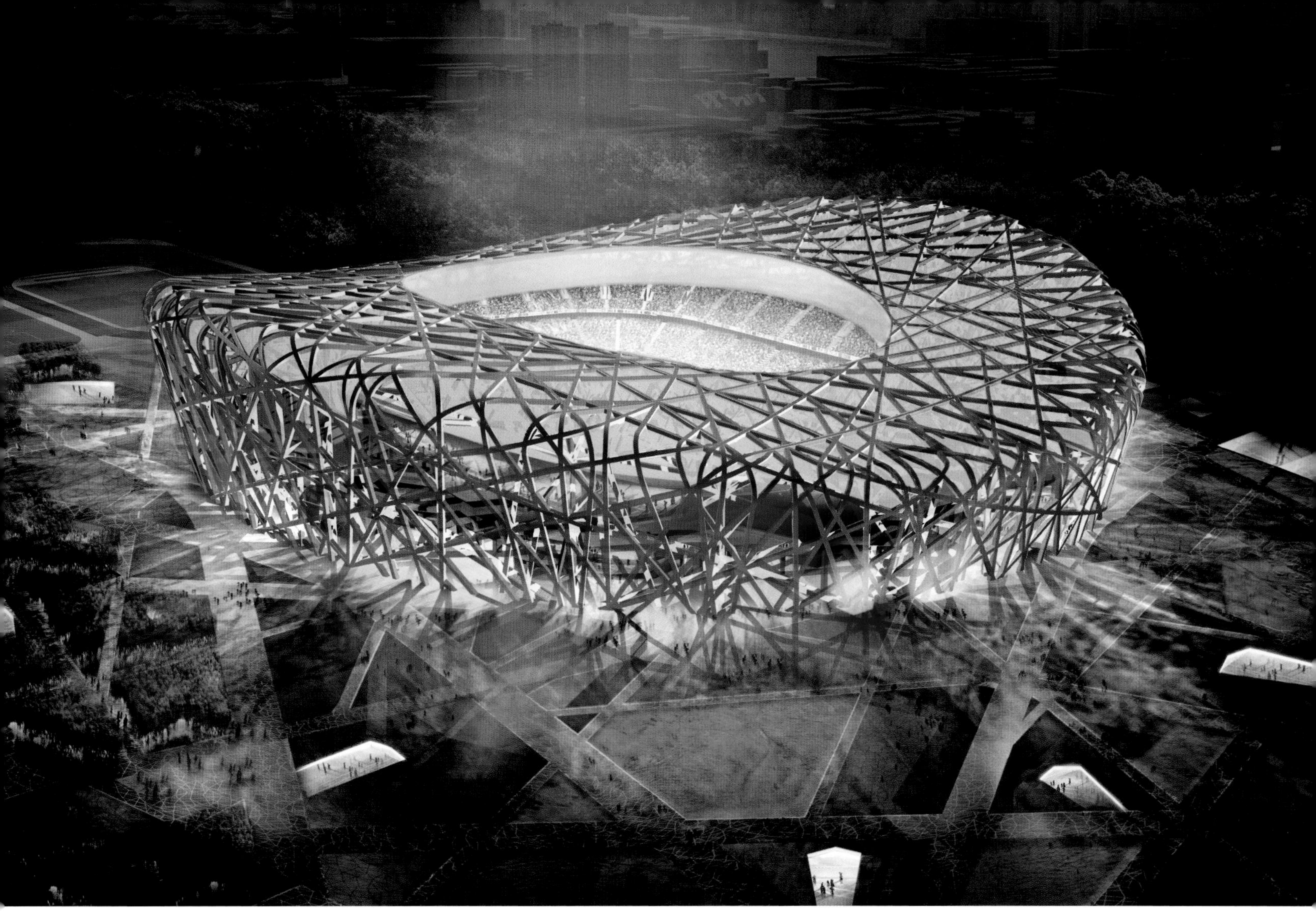

The bird's-nest effect of the structural members of the stadium makes it difficult to judge its true scale in the computer perspective above. The sections below render function and size more evident. Opposite page, bottom, construction photos taken early in 2007.

Die Konstruktionselemente des Stadions wirken wie ein Vogelnest, deshalb lassen sich in der Computerperspektive oben seine wahren Ausmaße nur schwer erkennen. Die Schnitte unten lassen Funktion und Größe klarer erscheinen. Gegenüberliegende Seite, unten: Fotos der Baustelle Anfang 2007.

L'effet de nid d'oiseau, donné par les poutres structurelles, rend difficile l'appréciation de l'échelle réelle dans l'image de synthèse ci-dessus. Les coupes ci-dessous en font mieux ressortir les fonctions et les dimensions. Page ci-contre, en bas, photos de chantier début 2007.

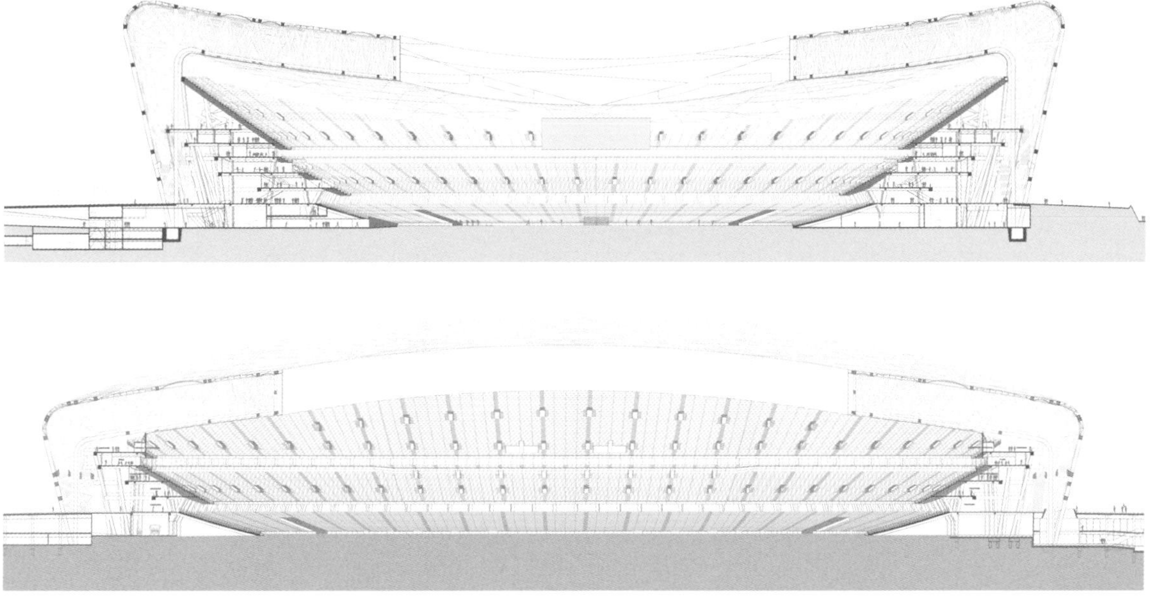

#7

ARATA ISOZAKI

ARATA ISOZAKI & ASSOCIATES
NOGIZAKA ATELIER
6-17, Akasaka 9-chome
Tokyo 107-0052
Japan

Tel: +81 3 3405 1526
Fax: +81 3 3475 5265
e-mail: info@isozaki.co.jp

Born in Oita City on the Island of Kyushu, Japan, in 1931, ARATA ISOZAKI graduated from the Architectural Faculty of the University of Tokyo in 1954 and established Arata Isozaki & Associates in 1963, having worked in the office of Kenzo Tange. Winner of the 1986 RIBA Gold Medal, he has been a juror of major competitions, such as that held in 1988 for the new Kansai International Airport. Notable buildings include: the Museum of Modern Art, Gunma (1971–74); the Tsukuba Center Building, Tsukuba (1978–83); the Museum of Contemporary Art, Los Angeles (1981–86); the Art Tower Mito, Mito (1986–90); the Team Disney Building, Florida (1990–94); the Center for Japanese Art and Technology, Cracow, Poland (1991–94); the B-con Plaza, Oita (1991–95); the Higashi Shizuoka Plaza Cultural Complex, Shizuoka; and Ohio's Center of Science and Industry (COSI), Columbus, Ohio. More recently, aside from the Yamaguchi Center for Arts and Media, Yamaguchi (2001–03), he has taken on a number of projects in Qatar, including the National Bank, the National Library, and the master plan for the Qatar Education City. Isozaki has also received a commission from the Aga Khan to develop the three new campuses of the University of Central Asia to be located in Tekeli, Kazakhstan; Naryn, Kyrgyz Republic; and Khorog, Tajikistan.

SHENZHEN CULTURAL CENTER

SHENZHEN, GUANGDONG 1997–2005

SITE AREA: 29 612 m²
FLOOR AREA: 33 663 m²
CLIENT: Shenzhen Bureau of Culture
COST: not disclosed

Arata Isozaki was selected for this project on the occasion of an international competition. The building features a 40-meter-high, 300-meter-long black granite wall that blocks out the sight and sound of an eight-lane highway. Spectacular glazed atria mark the concert hall or library entrance sequences. The complex polyhedrons that form the glazing are supported by tree-like columns that cast complex shadows in the space, enlivening it and giving it more depth than simpler structures might have. The facility consists of a main concert hall seating 1800 people, a smaller one with 400 seats, and a library, and it is located in the new urban center of the city. The library offers open access to most of its three million books and one million electronic documents. Isozaki's extensive experience in designing large cultural centers in Japan, and in other countries, such as Spain or the United States, means that calling on him was a "sure thing" as far as the authorities of Shenzhen were concerned. He has delivered more than an ordinary building with its strong black presence and shimmering interior light. The desire of a city like Shenzhen to have world-class facilities certainly meets with success in this new cultural center.

Arata Isozaki wurde für diesen Auftrag durch einen internationalen Wettbewerb ausgewählt. Das Gebäude zeichnet sich durch eine 40 m hohe und 300 m lange schwarze Granitwand aus, die Anblick und Geräuschkulisse einer achtspurigen Schnellstraße ausschaltet. Die jeweiligen Zugänge zu Konzerthalle und Bibliothek fallen durch imposante verglaste Vorhallen ins Auge. Die komplexen Polyeder, die die Verglasung strukturieren, werden von baumartigen Pfeilern getragen, die interessante Schatten in den Raum werfen, ihn dadurch beleben und ihm zu mehr Tiefe verhelfen, als es einfachere Strukturen vermocht hätten. Der Komplex besteht aus einer Hauptkonzerthalle mit 1800 Plätzen, einem kleineren Saal, in dem 400 Leute Platz finden, sowie einer Bibliothek und liegt im neuen urbanen Zentrum der Stadt. Die Bibliothek bietet freien Zugang zu mehr als drei Millionen Büchern und einer Million elektronischen Medien. Isozakis umfassende Erfahrung im Entwerfen bedeutender Kulturzentren in Japan und in anderen Ländern wie Spanien oder den Vereinigten Staaten hieß für die Verantwortlichen in Shenzhen, dass sie mit der Vergabe des Auftrags an ihn kein Risiko eingingen. Das Ergebnis ist mit seiner eindrucksvollen schwarzen Präsenz und der schimmernden Innenbeleuchtung mehr als ein gewöhnliches Gebäude. Der Wunsch einer Stadt wie Shenzhen nach Architektur von Weltklasse wird mit diesem neuen Kulturzentrum ganz sicher erfüllt.

C'est à l'issue d'un concours international que le projet d'Arata Isozaki a été sélectionné. Le bâtiment se signale par un mur de granit noir de 40 m de haut et 300 m de long qui bloque la vue et les nuisances sonores d'une autoroute à huit voies. De spectaculaires atriums de verre signalent l'entrée de la salle de concert et de la bibliothèque. Les polyèdres complexes qui constituent l'enveloppe sont soutenus par des colonnes arboriformes projetant des ombres complexes dans l'espace qu'ils animent et auquel ils donnent plus de profondeur qu'une ossature simple. Ce complexe situé dans le nouveau centre de la ville se compose d'une salle de concert principale de 1800 places, d'une de 400 places et d'une bibliothèque proposant trois millions de livres et un million de documents numérisés en accès libre. La longue expérience d'Isozaki dans la création de grands centres culturels au Japon, mais aussi en Espagne ou aux États-Unis, a pu rassurer les autorités de la ville Shenzen. À travers cette présence forte et sombre et ces volumes intérieurs vibrant de lumière, il a certainement réalisé bien plus qu'un équipement culturel ordinaire. Le désir d'une ville comme Shenzen de se doter d'équipements de classe internationale est comblé.

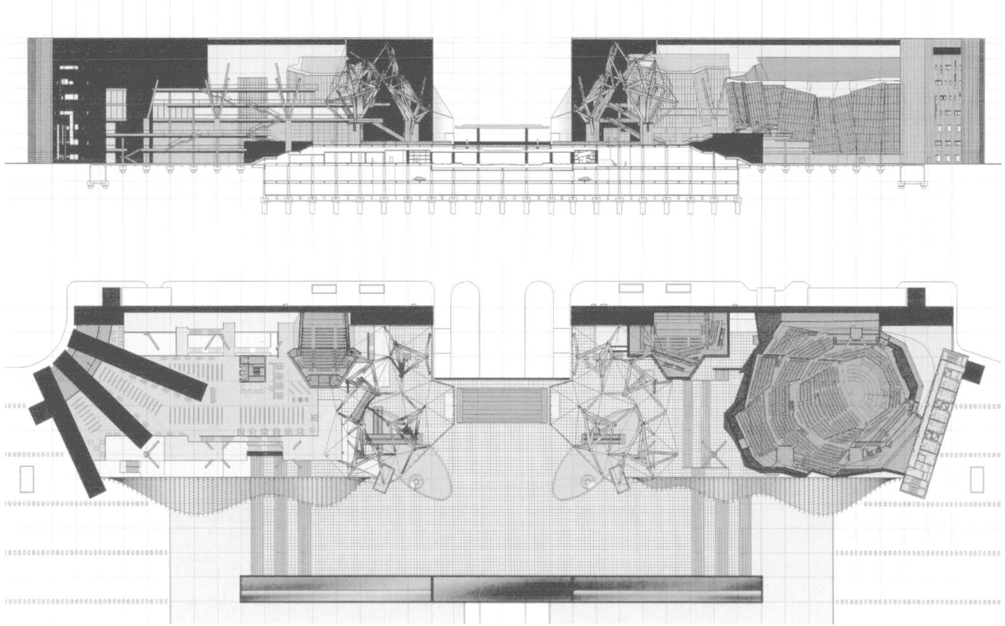

Perfectly familiar with the design of cultural centers or museums built in the United States or Japan, Isozaki brings a level of sophistication and architectural surprise to this complex that is not yet typical of China's new civic buildings.

Isozaki, der mit dem Bau von Kulturzentren oder Museen in den Vereinigten Staaten und Japan vertraut ist, stattete diesen Komplex mit einer für Chinas neue städtische Bauten noch untypischen Perfektion und architektonischen Finesse aus.

Familier des problèmes de conception de centres culturels ou de musées aux États-Unis ou au Japon, Isozaki atteint ici un degré de sophistication et de surprise encore rare dans les nouveaux bâtiments publics chinois.

The images emphasize the complexity of the design, with a spider-web pattern on the atrium windows and a maze of bridges crossing the void.

Die Abbildungen verdeutlichen die Komplexität des Entwurfs, mit einem Spinnwebmuster auf den Fenstern des Atriums und einem Gewirr von Brücken, die den leeren Raum überspannen.

Les photographies mettent en valeur la complexité du projet que manifestent le traitement en toile d'araignée des baies de l'atrium et le labyrinthe des passerelles dans le vide.

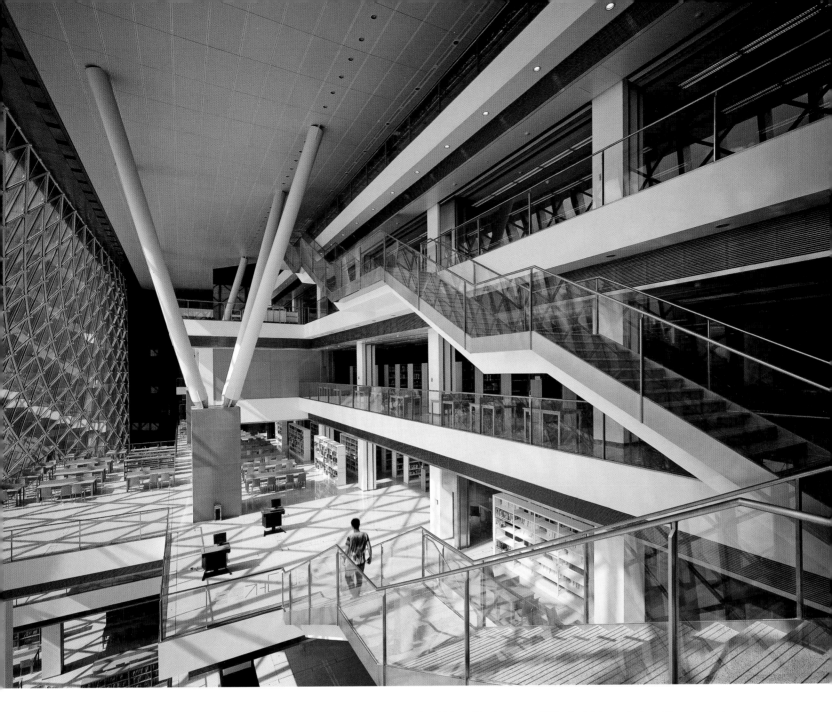

The elevation below, or perhaps even the lobby image above, demonstrates that the essential forms of the building are not overly complex, but that the architect has introduced movement and varying light patterns by playing on voids and an undulating, glazed façade.

Der Aufriss oder vielleicht sogar das Bild der Lobby oben veranschaulichen die nicht sonderlich komplizierte Grundform des Gebäudes. Durch das Spielen mit Leerstellen und eine gewellte Glasfassade hat der Architekt jedoch Bewegung und verschiedenartige Lichtmuster einfließen lassen.

L'élévation (ci-dessous), et peut-être même les images du grand hall (ci-dessus), montrent que les formes de base du bâtiment ne sont pas si complexes, mais que l'architecte a introduit un mouvement et divers effets d'éclairage en jouant sur les vides et l'ondulation de sa façade vitrée.

Isozaki has often changed styles in his career and here it is not easy to place him within the context of any given movement. Dramatic openings and spectacular shadow patterns animate his architecture here in any case.

Isozaki wechselte im Lauf seiner Karriere oft seinen Stil. Hier fällt es schwer, ihn in den Kontext einer bestimmten Bewegung einzuordnen. In jedem Fall wird seine Architektur von fulminanten Öffnungen und Schattenspielen aufgelockert.

Isozaki a souvent changé de style pendant sa carrière, et il n'est pas facile ici de le rattacher à un mouvement quel qu'il soit. Des ouvertures et des ombres spectaculaires animent magnifiquement l'ensemble de son projet.

#8

JIAKUN ARCHITECTS

JIAKUN ARCHITECTS
2-7F, Block 11
3# Yulin Nanlu
Chengdu, Sichuan 610041

Tel: +86 28 8556 8899
Fax: +86 28 8558 9491
e-mail: jkads@126.com
Web: www.jiakun.com

LIU JIAKUN graduated from the Department of Architecture of the Chongqing Institute of Architecture and Engineering and, after working in Tibet and Sinkiang, he established Jiakun Architects in 1999. The firm presently has 26 employees. Among Liu's works are: the Tibet Naqu Art Center; the Chengdu Culture Art School; the Qingpu Construction Exhibition Center (Shanghai); "Red Era" Entertainment Center, Chengdu, Sichuan (2001); the Lueyuan Stone Sculpture Art Museum, published here; the Sculpture Department of the Sichuan Fine Arts Institute, Chongqing (2004); the Motorola Chengdu Software Center; the Sichuan Anren Jianchuan Museum, Reception, and Dining Center for CIPEA, Nanjing (2006); and the Guangzhou Times Rose Garden, Guangzhou (2006). Liu states that "a good design equals using limited resources in a creative way."

LUEYUAN STONE SCULPTURE ART MUSEUM
CHENGDU, SICHUAN 2001–02

SITE AREA: 6670 m²
FLOOR AREA: 1037 m²
CLIENT: Xiangcai Securities Labor Union
COST: $ 355 000

This project is divided into four areas, with the most important being devoted to the museum itself, and the other three to parking, open exhibition and offices. Bamboo divides each part from the other. The museum display is designed around an atrium, and careful attention was paid to place gaps in the building blocks, allowing views of the landscape situated between the Fu River and the woods. Dedicated to the exhibition of a collection of Buddhist sculptures from the Han Dynasty (206 B.C.–A.D. 220) to the Song Dynasty (960–1125), the museum was designed in part to facilitate future changes, a constant habit in China. The architect refers to the concrete used in the project as "artificial stone." Liu Jiakun makes frequent reference to the poor quality of local construction, writing: "Because of the rude construction technology, it is very hard to assure the perpendicularity of the walls during the pouring of concrete. By laying interior brick walls first, these walls become the formwork for pouring the outer walls, and thus their perpendicularity is ensured. I hope to find out a way, an approach to contemporary architectural aesthetic ideals while feasible and proper in local conditions." The shale bricks used in this unusual way are not in fact visible in the museum, but are covered with a layer of concrete. Using this "soft layer," the architect suggests that future modifications of elements such as the technical conduits have been facilitated.

Dieses Projekt umfasst vier Areale: Auf dem wichtigsten befindet sich das eigentliche Museum, die übrigen drei werden als Parkfläche, für Freiluftausstellungen und für Büros genutzt. Die Bereiche sind durch Bambuspflanzen voneinander abgegrenzt. Das Museum gruppiert sich um ein Atrium, und es wurde darauf geachtet, zwischen den Baublöcken Lücken zu lassen, um Ausblicke auf die umgebende Landschaft zwischen dem Fluss Fu und der Bewaldung zu gestatten. Das Museum zeigt eine Ausstellung buddhistischer Skulpturen von der Han-Dynastie (206 v. Chr.–220 n. Chr.) bis zur Song-Dynastie (960–1125) und wurde zum Teil im Hinblick auf künftige Veränderungen geplant, eine in China verbreitete Gewohnheit. Der Architekt bezeichnet den bei diesem Projekt verwendeten Beton als »künstlichen Stein«. Dazu verwies Liu Jiakun häufig auf die schlechte Qualität der heimischen Bauweise. So schreibt er beispielsweise: »Aufgrund der primitiven Bautechnik ist es sehr schwierig, beim Gießen des Betons die lotrechte Stellung der Wände zu gewährleisten. Man hilft sich, indem zuerst innere Backsteinmauern errichtet werden, die beim Gießen des Betons als Schalungsform dienen und so die genaue Ausrichtung garantieren. Ich hoffe, einen Weg oder einen Ansatz zu den ästhetischen Idealen der zeitgenössischen Architektur zu finden, der bei den hiesigen Bedingungen machbar und zweckmäßig ist.« Die auf diese ungewöhnliche Weise verwendeten Schiefertonziegel sind in dem Museum nicht wirklich sichtbar, sondern werden von einer Betonschicht verdeckt. Nach Ansicht des Architekten erleichtert diese »weiche Schicht« künftige Veränderungen von Elementen wie etwa technische Leitungen.

Ce projet est divisé en quatre zones dont la plus importante est consacrée au musée organisé autour d'un atrium, et les trois autres à un parking, à un espace d'expositions en plein air et à des bureaux. Chaque partie est isolée des autres par des plantations de bambous. Une attention particulière a été portée aux vides entre les blocs qui constituent le bâtiment pour offrir des perspectives sur le paysage entre la rivière Fu et les bois. Consacré à la présentation d'une collection de sculptures bouddhiques s'étendant de la dynastie Han (206 av. J.-C.-220) à la dynastie Song (960–1125), le musée est conçu en prévision de futurs changements, habitude chinoise constante. Pour décrire le béton utilisé, l'architecte parle de « pierre artificielle ». Liu Jiakun fait par ailleurs de nombreuses références à la piètre qualité de la construction locale : « Parce que les technologies de construction sont encore primaires, il est très difficile d'assurer la perpendicularité des murs lors du coulage du béton. En commençant par monter d'abord les murs intérieurs en brique qui deviennent le coffrage partiel du mur extérieur, on est assuré de leur verticalité. J'espère découvrir une approche des idéaux esthétiques architecturaux contemporains qui soit réalisable dans ces conditions locales. » Les briques d'argile utilisées de cette façon inhabituelle ne sont pas visibles partout car elles sont enduites par endroits d'une couche de ciment. L'architecte pense que cette « couche molle » facilitera de futures modifications d'éléments comme celles des conduits techniques.

110°
35°
25°
95°
100°
110°

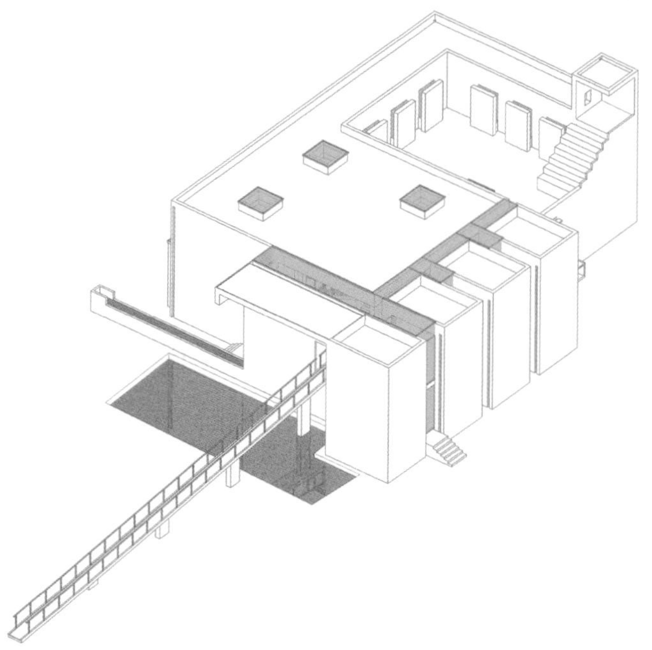

The roughness of the concrete employed by the architect and the repetitive towers forming the façade below might recall bunker design.

Die Rauheit des hier verwendeten Betons und die wiederkehrenden Türme, die die unten abgebildete Fassade prägen, erinnern entfernt an einen Bunker.

Le caractère brut du béton utilisé et la répétitivité des tours qui constituent la façade (ci-dessous) évoquent presque une esthétique de bunker.

A site plan (right) shows the corner location of the building, surrounded by greenery and approached by a footbridge (above).

Der Lageplan (rechts) zeigt die Ecklage des von Pflanzen umgebenen Gebäudes, das über eine Fußgängerbrücke zu erreichen ist (oben).

Le plan du site (à droite) montre l'implantation du bâtiment entouré de verdure et accessible par une passerelle (ci-dessus) dans un angle du terrain.

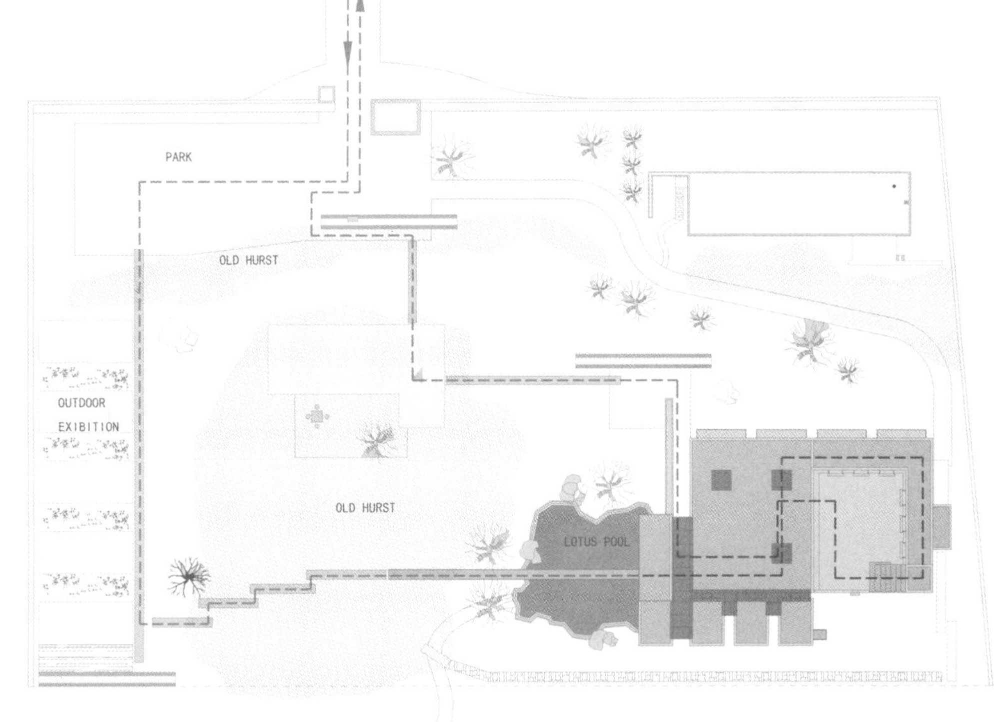

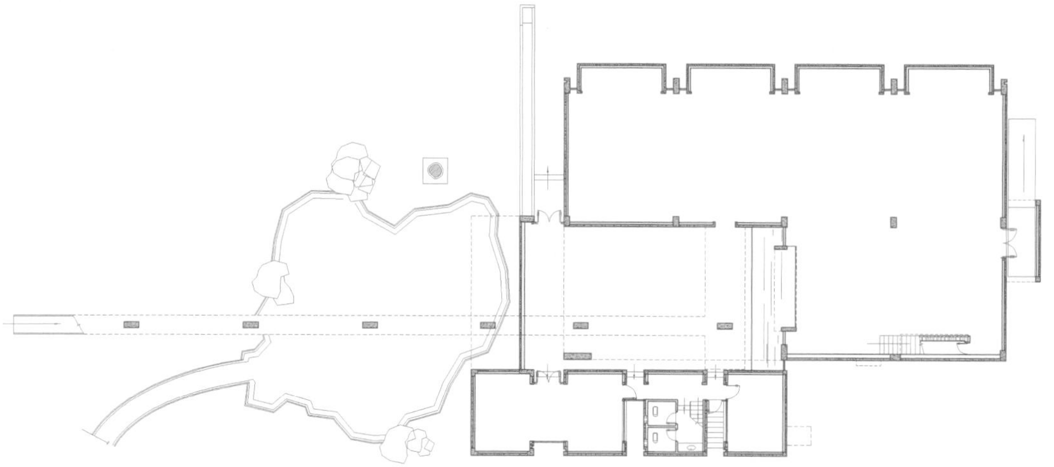

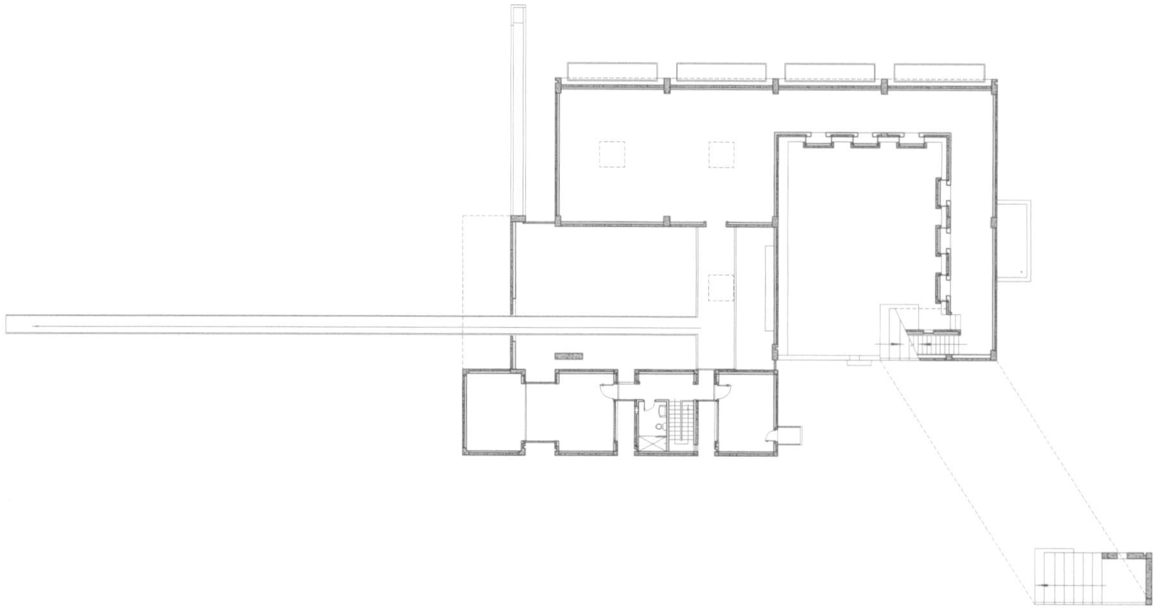

The roughness of the museum's walls contrasts voluntarily with the refinement of the sculptures displayed. Daylight penetrates the interior in an indirect manner.

Die Rauheit der Museumswände kontrastiert bewusst mit der Feinheit der ausgestellten Skulpturen. Tageslicht dringt auf indirekte Weise in das Innere ein.

L'aspect rugueux des murs du musée contraste volontairement avec le raffinement des sculptures exposées. La lumière naturelle pénètre à l'intérieur de manière indirecte.

30°
25°
110°

KENGO KUMA

KENGO KUMA & ASSOCIATES
2-24-8 BY-CUBE 2-4F Minamiaoyama
Minato-ku, Tokyo 107-0062
Japan

Tel: +81 3 3401 7721
Fax: +81 3 3401 7778
e-mail: kuma@ba2.so-net.ne.jp
Web: www.kkaa.co.jp

Born in 1954 in Kanagawa, Japan, **KENGO KUMA** graduated in 1979 from the University of Tokyo, with an M.Arch. In 1985–86, he received an Asian Cultural Council Fellowship Grant and was a Visiting Scholar at Columbia University, New York. In 1987, he established the Spatial Design Studio and, in 1991, he created Kengo Kuma & Associates. From 1998–99, he was a Professor at the Faculty of Environmental Information, Keio University and, since 2001, has been a Professor at the Faculty of Science and Technology at the same university. His work includes: the Gunma Toyota Car Show Room, Maebashi (1989); the Maiton Resort Complex, Phuket, Thailand; the Rustic, Office Building, Tokyo; Doric, Office Building, Tokyo; M2, Headquarters for Mazda New Design Team, Tokyo (all in 1991); Kinjo Golf Club, Club House, Okayama (1992); Atami Guest House, Guest House for Bandai Corp, Atami (1992–95); Karuizawa Resort Hotel, Karuizawa (1993); Tomioka Lakewood Golf Club House, Tomioka (1993–96); Kiro-san Observatory, Ehime (1994); Toyoma Noh-Theater, Miyagi (1995–96); and the Japanese Pavilion for the Venice Biennale, Venice, Italy (1995). He has also completed the Stone Museum (Nasu, Tochigi) and a Museum of Ando Hiroshige (Batou, Nasu-gun, Tochigi). More recently, he finished the Great Bamboo Wall guesthouse, Beijing, (2002); One Omotesando, Tokyo (2003); LVMH Osaka (2004); the Fukusaki Hanging Garden (2005); the Nagasaki Prefecture Art Museum (2005); Banraisha university facilities (Tokyo, 2005); The Scape, an apartment in Tokyo (2005); the Hoshinosato Nursing Home Annex (2005); Lotus House (2005); Z58 Building (Shanghai, 2003–06); Ginzan Onsen Fujiya Hotel (2006); and Y-Hutte House (2006), among others. Current projects include Dellis Cay Spa Resort (Turks and Caicos Islands); Suzhou Dwelling Project; 23 St James's Street, London; Tenerife Housing Project; Kenny Heights Museum in Kuala Lumpur; Modern Tea House Project in Frankfurt; and the New Sunlitun Project-N1 Boutique Hotel in Beijing.

ZHONGTAI BOX Z58 SHANGHAI 2003-06

SITE AREA: 961 m²
FLOOR AREA: 3159 m²
CLIENT: Zhongtai Lighting Group
COST: not disclosed

A multipurpose building including offices, a studio for lighting designers, and a guest house, the Zhongtai Box is located in eastern Shanghai next to a garden that was owned by the family of Sun Yatsen. Using an existing warehouse and adding a semi-outdoor atrium for the front portion of the property, Kuma arranged horizontal, mirror-finish, stainless-steel planter boxes in a louver pattern on the street side. Although he expected that the client, a large lighting and business firm, would reject the concept of renovation in a country that tends to want to build anew, he was pleased to discover that his idea of a kind of hanging garden opposite that of the Sun family was accepted. Kuma points out that this project, like his earlier Great Bamboo Wall house near the Great Wall, represents a "manifestation of the strong desire to get away from the practice of copying the West." Kengo Kuma has succeeded here as elsewhere in developing unique solutions to given architectural problems. "First," he says, "there is dialogue with the existing structure that stands on this site. We added glass, aluminum and greenery, while preserving the existing structure." As Kuma writes, dialogue is the theme of this project: "Dialogue with the existing things in the structure, and dialogue with time added character and richness to the structure. There is also dialogue with Fanyu Road which is in front of the building. A water feature and greenery are provided between the road and the building. The motivation for this was to create movement in the water and swaying of the green leaves through dialogue between them."

Die Zhongtai Box, ein Mehrzweckgebäude mit Büros, einem Studio für Lichtdesign und einem Gästehaus, liegt im Osten von Shanghai neben einem Garten, der früher der Familie von Sun Yatsen gehörte. Kuma, der ein vorhandenes Lagerhaus nutzte und im vorderen Teil der Liegenschaft ein halboffenes Atrium ergänzte, versah die Straßenseite mit horizontalen, verspiegelten Pflanzenkästen aus Edelstahl, die er lamellenförmig anordnete. Obgleich Kuma damit rechnete, dass der Auftraggeber, eine große Beleuchtungsfirma, in einem Land, das zu Neubauten tendiert, die Renovierung eines Altbaus ablehnen würde, stellte er zu seiner Freude fest, dass seine Idee eines hängenden Gartens gegenüber dem der Familie Sun akzeptiert wurde. Kuma weist darauf hin, dass dieses Projekt, wie sein zuvor erbautes »Großes Bambuswandhaus« in der Nähe der Chinesischen Mauer »Ausdruck des herrschenden Wunsches ist, von der Praxis, den Westen zu kopieren, abzukommen«. Hier, wie bereits andernorts, gelang es Kengo Kuma, für architektonische Probleme außergewöhnliche Lösungen zu entwickeln. Zum einen entsteht ein Dialog mit dem auf dem Gelände vorhandenen Bauwerk, dem er Glas, Aluminium und Begrünung hinzufügte. Wie Kuma ausführt, ist der Dialog das Leitthema dieses Projekts. »Dialog mit den vorhandenen Dingen im Bau und Dialog mit der Zeit verhalfen dem Gebäude zu Charakter und Gehalt. Außerdem besteht ein Dialog mit der an der Vorderseite des Gebäudes vorbeiführenden Fanyu-Straße. Zwischen Straße und Gebäude sind ein Wasserbecken und Bepflanzung vorgesehen. Durch den Dialog zwischen beiden soll Bewegung im Wasser und in den grünen Blätter erzeugt werden.«

Immeuble multifonctions contenant des bureaux, un studio pour des créateurs de luminaires et une maison d'hôtes, cette « Boîte Zhongtai » est située à l'est de Shanghai, non loin d'un jardin qui appartenait jadis à la famille de Sun Yat-Sen. Réutilisant un entrepôt existant et après voir ajouté un atrium semi-ouvert en partie avant, Kuma a disposé du côté de la rue des jardinières en acier inoxydable en miroir poli qui forment une sorte d'immense persienne. Alors qu'il s'attendait à ce que son client, une importante entreprise d'éclairage, rejette le concept même de rénovation dans un pays qui a tendance à vouloir tout reconstruire à neuf, il a eu l'heureuse surprise de découvrir que cette idée de « jardins » suspendus face à celui de la famille Sun était acceptée. Il fait remarquer que ce projet, comme sa Great Bamboo Wall House près de la Grande Muraille de Chine, représente « une manifestation du puissant désir de s'écarter des pratiques de copie de l'Occident ». Il a réussi, ici comme ailleurs, à apporter des solutions originales à des problèmes architecturaux précis. « Tout d'abord, écrit-il, a été créé un dialogue avec la construction existante sur le site. Nous avons apporté du verre, de l'aluminium et de la verdure, tout en préservant la structure existante. » Le dialogue est donc le thème de ce projet, comme le précise Kuma : « Le dialogue avec l'existant et le dialogue avec le temps qui a donné du caractère et de la richesse à la construction. Un dialogue s'ouvre aussi avec la route de Fanyu qui passe devant le bâtiment. Un dispositif d'eau et de plantes s'interpose maintenant entre la route et le bâtiment. Sa raison est de créer par les mouvements de l'eau et le balancement des feuilles un dialogue entre eux. »

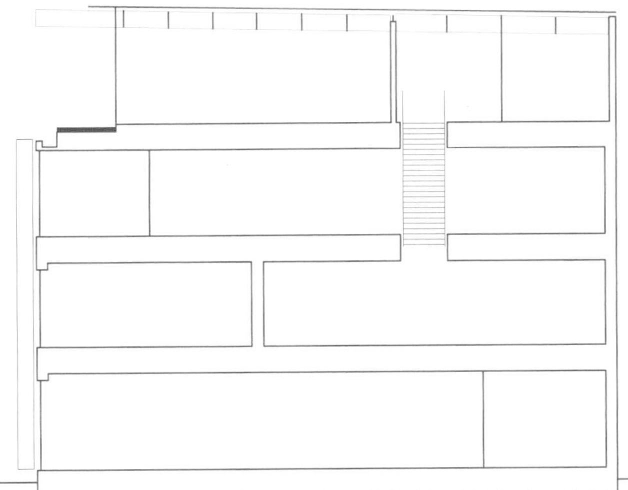

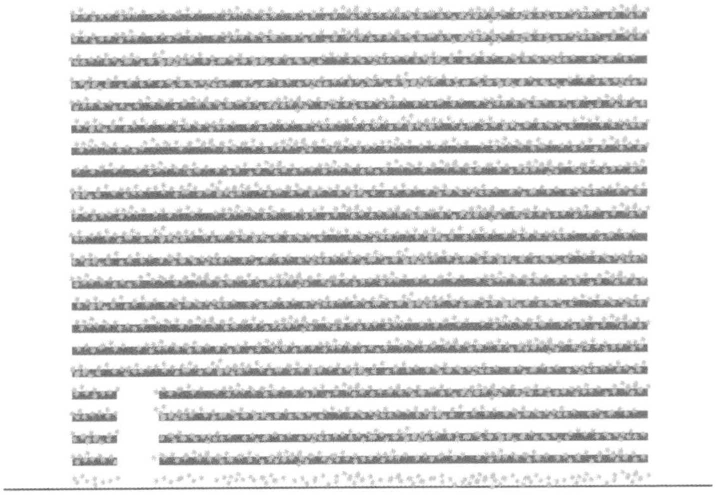

Called the Zhongtai Box, the building really does resemble a box, and yet the louvered surface and greenery introduced by Kengo Kuma give it an appearance that is anything but ordinary. Living spaces are seen below, and the section and elevation above show that the green façade conceals a quite simple floor plan.

Das »Zhongtai Box« benannte Gebäude ähnelt tatsächlich einem Kasten; die von Kengo Kuma verwendete lamellenförmige Oberfläche und die Bepflanzung verschaffen ihm jedoch ein keineswegs gewöhnliches Erscheinungsbild. Unten sind Wohnräume zu sehen, und Schnitt und Aufriss (oben) verraten, dass sich hinter der begrünten Fassade ein recht einfacher Grundriss verbirgt.

Appelé « Zhongtai Box », l'immeuble ressemble réellement à une boîte, même si sa façade habillée de persiennes et de verdure lui confère une apparence hors du commun. Les espaces de séjour (ci-dessous), la coupe et l'élévation (ci-dessus) montrent que la façade verte masque un plan au sol assez simple.

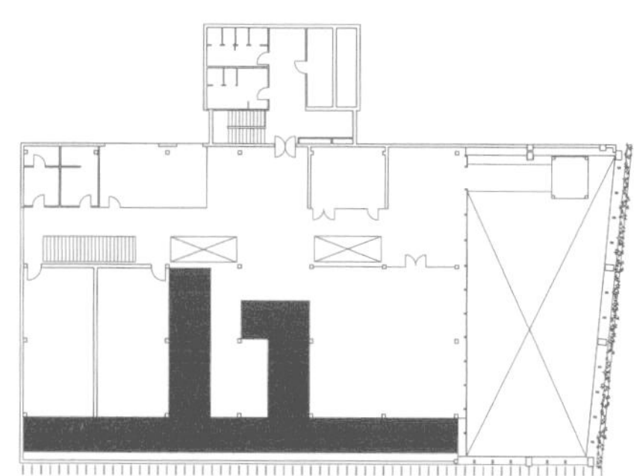

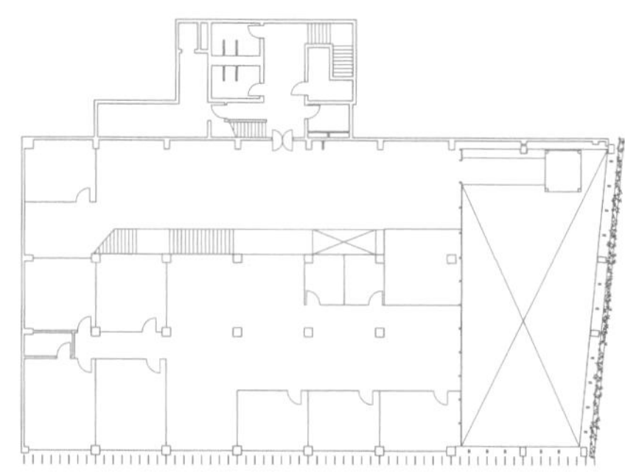

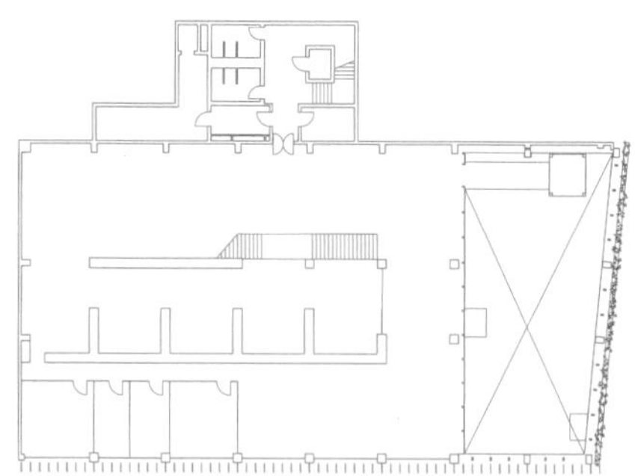

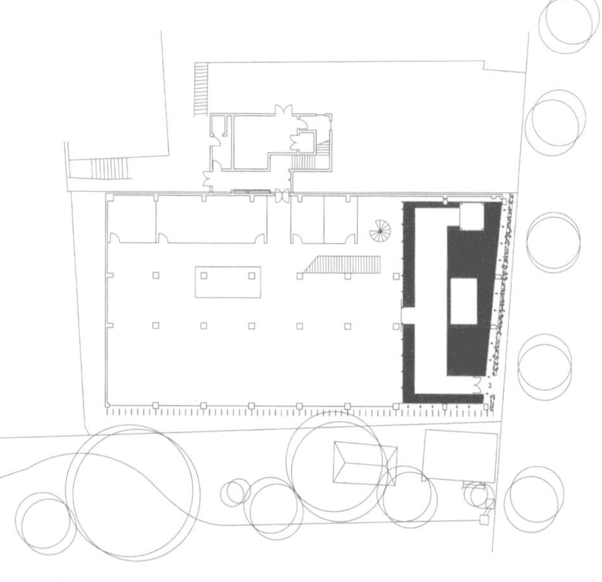

#10

LI XIAODONG ATELIER

LI XIAODONG
School of Architecture
Tsinghua University
Beijing 100 084

Tel: +86 10 6279 4237
Fax: +86 10 6277 0314
e-mail: xd-li@tsinghua.edu.cn

LI XIAODONG was born in 1963 in Beijing. He received his B.Arch degree (1984) from Tsinghua University in Beijing, and his M.Arch and Ph.D. from the Schools of Architecture of the Delft and Eindhoven Universities of Technology (1989–93). He is presently a Professor of Architecture at Tsinghua University and Chair of the Architecture Department there. He created his firm, Li Xiaodong Atelier, in 1997. He also teaches at the National University of Singapore. Aside from the Yuhu Elementary School, published here, he has worked on housing in Beijing and the renovation of the School of Architecture at Tsinghua University, Beijing (2005–06). Earlier work includes: the Cloudy Valley Hotel, Anhui Province (1984–86); the Drihoek shopping and residential complex, Amsterdam (1993–94); and the Delft Blaw housing project, Delft (1993–95). In 2000, he worked on the Singapore Zoo entrance and the Singapore Photographic Gallery. The Yuhu Elementary School won a UNESCO Asia-Pacific Award for the Protection of Cultural Heritage. Li Xiaodong won a RIBA award for the quality of his teaching in Singapore, and he has also published widely on cultural and urban studies, and on the history and theory of architecture.

YUHU SCHOOL AND COMMUNITY CENTER

LIJIANG, YUNNAN 2003–'04

FLOOR AREA: 800 m²
CLIENT: Yuhu Village
COST: $ 40 000
DESIGN TEAM: Li Xiaodong, Yeo Kangshua, Cheong Kenghua, Lim Guanxiong

Located at an altitude of over 2700 meters near the Jade Dragon Snow Mountain, the village of Yuhu is in the Naxi minority region in northwestern Yunnan Province. A primary school for the village had been built in 2001, but required enlargement. With the help of donations from Singapore, China, and the local government, Li Xiaodong undertook the study and construction of the extension using local materials, techniques, and resources. Intended for 160 students, the facility is divided into three small buildings arranged in a "Z" pattern around a maple tree. A staircase in reinforced concrete with timber steps is one marked departure from local architectural traditions, but it allowed the creation of supplementary classroom areas. A timber-frame structure was designed with local seismic conditions in mind, while local limestone and cobblestones were used extensively. Because of the danger of earthquakes, masonry elements are all non-load bearing. Traditional ornamentation or roof designs were reduced to the simplest possible expression, while retaining something of the spirit of the place.

Das Dorf Yuhu liegt auf einer Höhe von über 2700 m in einem von der Minorität der Naxi bewohnten Gebiet im Nordwesten der Provinz Yunnan, unweit vom Jadedrachen-Schneeberg. Eine 2001 im Dorf gebaute Grundschule musste erweitert werden. Mithilfe von Spenden aus Singapur, China und der Kommunalverwaltung übernahm Li Xiadong die Planung und Ausführung des Anbaus mit heimischen Materialien, Techniken und Hilfsmitteln. Die für 160 Schüler gedachte Einrichtung ist auf drei kleine Gebäude verteilt, die in Form eines Z um einen Ahornbaum angeordnet sind. Mit einer Treppe aus Stahlbeton mit Holzstufen weicht der Bau von heimischen Architekturtraditionen ab, aber die Treppe ermöglichte die Erschließung weiterer Klassenzimmer. Im Hinblick auf die hier herrschenden seismischen Bedingungen wurde der Bau als Holzrahmenkonstruktion errichtet, im Übrigen wurde ausgiebiger Gebrauch von heimischem Kalkstein und Kopfsteinen gemacht. Wegen der Erdbebengefahr sind sämtliche gemauerten Elemente nicht tragend. Traditionelle Schmuckelemente oder Dachgestaltungen wurden zwar auf die schlichtest mögliche Form reduziert, bewahren aber dennoch etwas vom Geist des Ortes.

Situé à plus de 2700 m d'altitude près de la Montagne du dragon de jade enneigée, le village de Yuhu fait partie de la région de la minorité Naxi, dans le nord-ouest de la province du Yunnan. L'école primaire, construite en 2001, devait être agrandie. Grâce à des donations venues de Singapour, de Chine et de l'administration locale, Li Xiaodong entreprit l'étude et la construction de cette extension en faisant appel aux matériaux, techniques et ressources trouvés sur place. Les installations conçues pour 160 élèves sont divisées en trois petits bâtiments disposés en « Z » autour d'un érable. L'escalier en béton armé à marches de bois, un des seuls écarts avec les traditions architecturales locales, a permis la création de classes supplémentaires. L'ossature en bois a été conçue en pensant aux conditions sismiques de la région et aucun élément en maçonnerie n'est porteur. Le calcaire et les galets locaux ont été abondamment employés. Le style traditionnel des toitures est réduit à sa plus simple expression, tout en conservant, d'une certaine manière, l'esprit du lieu.

The kind of contrasting, often rough, surfaces seen elsewhere in contemporary Chinese architecture have a different fundamental justification here, namely, that of the extremely remote setting of the school.

Die kontrastierenden, häufig rauen Oberflächen, die man andernorts in der zeitgenössischen Architektur Chinas antrifft, erhalten hier durch die extrem abgelegene Situation der Schule eine grundlegend andere Berechtigung.

Les surfaces souvent brutes et contrastées que l'on observe dans l'architecture contemporaine chinoise prennent ici un sens différent, lié à la situation géographique éloignée de cette école.

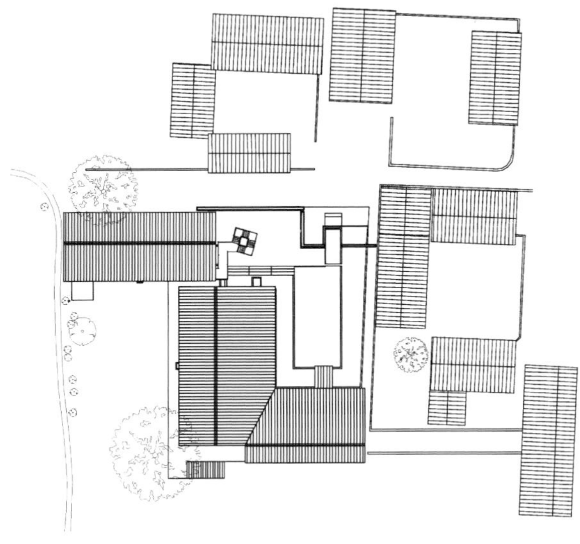

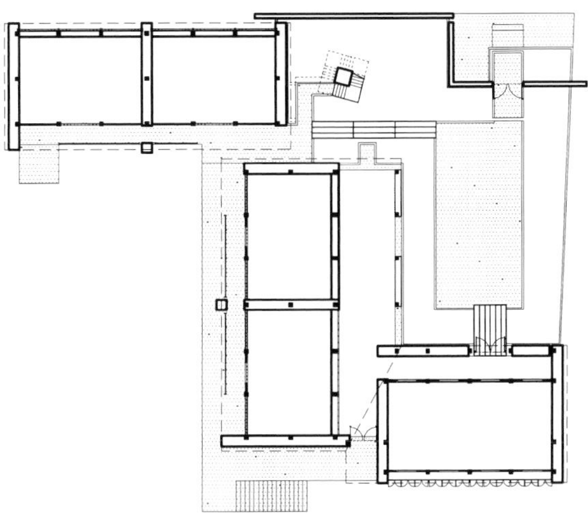

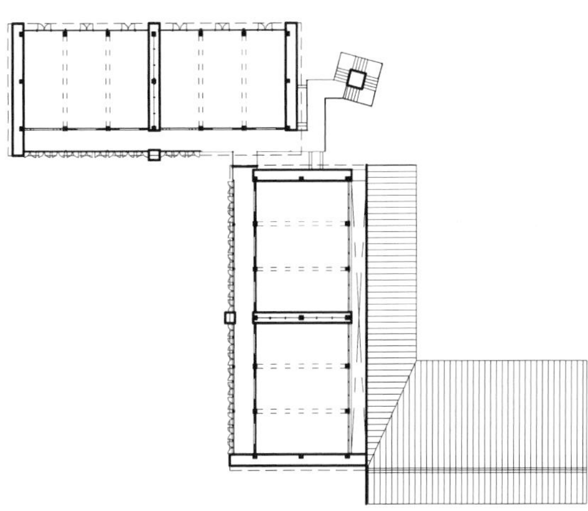

Roughly finished wood and stone come together with somewhat more unexpected glazed surfaces opening to the natural setting.

Grob bearbeitetes Holz und Stein treffen auf eher unerwartete verglaste Oberflächen, die sich zur umgebenden Landschaft öffnen.

Les habillages de bois brut et de pierre encadrent des plans vitrés inattendus, ouverts sur le cadre naturel.

#11

MAD

MAD LTD.
3rd floor West Building, No. 7
Banqiao Nanxiang
Beixinqiao, Beijing 100007

Tel: +86 10 6402 6632
Fax: +86 10 6402 3940
E-mail: office@i-mad.com
or mad-office@163.com
Web: www.i-mad.com

MAD is a Beijing-based architectural and design collaboration between Ma Yansong, Yosuke Hayano, and Dang Qun. MAD has received numerous international design awards for its projects, including the planned Absolute Tower in Toronto, Canada. The construction of the tower will make MAD the first Chinese architectural office to design an international landmark project. Ma obtained his M.Arch degree from Yale in 2002, where he received the Samuel J. Fogelson Memorial Award for Design Excellence. He worked with Zaha Hadid Architects and Eisenman Architects as a project designer and has taught at the Central Academy of Fine Arts in Beijing. Yosuke graduated from Waseda University in 2000 and received a Master's in Architectural Design at the Design Research Laboratory of the Architectural Association in (AA) London in 2003. After graduating from the AA, Hayano worked for Zaha Hadid Architects. Dang received her M.Arch degree from Iowa State University in 1999. Dang has been an assistant professor at Iowa State University and at Iowa State University's Foreign Studies Program in Rome (Italy), and a visiting professor at the Pratt Institute. She has also worked for several architecture firms in the United States on projects of different scales, and has received numerous awards. Their work includes: the Absolute Tower, Toronto; the Rising House and Hong Luo Clubhouse, both published here; and the Guangzhou Sun Plaza Biosciences facility in Guangzhou, due to start construction in 2007.

HONG LUO CLUBHOUSE

BEIJING 2004-06

BUILDING AREA: 487 m² INTERIOR AREA: 189 m²
CLIENT: private COST: not disclosed
DIRECTORS: Ma Yansong, Yosuke Hanayo
PROJECT ARCHITECT: Florian Pucher
DESIGN TEAM: Shen Jun, Christiaan Taubert, Marco Zuttioni, Yu Kui

Located in the Miyun area, about an hour's drive north of the center of Beijing, Hong Luo Lake is a rapidly growing residential area. 150 houses were built as part of the Hong Luo Villa project and MAD was asked to design a clubhouse or gathering place for home owners. Set on the lake itself, the clubhouse allows patrons to swim in a pool that floats in the lake. A wooden bridge offers access to the clubhouse from the area of the villas. The architects explain that "the architecture is physically and phenomenologically united to the natural landscape, lake, and mountains. The circulation, based on topography, landscaping, and environmental considerations, including lake conditions, mountain views, and the villa sites, determined the architectural form." The concrete roof of the structure is its most remarkable feature, aside from the actual site—it swoops down to the water itself and then rises to the sky, embodying the idea of "sanctuary and hope" that the community wishes to project to its city-dwelling clients.

Am etwa eine Autostunde nördlich des Zentrums von Peking in der Gegend von Miyun gelegenen Hong-Luo-See liegt ein schnell wachsendes Wohngebiet. Als Teil des Hong-Luo-Villa-Projekts entstanden 150 Häuser, und MAD erhielt den Auftrag, ein Club- oder Versammlungshaus für die neuen Bewohner zu entwerfen. Vom direkt am See liegenden Club erreichen die Gäste ein im See verankertes Schwimmbecken. Vom Areal der Villen gelangt man über einen hölzernen Steg ins Clubhaus. Die Architekten führen aus, dass »die Architektur sich physisch und phänomenologisch mit der Landschaft, dem See und den Bergen verbindet. Die Wegeführung, die auf Topografie, Bepflanzung sowie umweltrelevanten Überlegungen wie Zustand des Sees, Ausblicke auf die Berge und den Villengrundstücken basiert, bestimmte die architektonische Form.« Neben der Lage selbst ist das Betondach des Gebäudes sein eindrucksvollstes Merkmal – es reicht hinunter bis zum Wasser, um sich sodann zum Himmel zu erheben und verkörpert die Vorstellung von »Zuflucht und Hoffnung«, die die Gemeinde ihren städtischen Bewohnern vermitteln will.

Situé dans la zone de Miyun, à une heure de voiture environ au nord du centre de Pékin, le Lac de Hong Huo est une zone résidentielle en croissance rapide. Cent cinquante maisons ont été construites dans le cadre du projet Hong Luo Villa, et MAD a été chargé du clubhouse, lieu de réunions pour les propriétaires des maisons. Construit sur le lac, ce petit bâtiment, auquel on accède par une passerelle de bois, s'accompagne d'une piscine flottante. Selon le descriptif : « L'architecture est physiquement et phénoménologiquement unie au paysage naturel, au lac et aux montagnes. C'est la circulation reposant sur la topographie, l'aménagement paysager et des considérations environnementales, y compris l'état du lac, les vues sur les montagnes et les terrains des villas, qui a déterminé la forme architecturale. » En dehors de son site, le toit en béton du bâtiment est sa caractéristique la plus remarquable : il s'incline jusqu'à l'eau, puis s'élève vers le ciel, incarnant l'idée de « sanctuaire et d'espoir » que ce projet communautaire souhaite inspirer aux clients venus de la ville.

The folded plane that forms the roof of the building also becomes an interior wall in a gesture that is somewhat reminiscent of work seen in the West in recent years, but there is an austerity or simplicity here that sets the project apart.

Die aufgefaltete Fläche, die das Dach des Gebäudes bildet, wird auch zur Innenwand – ein Kunstgriff, der entfernt an Bauten erinnert, wie sie in den vergangenen Jahren im Westen entworfen wurden. Hier herrschen jedoch Strenge und Schlichtheit, die dem Projekt eine Sonderstellung verschaffen.

Le plan replié qui constitue la toiture se transforme en mur intérieur, gesterappelant certaines réalisations occidentales récentes qui s'accompagne ici d'une austérité et d'une simplicité remarquables.

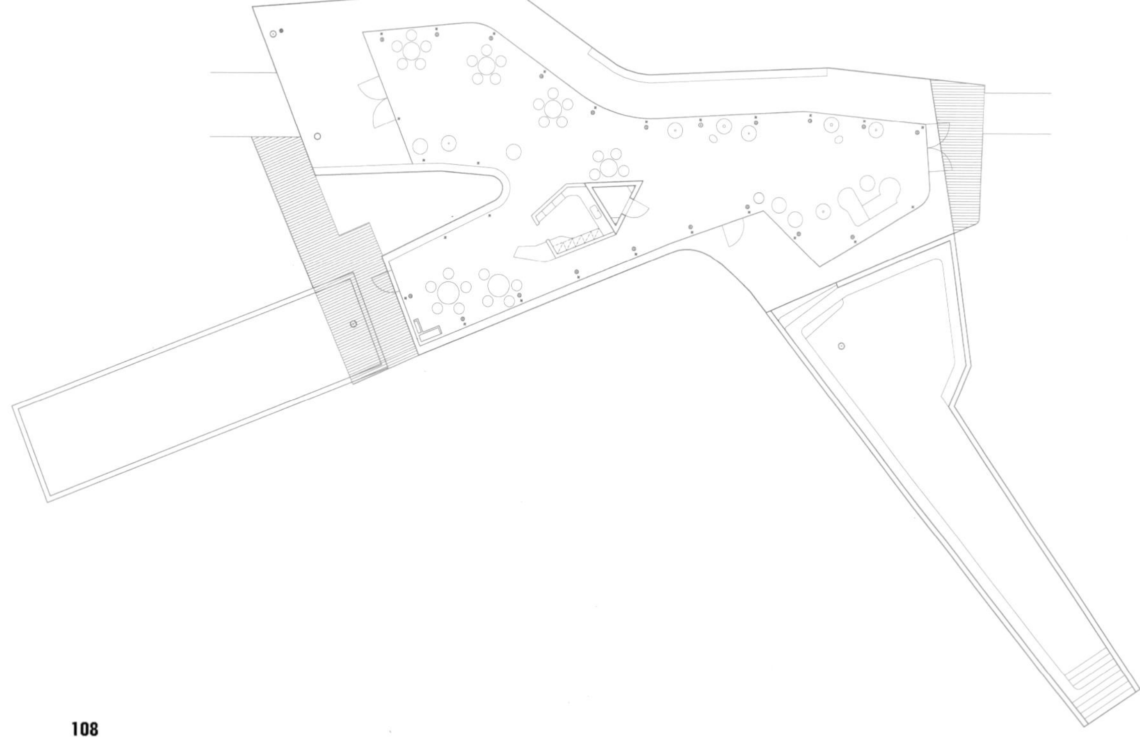

A concrete approach walk slices through the water and forms sharp lines that lead to the folding roof of the small building.

Ein Fußweg aus Beton durchschneidet das Wasser und betont die Linien, die zu dem Faltdach des kleinen Gebäudes führen.

La passerelle d'accès en béton franchit l'eau et constitue un axe rectiligne qui vient buter sur le toit replié du petit bâtiment.

#12

MADA S.P.A.M.

MADA S.P.A.M.
No. 2, Lane 134, Xinle Road
Xu Hui District
Shanghai 200031

Tel: +86 21 5404 1166
Fax: +86 21 5404 6646
E-mail: office@madaspam.com
Web: www.madaspam.com

MA QINGYUN graduated from Tsinghua University with a degree in Civil Engineering and Architecture in 1988. He worked briefly in a government historic preservation and urban planning office, before attending the Graduate School of Fine Art at the University of Pennsylvania, where he obtained his M.Arch in 1991. He became a certified architect in the state of Ohio in 1996 and worked in the office of KPF in New York (1991–95). He then established MADA s.p.a.m. (for strategy, planning, architecture, and media). Ma has taught at Harvard, Columbia, UPenn, the ETH in Zurich, the Berlage Institute, and the Berlin Technical University. He coordinated the first book by Rem Koolhaas and the Harvard Project on Cities, entitled *Great Leap Forward* (Taschen, 2001). Ma Qingyun is presently the Dean of the School of Architecture at USC. The firm's projects include: the Ningbo Culture Center, Ningbo (2000); Father's House, Xi'an (2004); the Ningbo Y-Town, published here; Chunshen Floating Street, Shanghai (2005); and the Xi'an TV Media Center (2005). As Ma writes, "We see architecture as a process that selects and configures material, technology, and finance. We see it as a construct of ideas, as well as products. We also see it as a form of knowledge gained through experiment and readjustment."

MADA S.P.A.M. OFFICE

SHANGHAI 2003–04

FLOOR AREA: 800 m^2
CLIENT: MADA s.p.a.m.
COST: not disclosed

The architects renovated a former kindergarten in Shanghai for their own use, but they took to heart the school's former name and made it part of their program. They explain, "The name Red Star may be the most frequently used term in the Chinese language during the years of the socialist regime. A famous movie called 'Shining Red Star' monumentalized this phrase in the heroic spirit of communist youth. With the late 60s and 70s baby boom, Red Star became one of the most popular names for Shanghai kindergartens and primary schools, the equivalent of today's chain brand." Intentionally maintaining the "banal" aspect of this early 1980s structure, the architects proceeded to wrap it in bamboo boards used in China for concrete formwork, framing the boards in stainless steel. Within, they have created a "free zone" that they describe as a cross between a production house and an exhibition space. A full-height entry with a skylight, which was formerly the location of a large staircase, penetrates the building and opens on to the three work floors. The architects see the reuse of such a fundamentally ordinary building as being part of the "legacy of continuous discontinuity of Shanghai." They conclude, "The office of MADA s.p.a.m. is not only obsessed with socialist nostalgia, but also fascinated by the opportunity to engage in the discourse of urban mutation caused by systematic obsolescence."

Die Architekten renovierten einen ehemaligen Kindergarten in Shanghai für ihre eigenen Zwecke, aber sie nahmen sich den früheren Namen der Einrichtung zu Herzen und machten ihn zu einem Teil ihres Programms. Dazu erklären sie: »Der Name ›Roter Stern‹ ist vermutlich der zu Zeiten des sozialistischen Regimes am häufigsten verwendete Begriff der chinesischen Sprache. Ein berühmter Film mit dem Titel ›Leuchtender Roter Stern‹ monumentalisierte diese Wendung im heroischen Geist der kommunistischen Jugend. Mit dem Babyboom der späten 60er- und 70er-Jahre wurde ›Roter Stern‹ zu einem der beliebtesten Namen für Kindergärten und Grundschulen in Shanghai, dem Gegenstück zu heutigen Markennamen.« Die Architekten behielten bewusst die »banalen« Aspekte des zu Beginn der 80er-Jahre entstandenen Gebäudes bei und verkleideten es mit Bambusbrettern, die man in China als Schalungsform für Beton verwendet; die Bretter wurden in Edelstahlrahmen eingefügt. Im Inneren schufen sie eine »freie Zone«, die sie als Mischung zwischen einer Fertigungshalle und einem Ausstellungsraum bezeichnen. Da, wo sich früher eine Treppe befand, durchstößt ein Eingang in ganzer Höhe mit einem Oberlicht das Gebäude und öffnet sich zu drei Bürogeschossen. Die Architekten sehen die Wiederverwendung eines solchen im Grunde gewöhnlichen Bauwerks als Teil des »Vermächtnisses einer kontinuierlichen Diskontinuität Shanghais«. Abschließend heißt es: »Das Büro von MADA s.p.a.m. ist nicht nur von sozialistischer Nostalgie besessen, sondern auch fasziniert von der Möglichkeit, sich an dem Diskurs über den urbanen Wandel zu beteiligen, der durch die systematischeVernachlässigung verursacht wurde.«

Bien que ce soit pour leur propre usage que les architectes ont rénové cet ancien jardin d'enfants de Shanghai, ils ont tenu à conserver son nom et à l'intégrer dans leur programme. « La dénomination d'Étoile rouge est peut-être l'une des plus utilisées dans la langue chinoise sous le régime communiste. Un célèbre film intitulé « L'Étoile rouge étincelante » l'avait institutionnalisé dans l'esprit de la jeunesse communiste. Avec l'explosion démographique de la fin des année 1960 et des années 1970, « Étoile rouge » est devenue l'une des dénominations les plus populaires des jardins d'enfants et des écoles primaires de Shanghai, l'équivalent actuel d'une marque de chaîne. » Conservant volontairement l'aspect « banal » de ce bâtiment du début des années 1980, les architectes l'ont enveloppé de lattes de bambou utilisées en Chine pour les coffrages à béton, mais tenues dans des cadres en acier inoxydable. À l'intérieur, ils ont créé une « zone libre » décrite comme un croisement de maison de production et d'espace d'expositions. Une entrée sous verrière occupe toute la hauteur d'une ancienne cage d'escalier, pénètre le bâtiment et ouvre sur les trois niveaux de bureaux. Pour les architectes, cette réutilisation d'un immeuble aussi fondamentalement ordinaire fait partie de « l'héritage de discontinuité continue de Shanghai ... Les bureaux de MADA ne sont pas seulement obsédés par la nostalgie du socialisme, ils sont également fascinés par l'opportunité de participer au débat sur la mutation urbaine que provoque une obsolescence systématique. »

红
托儿所

Few details actually reveal that the MADA s.p.a.m. offices used to be a school. Cladding and the varied glazing, on the contrary, give the impression that this is a new building. Elevations to the right reveal the institutional aspect of the former school more clearly.

Nur wenige Einzelheiten lassen erahnen, dass es sich bei dem Büro von MADA s.p.a.m. früher um eine Schule handelte. Die Verkleidung und die variablen Glasflächen erwecken im Gegenteil den Eindruck, es handele sich um einen Neubau. Die Aufrisse rechts zeigen deutlicher den Charakter der ehemaligen Schule.

Seuls quelques détails révèlent que les bureaux de l'agence MADA s.p.a.m. étaient naguère une école. L'habillage et les baies vitrées donnent au contraire l'impression qu'il s'agit d'un bâtiment neuf. Les coupes (à droite) expriment plus clairement les aspects fonctionnels de l'ancienne école.

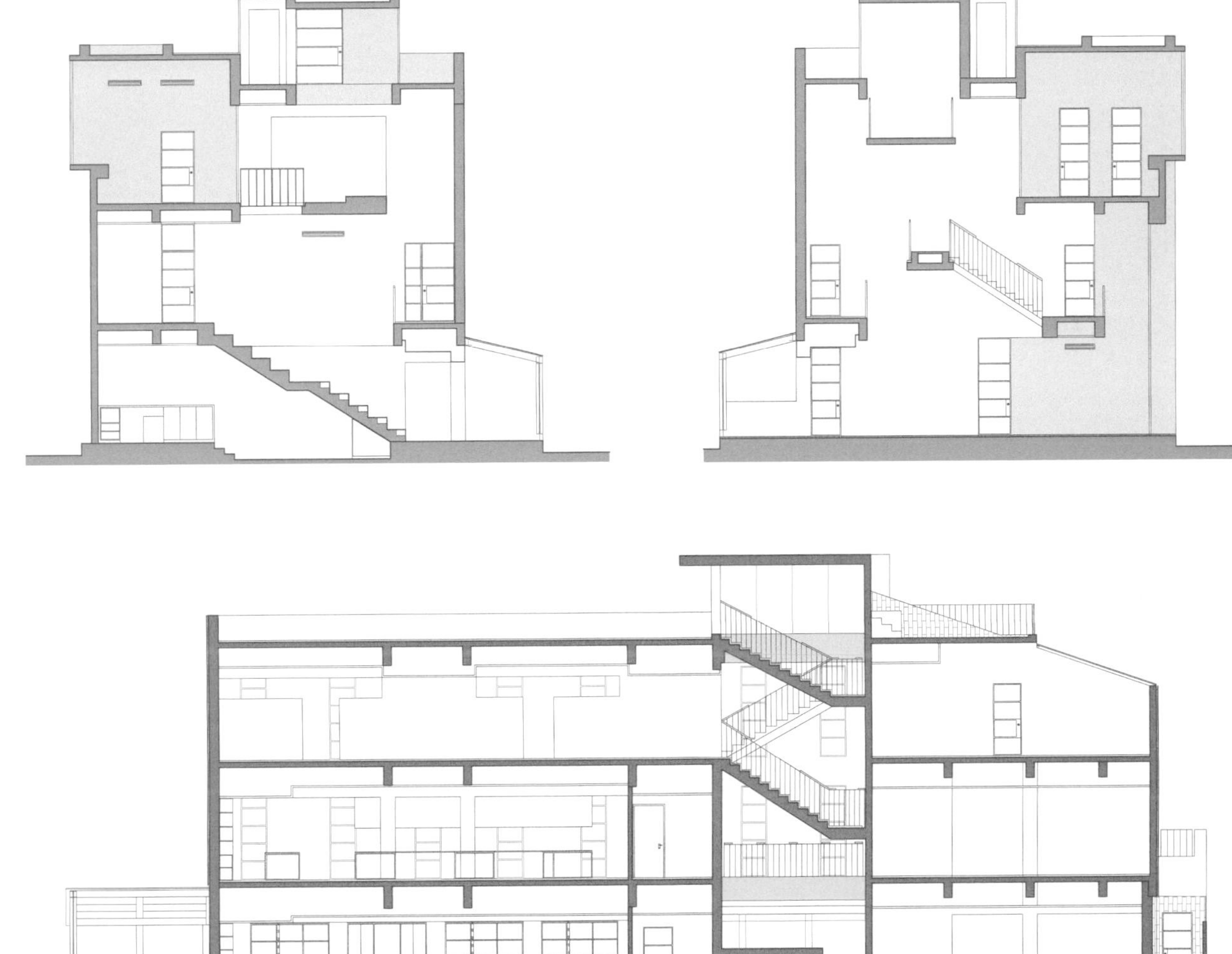

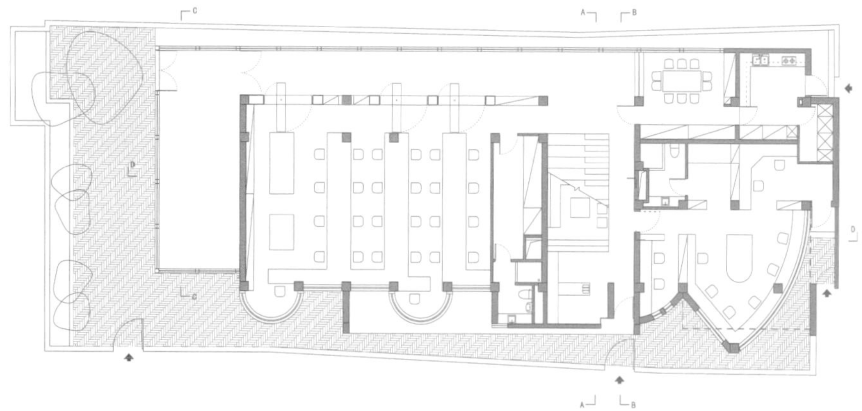

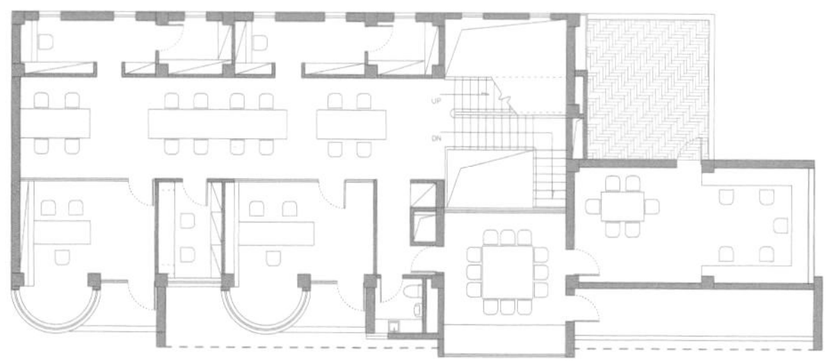

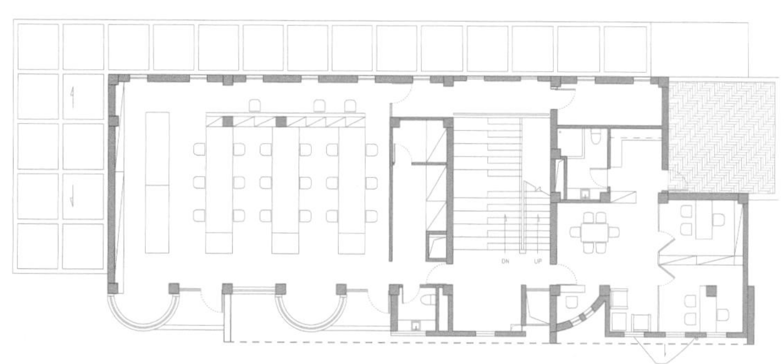

Inserted into the rapidly changing Shanghai skyline, the offices stand out and contrast markedly with the relatively disordered neighborhood. The entrance and stair void (above) penetrates the building and links its floors.

Der in die sich rasant verändernde Skyline Shanghais eingefügte Bürobau fällt auf und steht in deutlichem Kontrast zum eher regellosen Umfeld. Eingang und Treppenhaus (oben) durchdringen das Gebäude und verbinden die Geschosse.

Inscrits dans le panorama urbain de Shanghai, qui affiche une évolution rapide, ces bureaux se remarquent et contrastent avec un voisinage relativement confus. L'entrée et la cage d'escalier (ci-dessus) pénètrent profondément dans le bâtiment et relient ses niveaux entre eux.

JADE VILLAGE
LANTIAN, XI'AN, SHAANXI 2005

SITE AREA: 319 m^2
FLOOR AREA: 109 m^2
CLIENT: Jade Valley Wine and Resort Co. Ltd.
COST: not disclosed

In a most unusual project description, MADA cites "local peasants" as consultants on the project and "old local Lantian craftsmen led by Qingcai Zhang and Jingtan Zhou" as the builders of this brick masonry and wood resort structure. The Well Hall, as it is called, is a "probe piece for a larger project developed by MADA in connection with Jade Valley Wine and Resort Co. Ltd. to create a mixed-use tourism project with a hotel, time-share B&B and winery together with a small agricultural museum." The concept of this first structure does not so much seek to imitate or use local architecture directly as it does to employ craftsmen and subtly subvert the process to make them create something other than what they might have intended. As MADA explains, "In the project the architect has remodeled the residential quarter and social quarter of a traditional courtyard home, altered the interior spatial formation, changed brick course work and readjusted the fenestration schemes. Both red and gray bricks are used, but they are fabricated instead of laid. Red brick is used for interior and gray for exterior. In another instance, the height of the traditional typology on which this building is based is stretched substantially, almost in a Photoshop way, first to respond to the scale of the landscape which is grand and alien to local residential senses, and then to engender a life that is equally alien to the local scene."

In einer höchst ungewöhnlichen Projektbeschreibung führt MADA »einheimische Bauern« als Projektberater und »alte Handwerker aus Lantian unter Führung von Qingcai Zhang und Jingtan Zhou« als Erbauer dieses Gebäudes aus Backsteinmauerwerk und Holz an. Bei der sogenannten Well Hall handelt es sich um einen »Testbau für ein umfassenderes Projekt, das von MADA in Verbindung mit der Jade Valley Wine and Resort Co. Ltd. entwickelt wurde, um eine touristische Mehrzweckanlage mit Hotel, time-share Bed & Breakfast und Weinkellerei mit einem kleinen landwirtschaftlichen Museum zu erstellen«. Bei dem Konzept dieses ersten Gebäudes ging es nicht so sehr darum, ortsspezifische Architektur unmittelbar nachzuahmen oder zu verwenden, sondern vielmehr darum, die Handwerker einzubeziehen und den Arbeitsprozess subtil zu unterwandern, um etwas anderes zu schaffen, als sie vielleicht ursprünglich beabsichtigten. MADA erläutert: »Bei dem Projekt hat der Architekt die Wohn- und Gesellschaftsräume eines traditionellen Hofhauses neu gestaltet, die innere Raumaufteilung umgewandelt, die Schichtung der Backsteine geändert sowie die Fenster neu angepasst. Es wurden sowohl graue wie rote Ziegel verwendet, aber sie werden gefertigt anstatt (nur) verlegt. Rote Steine kamen innen, graue außen zum Einsatz. Außerdem wurde die Höhe des traditionellen Bautyps, auf dem dieses Gebäude basiert, erheblich gestreckt, beinahe nach Art eines digitalen Bildbearbeitungsprogramms, um sich dem Maßstab der Landschaft anzupassen, was für das lokale Verständnis von Wohnen ebenso imposant wie fremdartig ist, und eine Lebensart zu erzeugen, die der heimischen Szene gleichermaßen fremd ist.«

Dans un descriptif de projet très inhabituel, l'agence MADA cite « les paysans locaux » comme consultants et « les vieux artisans locaux de Lantian dirigés par Qingcai Zhang et Jingtan Zhou » comme constructeurs de cet hôtel de loisirs en maçonnerie de briques et en bois. Le Well Hall est le « prototype d'un projet plus vaste mis au point par MADA en connexion avec la Jade Valley Wine and Resort Co. Ltd. pour créer un ensemble touristique mixte comprenant un hôtel, des chambres d'hôtes en propriété temporaire, un chais et un petit musée d'agriculture ». Le concept de ce premier bâtiment ne cherche pas tant à imiter directement ou à utiliser l'architecture locale qu'à faire appel à des artisans locaux et subvertir subtilement leur processus de travail afin de les amener à créer quelque chose d'autre que ce qu'ils étaient naturellement incités à faire. Comme le précise l'agence : « Dans ce projet, nous avons remodelé la partie résidentielle et la partie de réception d'une maison à cour traditionnelle, modifié sa répartition spatiale intérieure et l'appareillage de brique et réajusté le fenêtrage. Des briques rouges pour l'intérieur et grises pour l'extérieur ont été utilisées, mais appareillées plutôt que posées. Autre exemple, la hauteur de type traditionnel dont s'inspire ce bâtiment est fortement étirée, comme on le ferait avec le logiciel Photoshop, pour répondre, d'une part, à l'échelle splendide du paysage qui n'est pas prise en compte par les traditions de l'habitat local et, d'autre part, pour susciter une vie qui est tout aussi étrangère à la scène locale. »

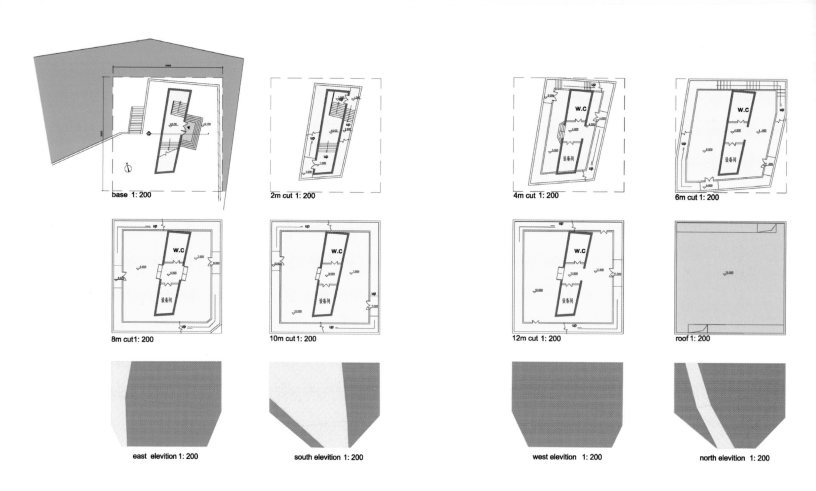

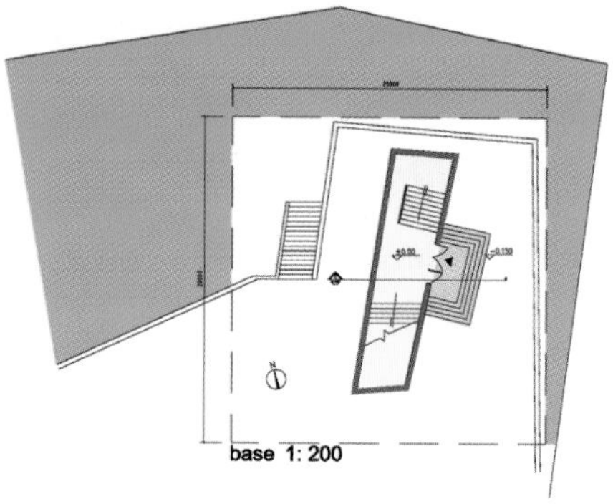

base 1: 200

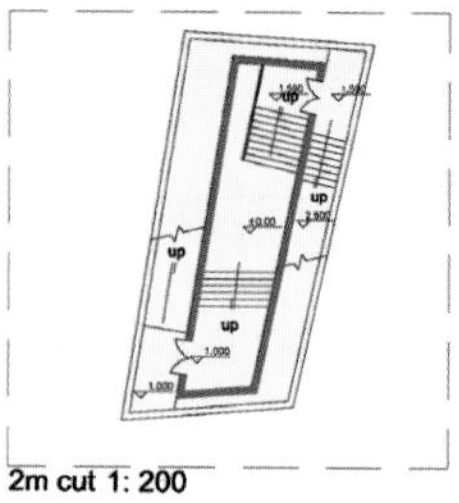

2m cut 1: 200

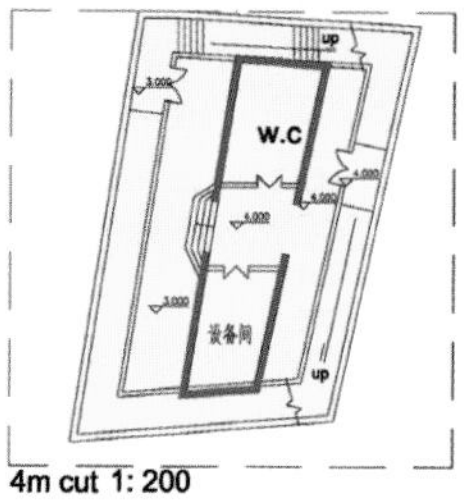

4m cut 1: 200

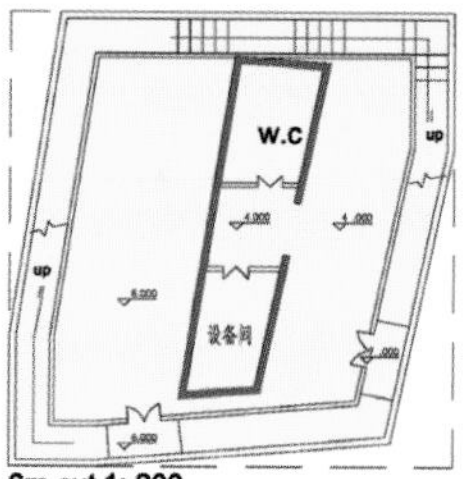

6m cut 1: 200

8m cut1: 200

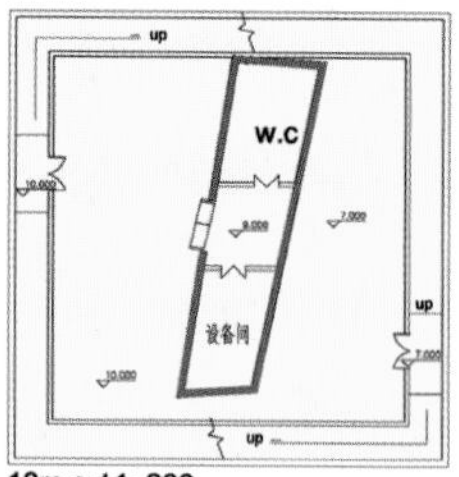

10m cut1: 200

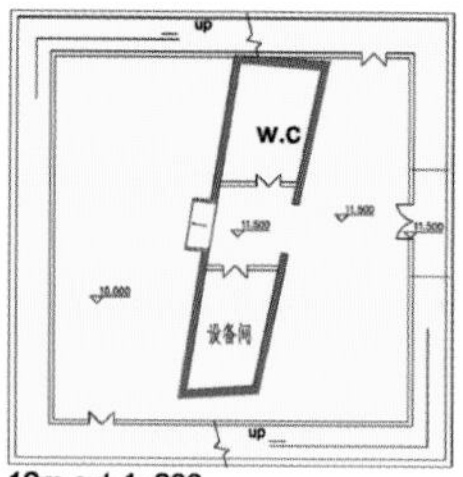

12m cut 1: 200

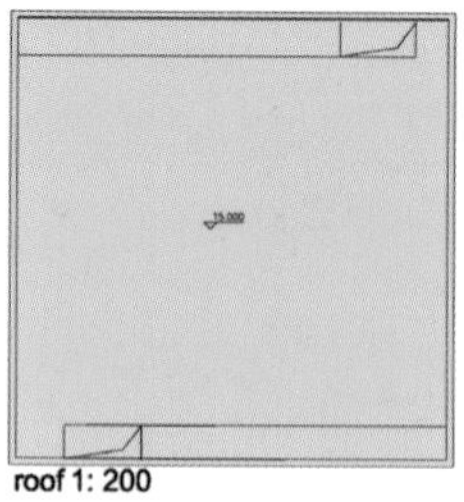

roof 1: 200

east elevition 1: 200

south elevition 1: 200

west elevition 1: 200

north elevition 1: 200

Playing on the typology of the traditional courtyard home, the architects have in fact developed quite modern forms with a distinct connection to China's past.

Indem sie mit dem Typus des traditionellen Hofhauses spielten, entwickelten die Architekten ganz moderne Formen mit deutlichen Anklängen an Chinas Vergangenheit.

En jouant sur la typologie traditionnelle de la maison à cour, les architectes ont en fait mis au point des formes assez modernes, non sans connexion avec le passé de la Chine.

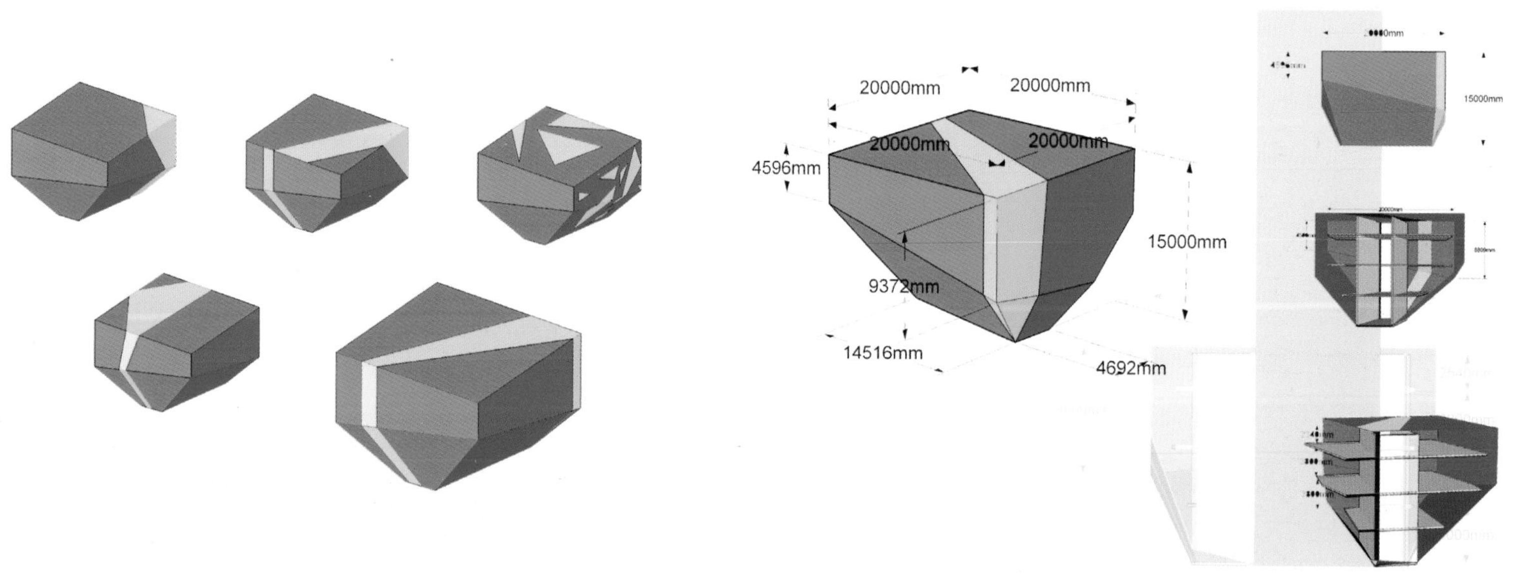

Alternating gray and red bricks animate the surface of the building but preserve a kind of roughness or sense of enclosure that underlines the links to the past.

Die abwechselnde Verwendung grauen und roten Backsteins belebt die Außenflächen der Gebäude, bewahrt jedoch eine Art Rauheit oder ein Gefühl des Umbautseins, das die Verbindung zur Vergangenheit unterstreicht.

L'alternance de briques rouges et grises anime la façade, mais maintient une sorte de brutalité ou de sentiment de clôture qui souligne les liens avec le passé.

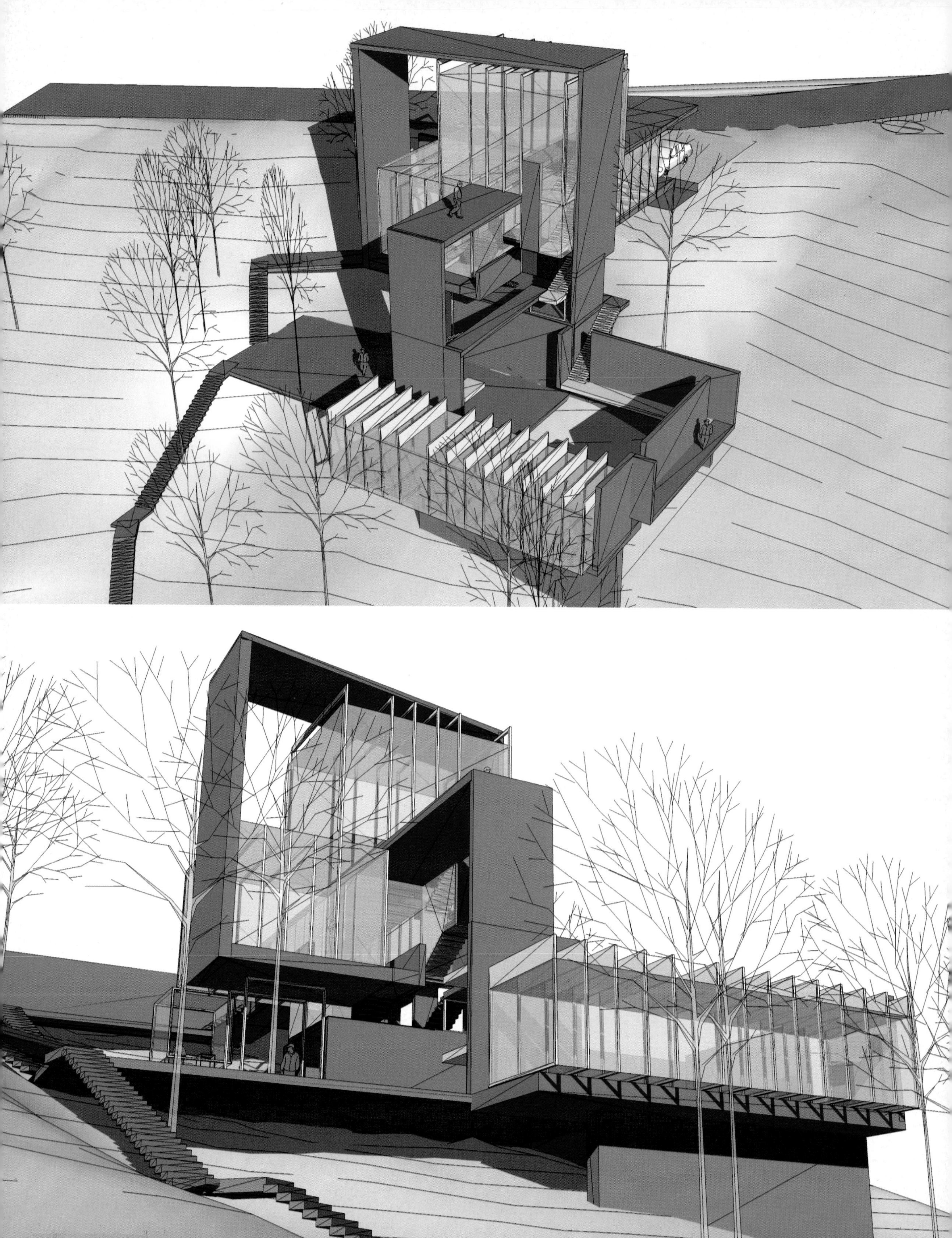

#13

NODE – ARCHITECTURE

NODE – ARCHITECTURE
4/F, N5 Puzhou High-Tech
Development Park
Nansha, Guangzhou 511458
Tel: +86 20 3468 0361
Fax: +86 20 3468 0301

3603, West Tower, 36/F
Shun Tak Centre
200 Connought Road Central
Sheung Wan Hong Kong SAR
Tel: +852 2137 2680
Fax: +852 2137 2690
E-mail: node@nodeoffice.com
Web: www.nodeoffice.com

LIU HENG was born in 1967 in Guangzhou. She obtained her Bachelor of Science in Architecture degree from the Huazhong University of Science and Technology in Wuhan (1989), and her M.Arch from the University of California at Berkeley (1994). She is a Doctor of Design candidate at the Harvard Graduate School of Design. Beginning in 1995, she was a project architect for the Fok Ying Tung Foundation. She is the principal and founder of NODE – Architecture. As she explains, NODE stands for Nansha Original DEsign (or NO DEsign) and was established in early 2004. It is an architectural practice based in Nansha, which grew out of a series of projects associated with the Fok Foundation of Hong Kong, and it presently consists of 10 architects and designers. She has worked extensively on a joint venture between the Fok Ying Tung Foundation of Hong Kong and the Guangzhou government intended to develop a "modern resort and high-tech city with international standards" at the mouth of the Pearl River on a 22-square-kilometer site. Among her projects are: the Depin Bookstore (2002); PRD World Trade Center (2004–06); Nansha Grand Hotel Health Center (2004–06); Lujin Housing complex (2004–); and the Nansha Yacht Club (2005–), all located in Nansha. Current projects include the Times Branch of the Guangdong Museum of Art in Guangzhou (with Rem Koolhaas and Alain Fouraux).

ARTIST STUDIO
PUKOU DISTRICT, NANJING, JIANGSU 2004–07

SITE AREA: 3125 m² FLOOR AREA: 398 m²
CLIENT: private COST: not disclosed
PROJECT TEAM: Liu Heng (principal), Huang Jie-Bin

Part of the CIPEA (China International Practical Exhibition of Architecture), Liu Heng's project is one of 24 buildings being designed by 10 Chinese architects (including Ai Wei Wei, MADA s.p.a.m., and Zhang Lei) and 10 foreign architects (amongst them, Steven Holl, Arata Isozaki, Mathias Klotz, David Adjaye, Luis Mansilla, Sean Godsell, Odile Decq, and Kazuyo Sejima). The essential idea of this design is a 4.8-meter-wide, 175-meter-long linear plane of steel that "folds up and down, left and right, and forms a series of intimate spaces, running from the upper hill to the lower lake." Inspired by an artist who is a friend of the architect, Song Dong, the house develops itself around the concept of 13 characters—"the blurred; the empty | in-between; in | out; land- | -scape; to stop | to walk | to run | to fly; to construct | to de-construct." Although the precise idea of the 13 characters may not be obvious to those who do not read Chinese, the basic concept of a folded plane forming a house is perfectly legible in this innovative, modern, and open house.

Als Teil der CIPEA (Internationale Ausstellung angewandter Architektur Chinas) ist Liu Hengs Projekt eines von 24 Gebäuden, die von zehn chinesischen Architekten, darunter Ai Wei Wei, MADA s.p.a.m. und Zhang Lei, und von zehn ausländischen Architekten, darunter Steven Holl, Arata Isozaki, Mathias Klotze, David Adjaye, Luis Mansilla, Sean Godsell, Odile Decq und Kazuyo Sejima, entworfen wurden. Die wesentliche Idee dieses Entwurfs besteht darin, dass eine 4,8 m breite und 175 m lange lineare Stahlfläche »sich nach oben und unten sowie nach links und rechts faltet und eine Reihe intimer Räume bildet, die vom oberen Hügel bis zum unten gelegenen See reicht«. Inspiriert von Song Dong, einem mit der Architektin befreundeten Künstler, entwickelt sich das Haus um den Begriff von 13 Schriftzeichen – »dem Verschwommenen; dem Leeren; dem Dazwischen; drinnen; draußen; Land-; -schaft; stehenbleiben; gehen; laufen; fliegen; bauen; abbauen«. Wenngleich der genaue Charakter der 13 Schriftzeichen, sich denen, die kein Chinesisch lesen können, nicht erschließen mag, ist doch die Grundidee einer gefalteten Fläche, die ein Haus bildet, anhand dieses innovativen, modernen und offenen Hauses gut verständlich.

Réalisé dans le cadre de la CIPEA (China International Practical Exhibition of Architecture), le projet de Liu Heng fait partie de vingt-quatre constructions conçues par dix architectes chinois, dont Ai Wei Wei, MADA s.p.a.m. et Zhang Lei, et dix étrangers, dont Steven Holl, Arata Isozaki, Mathias Klotz, Davide Adjaye, Luis Mansilla, Sean Godsell, Odile Decq et Kazuyo Sejima. L'idée de base est celle d'un bandeau d'acier de 175 m de long et 4,8 m de large qui « se plie à la verticale, à l'horizontale, vers la gauche ou vers la droite pour constituer une succession d'espaces intimes, descendant du sommet de la colline jusqu'au lac ». Inspirée par un artiste ami de l'architecte, Song Dong, cette maison se développe autour d'un concept qui s'exprime à travers treize caractéristiques : « le flou, le vide/ entre deux ; dedans-dehors / terre-paysage ; arrêter, marcher, courir, voler / construire, déconstruire ». Bien que le contenu précis de ces éléments ne soit pas évident pour ceux qui ne lisent pas le chinois, le concept de base d'un plan qui se plie pour former une maison est parfaitement lisible dans cette maison moderne ouverte et novatrice.

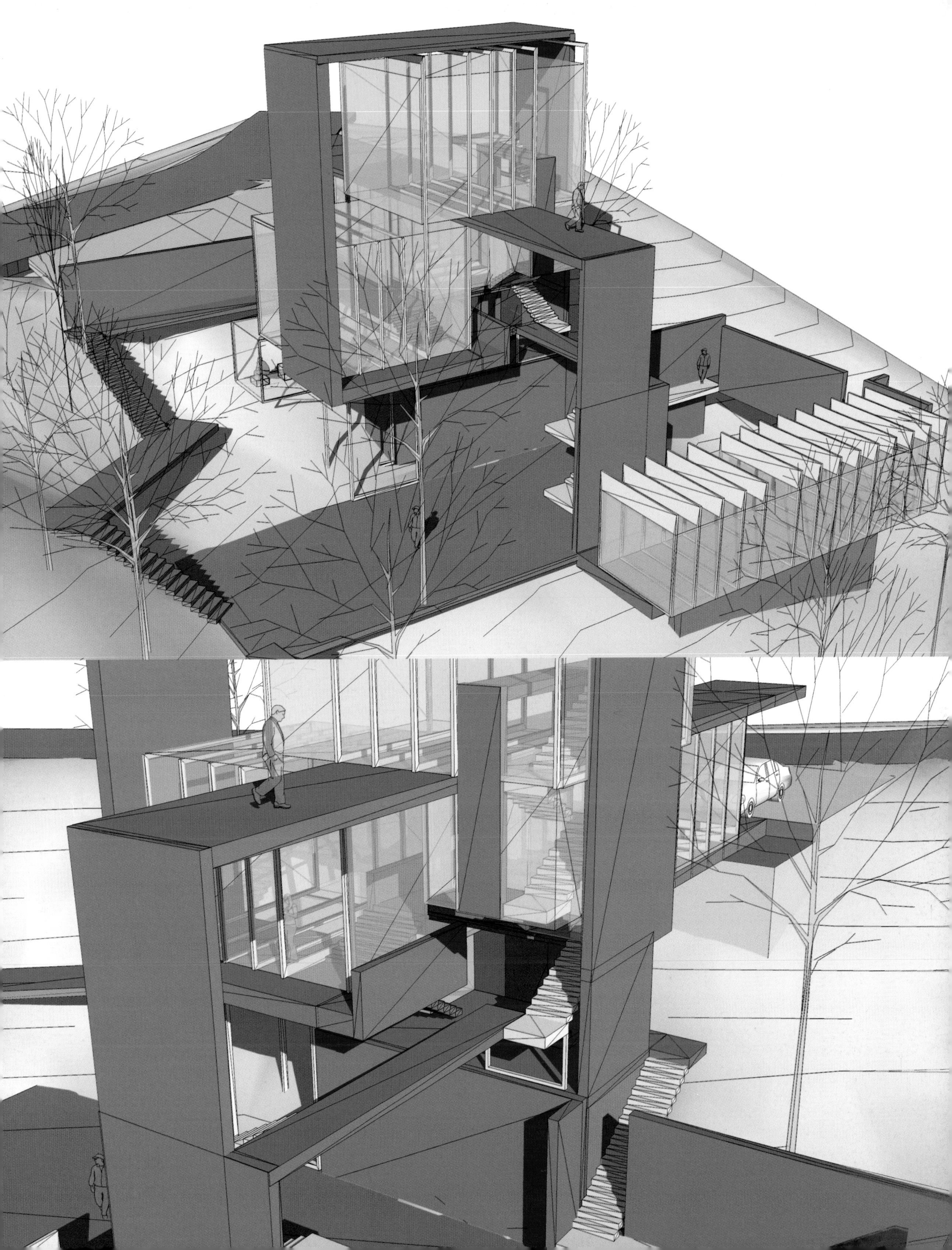

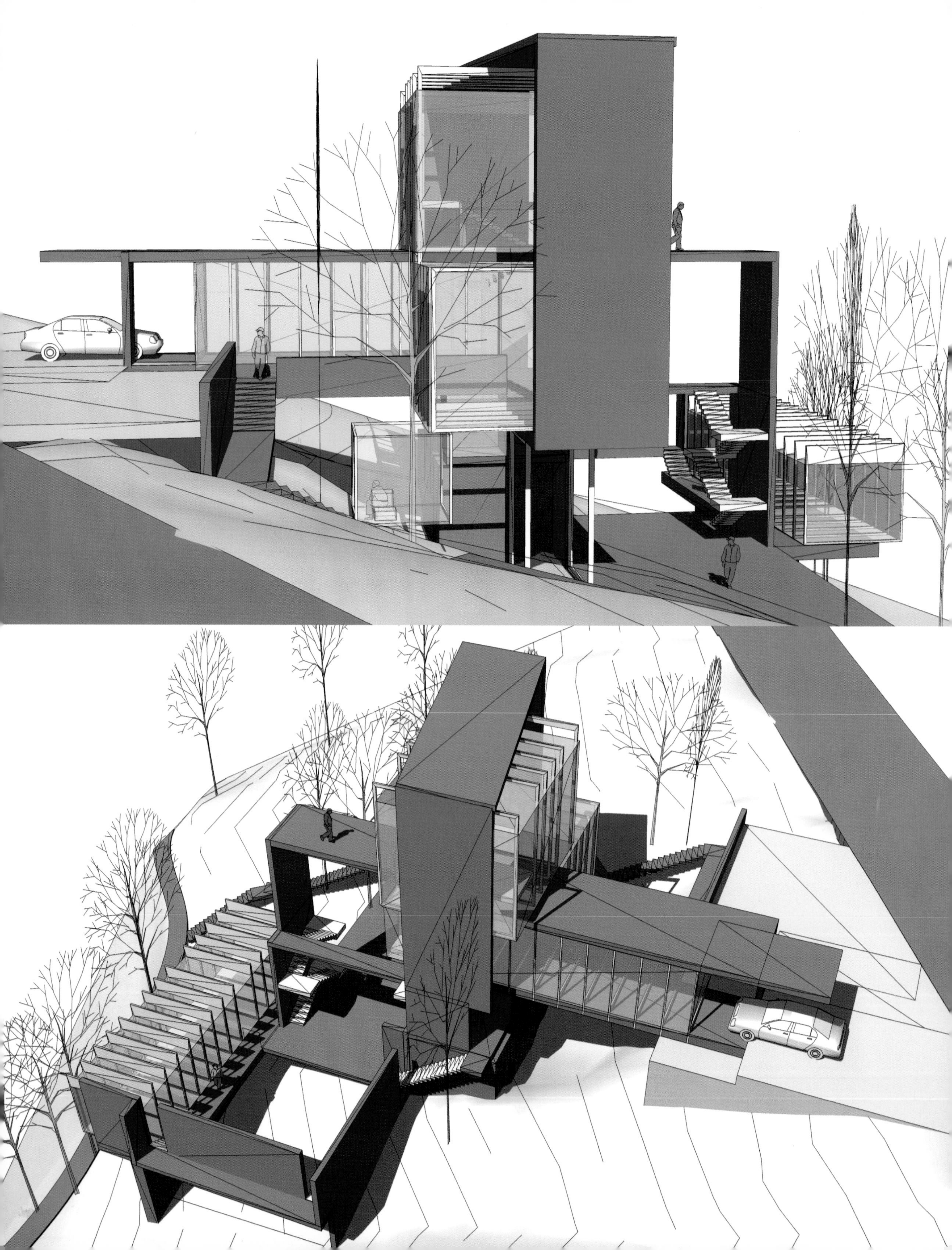

The assemblage of rectangular forms visible in the plans to the right does not reveal the most unusual aspect of the structure – its conception as a continuous folding plane.

Die auf dem Lageplan rechts zu erkennende Ansammlung rechteckiger Formen ist nicht der ungewöhnlichste Aspekt der Anlage – dies ist ihr Entwurf als fortlaufend gefaltete Fläche.

L'assemblage de formes rectangulaires, visible sur les plans de droite, ne traduit pas l'aspect le plus intéressant de cette structure, à savoir sa conception en ruban continu.

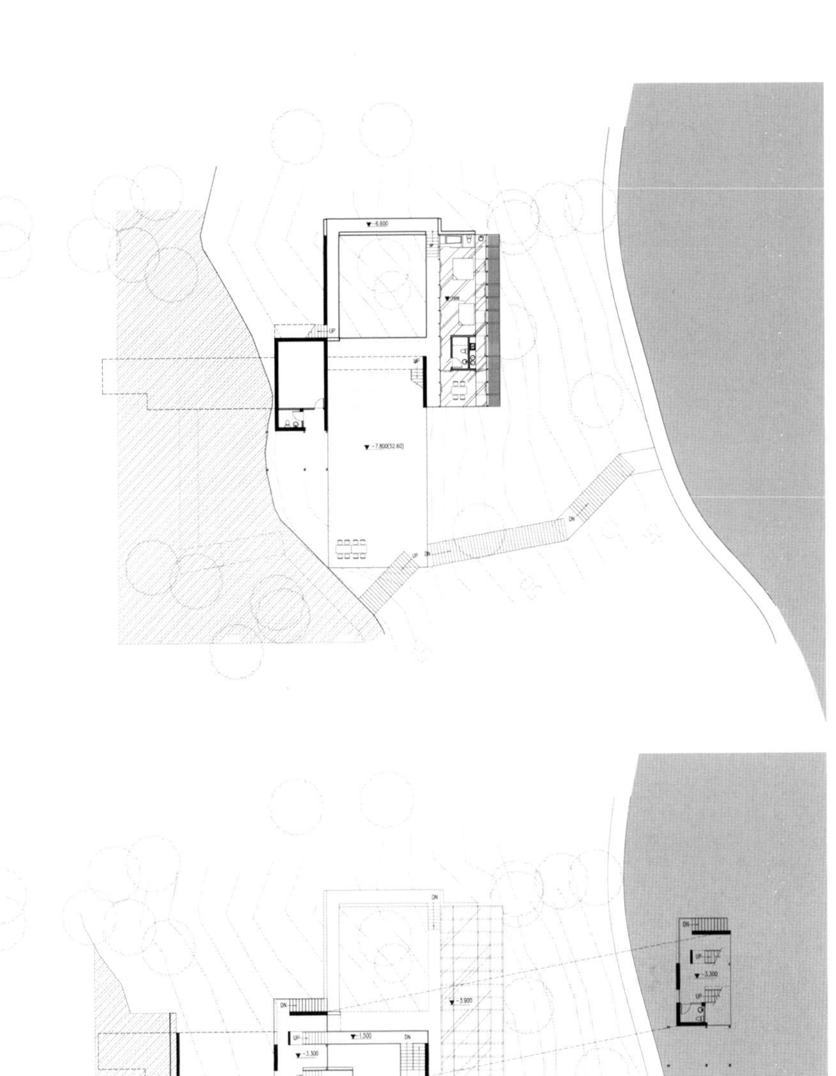

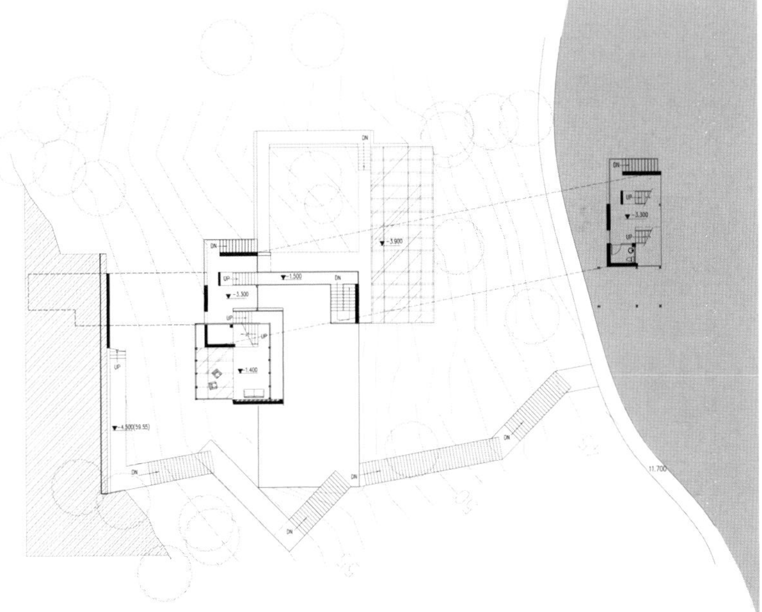

Computer perspectives show the dramatic contrast between open or glazed surfaces and the massive steel containing walls that form the house.

Computerperspektiven zeigen den deutlichen Kontrast zwischen offenen und verglasten Oberflächen sowie die wuchtigen stahlverstärkten Wände, die das Haus bilden.

Ces perspectives par image de synthèse illustrent le contraste spectaculaire entre les surfaces ouvertes ou vitrées et les murs en acier massif qui constituent la maison.

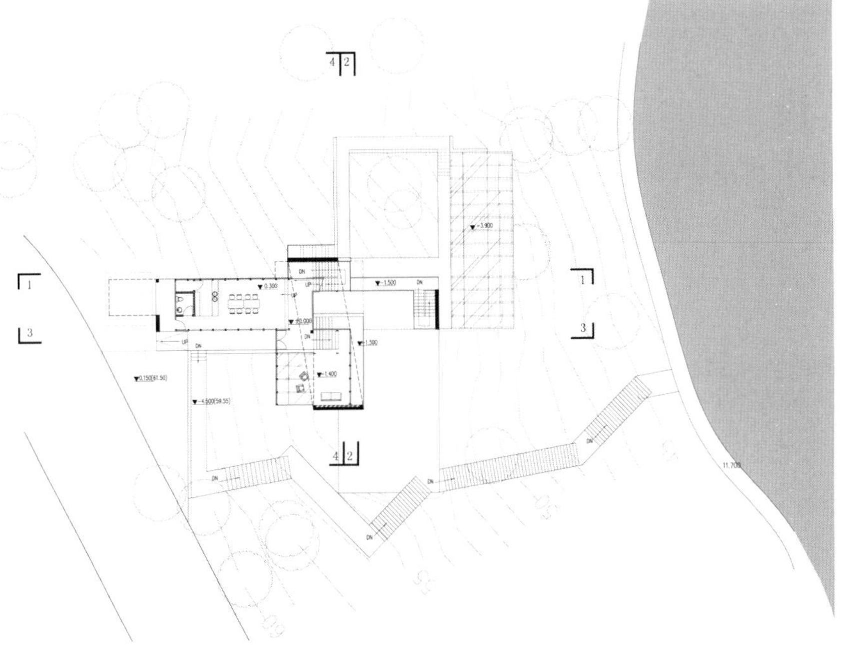

#14

OMA / REM KOOLHAAS

OFFICE FOR METROPOLITAN ARCHITECTURE
Heer Bokelweg 149
3032 AD Rotterdam
The Netherlands

Tel: +31 10 243 8200
Fax: +31 10 243 8202
E-mail: office@oma.nl
Web: www.oma.nl

REM KOOLHAAS created the Office for Metropolitan Architecture in 1975 together with Elia and Zoe Zenghelis and Madelon Vriesendorp. Born in Rotterdam in 1944, Koolhaas tried his hand as a journalist for the *Haagse Post* and as a screen-writer before studying at the Architectural Association (AA) in London. He became well known after the 1978 publication of his book *Delirious New York*. OMA is lead today by six partners: Rem Koolhaas, Ole Scheeren, Ellen van Loon, Reinier de Graaf, Floris Alkemade and Managing Director Victor van der Chijs. Their built work includes a group of apartments at Nexus World, Fukuoka (1991), and Villa dall'Ava, Saint-Cloud, France (1985–91). Koolhaas was named head architect of the Euralille project in Lille in 1988, and has worked on a design for the new Jussieu University Library in Paris. His 1400 page book *S,M,L,XL* (Monacelli Press, 1995) has more than fulfilled his promise as an influential writer. He won the 2000 Pritzker Prize and the 2003 Praemium Imperiale Award for architecture. More recent work of OMA includes a house, Bordeaux, France (1998); the campus center at the Illinois Institute of Technology, Chicago; the new Dutch Embassy in Berlin; as well as the Guggenheim Las Vegas and Prada boutiques in New York and Los Angeles. OMA completed the Seattle Public Library in 2004, and participated in the Samsung Museum of Art (Leeum) in Seoul with Mario Botta and Jean Nouvel. Current work includes the design of OMA's largest project ever—the 575 000-square-meter Headquarters and Cultural Center for China Central Television (CCTV) in Beijing, published here; the 1850-seat Porto Concert Hall, Porto; and the New City Center for Almere, The Netherlands, for which the firm has drawn up the master plan.

CCTV HEADQUARTERS, TVCC CULTURAL CENTER

BEIJING 2005–08

SITE AREA: 20 hectares in new Central Business District
FLOOR AREA: CCTV total 465 000 m^2, TVCC total 95 000 m^2
CLIENT: China Central Television (CCTV)
COST: € 750 million
PARTNERS IN CHARGE: Rem Koolhaas, Ole Scheeren

With the CCTV Headquarters in Beijing OMA and Rem Koolhaas have taken a radically different approach than other designers might have employed. As they write, "Instead of competing in the hopeless race for ultimate height—dominance of the skyline can only be achieved for a short period of time, and soon another, even taller building will emerge—the project proposes an iconographic constellation of two high-rise structures that actively engage the city space: CCTV and TVCC." A common production platform is the base for the two linked towers, and they are joined at the top, creating a "cantilevered penthouse for the management." "A new icon is formed ...", say the designers, "not the predictable two-dimensional tower 'soaring' skyward, but a truly three-dimensional experience, a canopy that symbolically embraces the entire population. The consolidation of the TV program in a single building allows each worker to be permanently aware of the nature of the work of his co-workers—a chain of interdependence that promotes solidarity rather than isolation, collaboration instead of opposition. The building itself contributes to the coherence of the organization." The CCTV tower will be partially visible to the public admitted to a dedicated "loop" allowing views of the production process and the city itself. The Television Cultural Center (TVCC) will be entirely open to the public and includes a 1500-seat theater, a ballroom, cinemas, recording studios and exhibition areas. The international broadcasting center for the 2008 Olympic Games and a five-star hotel will also be accommodated in the building. Much as they did in the case of the Seattle Central Library, the architects have taken on not only the specific functions requested in this instance, but also the very idea of the building typology involved.

OMA und Rem Koolhaas näherten sich dem Auftrag für die CCTV-Zentrale mit einem radikal anderen Ansatz als andere Büros. Sie führen dazu aus: »Anstatt sich an der hoffnungslosen Jagd nach der ultimativen Höhe zu beteiligen – die Beherrschung der Skyline bleibt immer nur für kurze Zeit bestehen bis bald ein anderes, noch höheres Gebäude entsteht – sieht das Projekt eine ikonografische Konstellation zweier Hochhäuser vor, die aktiv den Stadtraum in Anspruch nehmen: CCTV und TVCC.« Eine gemeinsame Produktionsebene ist die Basis der beiden miteinander verbundenen Türme, die darüber hinaus auch am oberen Ende verbunden sind, so dass »ein auskragendes Penthouse für die Führungskräfte« entsteht. »Eine neue Ikone wird gestaltet«, sagen die Designer, »nicht der zu erwartende, zweidimensionale, sich himmelwärts ›erhebende‹ Turm, sondern eine wirklich dreidimensionale Erfahrung, ein Baldachin, der symbolisch die ganze Einwohnerschaft umfasst ... Die Zusammenführung des Fernsehprogramms in einem einzigen Gebäude fördert bei jedem hier Beschäftigten das Bewusstsein für die Art der Arbeit seiner Kollegen – eine Kette von gegenseitigen Abhängigkeiten, die Solidarität, nicht Isolation, Zusammenarbeit, nicht Opposition fördert. Das Gebäude trägt selbst zur Kohärenz der Organisation bei.« Der CCTV-Tower wird für Besucher teilweise zugänglich sein, sie erhalten Zutritt zu einem sogenannten Ring, von dem aus man die Fernsehproduktion und die Stadt selbst überschauen kann. Das Fernsehkulturzentrum (TVCC), zu dem ein Theater mit 500 Plätzen, ein Ballsaal, Kinos, Aufnahmestudios und Ausstellungsflächen gehören, wird allen offen stehen. Außerdem werden in dem Gebäude das internationale Sendezentrum für die Olympischen Spiele 2008 sowie ein Fünf-Sterne-Hotel Platz finden. Ähnlich wie bei der Zentralbibliothek in Seattle, haben sich die Architekten nicht nur auf die in diesem Fall geforderten spezifischen Funktionen eingelassen, sondern auch auf die eigentliche Gebäudetypologie.

L'agence OMA et Rem Koolhaas ont abordé le projet du siège de CCTV à Pékin selon une approche radicalement différente de celle qu'auraient pu employer d'autres architectes. Comme ils l'expliquent : « Au lieu de concourir dans une compétition pour la plus grande hauteur, qui est sans espoir – dominer le panorama urbain ne dure que peu de temps, bientôt un immeuble encore plus haut apparaît – le projet propose une constellation iconographique de deux immeubles de grande hauteur qui dialoguent activement dans le paysage : CCTV et TVCC. » Une plate-forme de production commune sert de base à ces deux tours qui se rejoignent à leur sommet, occupé par « une penthouse en porte-à-faux destinée à la direction ». « Une nouvelle icône est née ..., ajoutent les concepteurs, non celle de la tour prévisible en deux dimensions « jaillissant » vers le ciel, mais celle d'une création authentiquement tridimensionnelle, un auvent qui symboliquement s'étend sur toute la population ... La consolidation des programmes de télévision dans un immeuble unique permet à chaque employé d'être en permanence conscient de la nature du travail de ses collègues – une chaîne d'interdépendances qui met en avant la solidarité plutôt que l'isolement, la collaboration plutôt que l'opposition. L'immeuble lui-même contribue à la cohérence de l'entreprise ». La tour CCTV sera partiellement visible au public admis dans une « boucle » qui permet d'observer le processus de production et la ville. Le Centre culturel de la télévision (TVCC) sera entièrement ouvert au public et comprendra une salle de spectacles de 1 500 places, une salle de bal, des cinémas, des studios d'enregistrement et des espaces d'expositions. Le Centre international de diffusion des Jeux olympiques de 2008 et un hôtel 5 étoiles seront également aménagés dans le même immeuble. En grande partie comme ils l'ont fait pour la Bibliothèque centrale de Seattle, les architectes ont pris en compte non seulement les fonctions spécifiques attendues, mais aussi la typologie même de ce type particulier de bâtiment.

The enormous forms of the CCTV building appear to lean into each other, supporting one another and hanging in good part, over empty space.

Die gewaltigen Formen des CCTV-Gebäudes scheinen sich stützend aneinander anzulehnen und hängen dabei zu einem erheblichen Teil über dem freien Raum.

Les énormes masses de l'immeuble CCTV semblent s'incliner l'une vers l'autre ou se soutenir mutuellement, suspendues en grande partie au-dessus du vide.

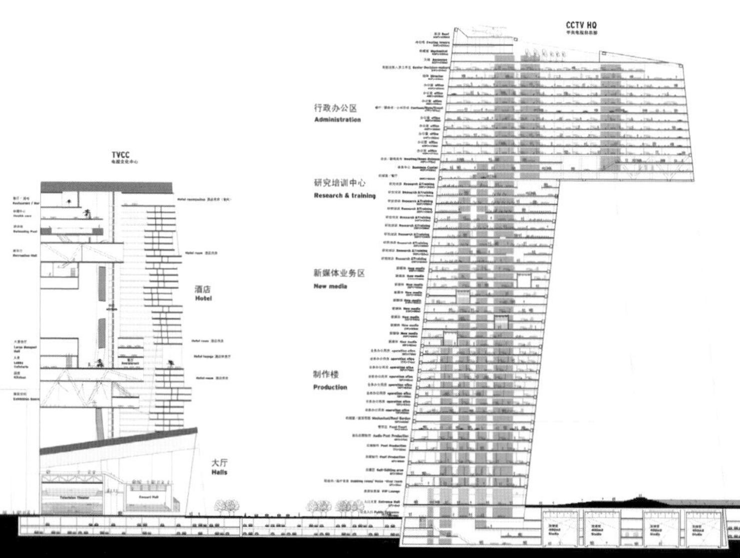

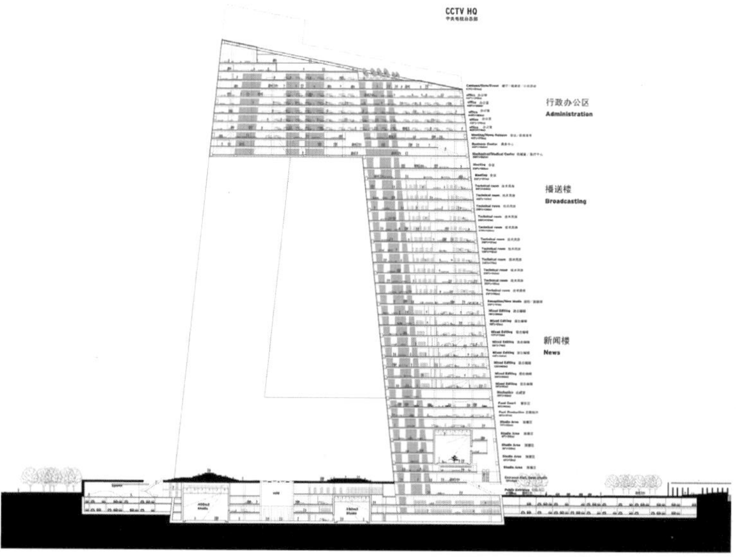

The great complexity of the design and its various functions is revealed in the axonometric view to the right.

Anhand der Axonometrie (rechts) sind die große Komplexität des Entwurfs und seine verschiedenen Funktionen zu erkennen.

La grande complexité de ce projet et de ses diverses fonctions s'exprime dans la vue axonométrique de droite.

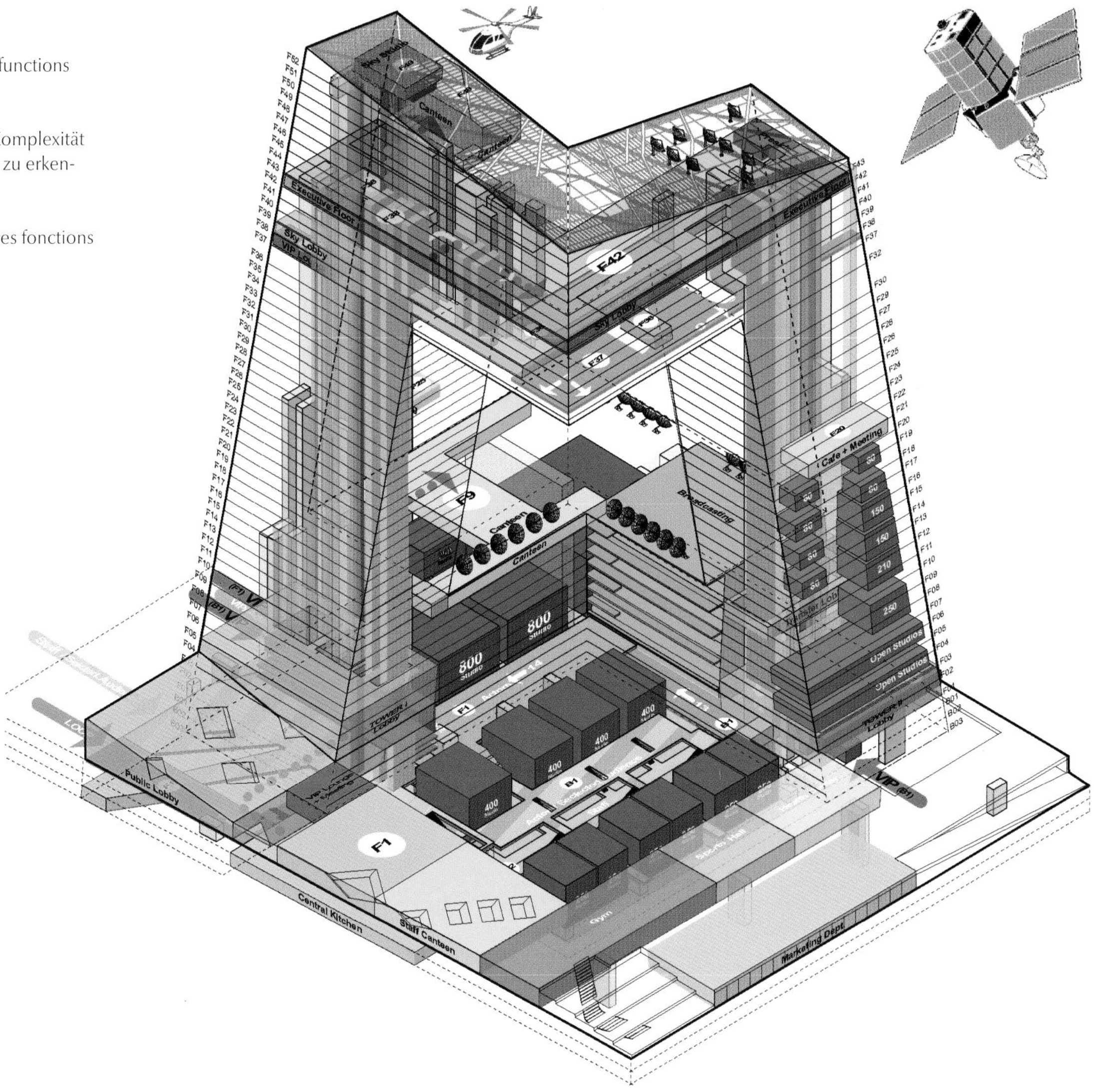

The shapes of the CCTV tower are arguably nothing like any building on this scale ever erected before. Below, construction photographs taken early in 2007.

Die Formgebung des CCTV-Turms ähnelt keinem je in dieser Größenordnung realisierten Gebäude. Unten: Fotos der Baustelle Anfang 2007.

Les formes de l'immeuble CCTV n'ont rien à voir avec tout ce qui a pu être construit à cette échelle jusqu'ici. Ci-dessous : photos de chantier prises début 2007.

#15

PEI ZHU

STUDIO PEI ZHU
B-413 Tian Hai Business Center
No. 107 Donsi Street
Beijing 100007

Tel: +86 10 6401 6657
Fax: +86 10 6403 8967
E-mail: office@studiozp.com

PEI ZHU was born in Beijing, in 1962. He received his M.Arch degree from Tsinghua University, and Master of Architecture and Urban Design degree from the University of California at Berkeley. He has worked with the large American firm RTKL Associates, and as an associate professor at Tsinghua University. He is the principal architect and founder of Studio Pei Zhu and, prior to opening this office in 2005 in Beijing, he was a founding partner and design principal of URBANUS (2001–04). He has been involved in major projects in the United States, as well as projects in China, such as Shanghai Science Land, a science museum; Digital Beijing, an Olympic project for Beijing 2008, published here; and Blur Hotel, a design hotel in the center of Beijing.

DIGITAL BEIJING
BEIJING
2005–07

FLOOR AREA: 98 000 m² CLIENT: Government of Beijing
COST: not disclosed ARCHITECTS: Studio Pei Zhu, URBANUS
PROJECT DESIGNERS: Pei Zhu, Tong Wu, Hui Wang
PROJECT TEAM: Liu Wentian, Li Chuen, Lin Lin, Tian Qi

Located opposite Herzog & de Meuron's Olympic Stadium on the Olympic Green, Digital Beijing was designed by Pei Zhu and his former firm, URBANUS, as the control and data center for the 2008 Games. Subsequently, the building is due to be used as a "virtual museum and exhibition center for digital products." The architect describes this large and imposing reinforced concrete and steel frame building as being an exploration of the impact of electronics on architecture. More specifically, he writes, "The concept for Digital Beijing was developed through reconsideration and reflection on the role of contemporary architecture in the information era. Resembling that omnipresent symbol, the bar code, the building emerges from a serene water surface. The façade itself is detailed to resemble an integrated circuit board. The abstracted mass of the building, reflecting the simple repetition of 0 and 1 in its alternation between void and solid, recreates on a monumental scale the microscopic underpinnings of life in the digital age to form a potent symbol of the Digital Olympics and the Digital Era. In the future, it is expected that the building will be constantly under renovation as it evolves to keep pace with technology."

Das direkt gegenüber dem von Herzog & de Meuron entworfenen Olympiastadion auf dem olympischen Rasen gelegene Digital Beijing wurde von Pei Zhu und seinem ehemaligen Büro Urbanus als Kontroll- und Datenzentrum für die Spiele 2008 entworfen. Danach soll der Bau als »virtuelles Museum und Ausstellungszentrum für digitale Produkte« genutzt werden. Der Architekt versteht seinen großräumigen, imposanten Stahlskelettbau als Testfall zur Erforschung der Auswirkungen von Elektronik auf die Architektur. Dazu schreibt er: »Das Konzept für Digital Beijing entstand beim Prüfen und Nachdenken über die Rolle der zeitgenössischen Architektur im Informationszeitalter. Das dem allgegenwärtigen Symbol des Strichcodes ähnelnde Bauwerk erhebt sich aus einer unbewegten Wasserfläche. Dank ihrer Gliederung erinnert die Fassade an eine integrierte Schaltplatine. Der Baukörper, der durch den Wechsel zwischen Lücke und Masse die einfache Wiederholung von 0 und 1 widerspiegelt, gestaltet in gewaltigem Maßstab den mikroskopischen Unterbau des Lebens im digitalen Zeitalter. Er wird so zu einem machtvollen Symbol der digitalen Olympischen Spiele und der digitalen Epoche. Für die Zukunft ist damit zu rechnen, dass sich das Gebäude ständig im Umbau befinden wird, um mit der sich weiterentwickelnden Technik Schritt zu halten.«

Élevé sur la Pelouse olympique face au Stade olympique d'Herzog & de Meuron, « Pékin Numérique » a été conçu par Pei Zhu et son ancienne agence, Urbanus. Ce Centre de contrôle et de traitement des données numériques des Jeux olympiques de 2008 devrait, par la suite, servir de « musée virtuel et de centre d'expositions pour produits numériques ». L'architecte décrit cette vaste et imposante construction en béton armé à ossature d'acier comme une recherche sur l'impact de l'électronique sur l'architecture. Plus précisément, il écrit : « Le concept de Digital Beijing a été mis au point par le réexamen et la réflexion sur le rôle de l'architecture contemporaine à l'ère de l'information. Faisant penser au symbole omniprésent du code-barre, l'immeuble émerge d'un plan d'eau. La façade elle-même ressemble à un circuit imprimé. La masse abstraite du bâtiment, qui reflète la répétition binaire de 0 et de 1 dans son alternance de vides et de pleins, recrée à une échelle monumentale la face cachée microscopique de la vie à l'ère numérique pour créer un symbole puissant des Jeux olympiques de l'Ère numérique. Dans le futur, nous espérons que l'immeuble sera en réaménagement permanent pour pouvoir évoluer au rythme de la technologie. »

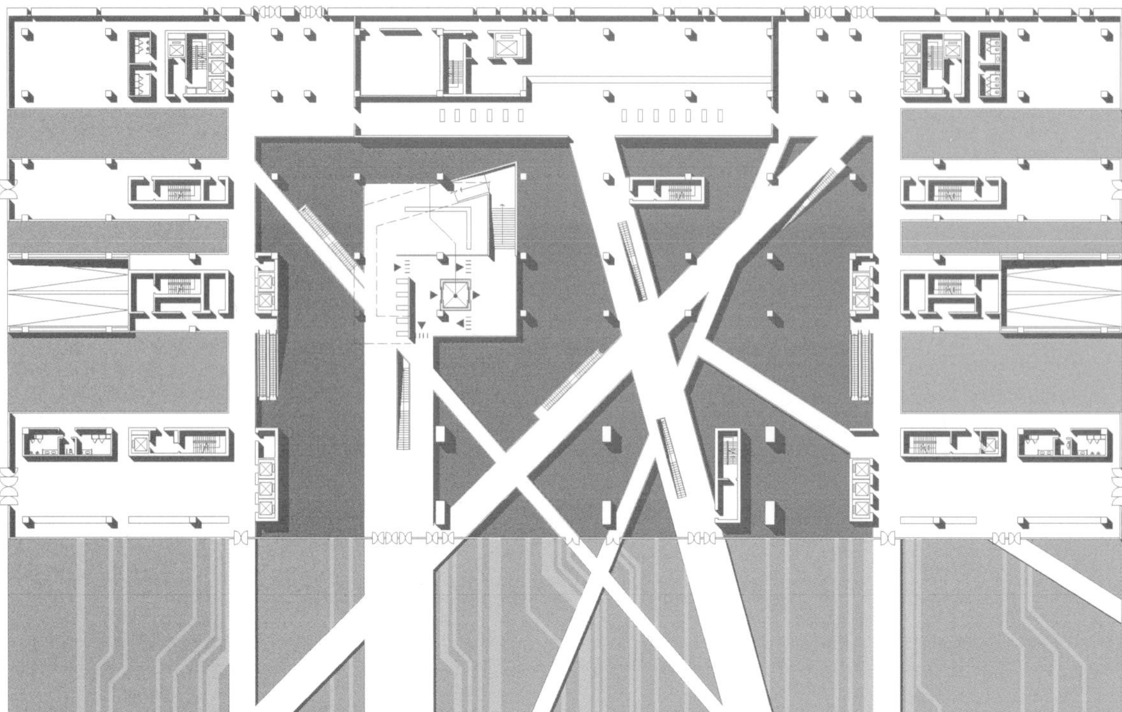

The basic rectangular floor plan is pierced in several locations. Interior view shows a suspended bridge and ramps (right).

Der im Wesentlichen rechteckige Grundriss ist an verschiedenen Stellen durchbrochen. Auf der Innenansicht (rechts) sind eine hängende Brücke und Rampen zu sehen.

Le plan rectangulaire s'ouvre en plusieurs endroits. Vue intérieure d'une passerelle et de rampes (à droite).

#16

URBANUS ARCHI-TECTURE & DESIGN

URBANUS ARCHITECTURE & DESIGN, INC.
Building E-6, 2nd Floor
Huaqiaocheng Dongbu
Industrial Zone
Nanshan District,
Shenzhen 518053

Tel: +86 755 8609 6345
Fax: +86 755 8610 6336
E-mail: office@urbanus.com.cn
Web: www.urbanus.com.cn

LIU XIAODU is one of the founding partners of URBANUS. Prior to establishing the office, Liu was a project architect and project designer at Design Group Inc., Columbus, Ohio, and Stang & Newdow Inc. in Atlanta, Georgia. He received his B.Arch degree from Tsinghua University (1985), and M.Arch from Miami University, Oxford, Ohio (1997). He has six years of teaching experience at Tsinghua University. Prior to co-founding URBANUS, MENG YAN was a project architect and designer at Kohn Pedersen Fox Associates PC; Meltzer Mandl Architects in New York; Brown & Bills Architects in Dayton, Ohio; and Yong-mao Architects and Engineers in Beijing. WANG HUI, another co-founder of the firm, worked with Gruzen Samton Architects; Gensler; and Gary Edward Handel +Associates. Like his two partners, he was educated at Tsinghua University and Miami Univerisity. Their completed works include: Diwang Park A, Shenzhen (2000); CRL and Constellation Development Sales Office, Beijing (2003); OCT Contemporary Art Terminal, Shenzhen (2004); Xinhai Garden Residential Development, Shenzhen (2004); Metro Office Tower, Shenzhen (2005); Teda Vanton U-Club, Tianjin (2005); and Diwang Park B, Shenzhen (2005). Current projects include: Shenzhen International Yacht Club, Shenzhen (2006); Public Art Plaza, Shenzhen (2006); Dafen Art Museum, published here; Shanghai Multimedia Valley Office Park, Shanghai (2007); Digital Beijing (with Studio Pei Zhu), published here; and the Nanyou Shopping Park, Shenzhen (2007).

GANGSHA VILLAGE
SHENZHEN, GUANGDONG 2005–

SITE AREA: 17 hectares
FLOOR AREA: 400 000 m²
COST: not disclosed
PARTNERS IN CHARGE: Liu Xiaodu, Meng Yan
CO-DESIGNERS: Huang Weiwen, Zhang Jianhui

Based in part in Shenzhen, the architects have taken a direct interest in the rapid development of the city. As they explain, "In 1979 Shenzhen was a remote border town with a population of 20 000. It reached a population of eight million and an average GDP of 20 billion USD in 2002. Its population has grown 400 times and the GDP has grown 500 times in 22 years." Looking ahead to continuing development, they have proposed a strategy for "rehabilitation versus total reconstruction" of four areas in the city: Fuxin Village, Xinzhou Village, the Dafen Art Museum in Dafen Village, and Gangsha Village. As they explain this latter intervention, "The Heyuan block of Gangsha village has a land area of 17 hectares. The block had a housing area of 270 000 square meters in 1996. By 2001, the total area had increased to over 400 000 square meters. It is located in the future Core Business District (CBD) in Shenzhen, thus facing tremendous rehabilitation pressure. Through partial demolition, infilling, stitching and adding public facilities on the roofs, this dynamic rehabilitation will fix the existing dense buildings and fragmented public spaces. It will also lay out better defined commercial streets, service roads, and courtyard-type public spaces. This renovation strategy will also dramatically improve the commercial, housing, transportation and community facilities in order to generate the highest possible increase in property value, and simultaneously maintain the intricate social structure of the existing neighborhood."

Die teilweise in Shenzhen ansässigen Architekten nehmen unmittelbaren Anteil an der rapiden Entwicklung der Stadt. Sie erläutern dazu: »Im Jahr 1979 war Shenzhen eine abgelegene Grenzstadt mit 20 000 Einwohnern. 2002 war die Einwohnerschaft auf acht Millionen angewachsen mit einem durchschnittlichen Bruttoinlandsprodukt von 20 Milliarden Dollar. Die Bevölkerung ist in 22 Jahren um das 400-fache, das Bruttoinlandsprodukt um das 500-fache gewachsen.« Angesichts der anhaltenden Entwicklung sprachen sie sich für eine Strategie der »Sanierung anstelle völliger Neubebauung« für vier Stadtteile aus: Fuxin, Xinzhou, eine Konzeption für das Kunstmuseum in Dafen sowie ein »Vorschlag für die dynamische Sanierung von Gangsha«. Sie erläutern diese Maßnahme folgendermaßen: »Das Heyuan-Viertel von Gangsha umfasst ein Gelände von 17 ha. 1996 hatte das Viertel eine Wohnfläche von 270 000 m². 2001 war die Gesamtfläche auf über 400 000 m² angewachsen. Sie liegt im künftigen zentralen Geschäftsviertel von Shenzhen und ist somit erheblichem Sanierungsdruck ausgesetzt. Durch partiellen Abriss, das Füllen von Lücken und das Ergänzen öffentlicher Einrichtungen auf den Dächern wird diese dynamische Sanierung die vorhandene dichte Bebauung und die bruchstückhaften öffentlichen Räume instandsetzen. Darüber hinaus werden klarer bezeichnete Geschäftsstraßen, Nebenstraßen sowie innenhofartige öffentliche Räume geplant. Diese Sanierungsstrategie wird auch die Gewerbe-, Wohn-, Verkehrs- und Gemeinschaftseinrichtungen deutlich verbessern, um eine maximale Wertsteigerung der Liegenschaften zu bewirken und gleichzeitig die komplizierte Sozialstruktur der bestehenden Wohnviertel zu bewahren.«

Également installés à Shenzen, les architectes se sont directement intéressés au développement rapide de cette ville. Comme ils l'expliquent : « En 1979, Shenzen était une lointaine ville-frontière de 20 000 habitants. Elle a atteint une population de 8 millions d'habitants et un produit local brut de 20 milliards de dollars en 2002. Sa population a donc été multipliée par 400 et ses ressources par 500 en vingt-deux ans. » En prévision de la poursuite de ce développement, l'agence a proposé une stratégie de « réhabilitation à l'opposé d'une reconstruction totale » de quatre zones urbaines : le village de Fuxin, le village de Xinzhou, une « proposition pour le Musée d'art de Dafen dans le village éponyme et une proposition pour la réhabilitation dynamique du village de Gangsha ». Ainsi que l'expliquent les architectes : « Le secteur d'Heyuna dans le village de Gangsha représente une surface de 17 hectares. En 1996, 270 000 m² avaient été construits. En 2001, cette surface dépassait 400 000 m². Il est situé dans le futur CBD (Core Business District), le quartier central des affaires de Shenzen, et doit donc faire face à une pression énorme pour sa réhabilitation. Par des démolitions partielles, des insertions, des adjonctions et en ajoutant des équipements publics sur les toits, cette réhabilitation dynamique fixe les immeubles densément peuplés existants et les espaces publics fragmentés. Elle permet également de développer un meilleur plan pour les rues commerçantes, les voies de service et les espaces publics de type « cour ». Cette stratégie de rénovation améliorera spectaculairement la qualité des équipements commerciaux, des logements, des transports et des services communs pour offrir la valeur de propriété immobilière la plus élevée possible tout en maintenant la structure sociale complexe du quartier existant. »

中国凤凰大厦
8305 8888
PRESERVE.
INTRUDE.

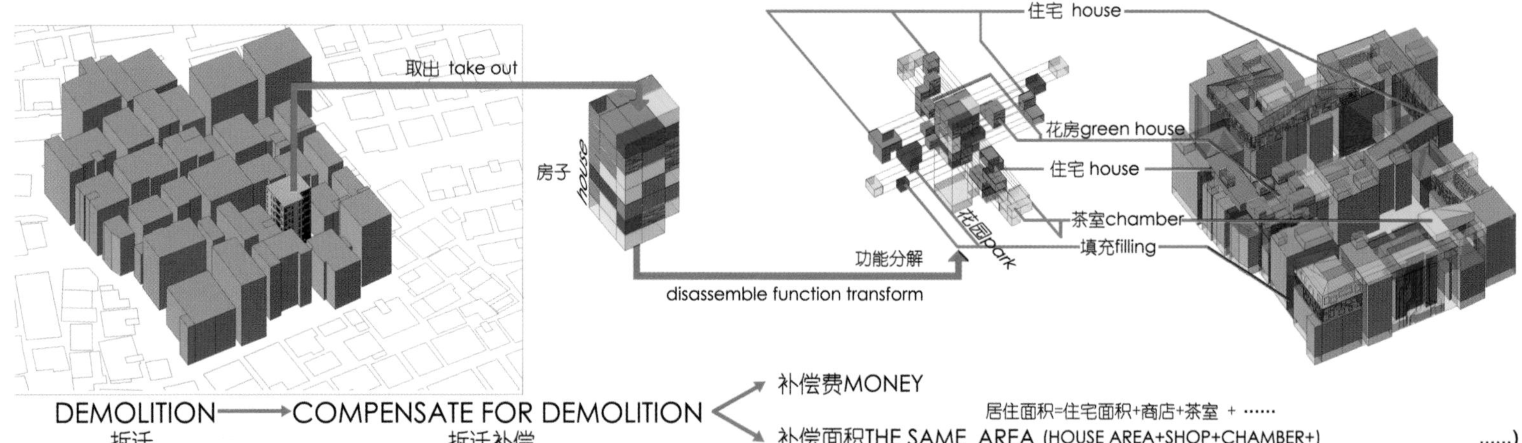

The response of Urbanus to the density of this area in the future Core Business District of Shenzhen is to reweave its circulation patterns, adding a layer of bridges, passages or public facilities that are intended to simplify the movement of residents and improve the quality of life.

Urbanus reagierte auf die dichte Bebauung im künftigen zentralen Geschäftsviertel von Shenzhen mit einer Neuordnung der Wegeführung, indem eine Ebene mit Brücken, Passagen oder öffentlichen Einrichtungen ergänzt wurde, die die Fortbewegung der Bewohner vereinfachen und die Lebensqualität verbessern sollen.

La réponse d'Urbanus au problème de la densité du futur quartier central des affaires de Shenzen est de « retisser » les circulations par l'ajout d'une strate de ponts, de passages et d'équipements publics qui veut simplifier les déplacements des résidents et améliorer leur confort de vie.

The architects are (rightly) concerned not only with appearances but with the function and value of the real estate that they are proposing to improve. Their work in this area only makes sense if they can upgrade the quality of life, thus also potentially raising investment.

Die Architekten beschäftigen sich (zu Recht) nicht nur mit dem Erscheinungsbild, sondern auch mit Funktion und Wert der Immobilien, die sie optimieren wollen. Ihre Tätigkeit in diesem Viertel ist nur dann sinnvoll, wenn es ihnen gelingt, die Lebensqualität und dadurch auch die Investitionen potentiell zu steigern.

Les architectes sont à juste titre concernés par l'aspect mais par aussi par la fonction et la valeur du parc immobilier qu'ils proposent d'améliorer. Leur travail ne prend son sens que s'ils sont capables d'améliorer le niveau de qualité de vie, accroissant ainsi potentiellement la valeur de l'investissement.

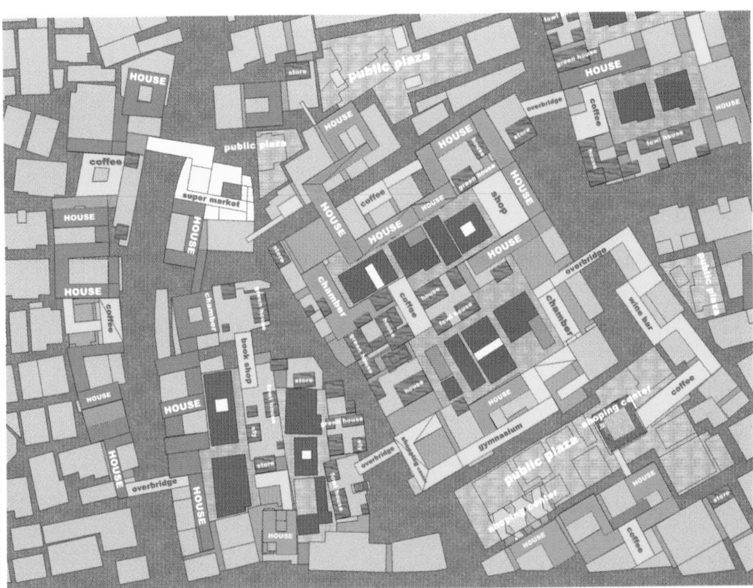

DAFEN ART MUSEUM SHENZHEN, GUANGDONG 2006 –

SITE AREA: 11 300 m² FLOOR AREA: 16 866 m²
COST: not disclosed PARTNERS IN CHARGE: Liu Xiaodu, Meng Yan
PROJECT ARCHITECTS: Fu Zhuoheng, Chen Yaoguang

The Dafen Village area is well known in China for its oil painting replica workshops that export to Europe, America, and Asia. The production of the area has long been considered to be a "strange mixture of art, bad taste and commercialism," according to the architects. Their goal has been to reinterpret this image with an innovative approach that seeks to "hybridize" different programs, including oil painting galleries, shops, commercial spaces, and studios. Pathways through the building's public spaces encourage interaction with the community. Their strategy is actually quite daring, as the architects acknowledge when they confront their project with the typical idea of a museum. As they write, "The walls of a traditional museum clearly define the boundary between the art world and the outside world. Its exclusiveness protects the museum's content from the reality of daily life on the outside. But here the name 'museum' can hardly describe the contents of the new building, which will be located in Dafen Village, or at least it contains much more than a typical museum is willing or capable to include. The irony is that in a place unimaginable for a typical art museum, we hope it can host the most avant-garde contemporary art shows, and at the same time can include the local new vernacular pop art. It should be a highly mixed building, a hybrid container."

In China kennt man die Gegend um Dafen wegen der hier ansässigen Werkstätten, in denen Repliken von Ölgemälden angefertigt und dann nach Europa, Amerika und Asien exportiert werden. Den Architekten zufolge wird die Produktion dieser Gegend seit Langem für eine »seltsame Mischung aus Kunst, schlechtem Geschmack und Kommerz« gehalten. Ziel war es, dieses Image durch einen innovativen Ansatz umzudeuten im Versuch, verschiedene Funktionen wie Gemäldegalerien, Läden, Gewerberäume und Ateliers miteinander zu verbinden. Fußwege durch die öffentlichen Bereiche des Gebäudes fördern die Interaktion mit der Kommune. Ihre Vorgehensweise ist recht gewagt, was die Architekten einräumen, wenn sie ihr Projekt mit einem typischen Museumsbau vergleichen. Dazu schreiben sie: »Die Wände eines herkömmlichen Museums bezeichnen klar die Grenze zwischen der Welt der Kunst und der Außenwelt. Seine Exklusivität schützt den Inhalt des Museums vor der draußen herrschenden Realität des Alltags. In diesem Fall aber ist die Bezeichnung ›Museum‹ für den Gehalt des neuen Gebäudes, das in Dafen entsteht, kaum zutreffend, oder es enthält zumindest viel mehr, als ein typisches Museum willens oder bereit ist aufzunehmen. Ironischerweise wird es an einem für ein herkömmliches Kunstmuseum völlig inakzeptablen Ort höchst avantgardistische Ausstellungen zeitgenössischer Kunst zeigen und gleichzeitig die heimische neue Pop-Art beherbergen. Es soll ein höchst vielgestaltiges Gebäude, ein hybrides Behältnis werden.«

La région du village de Dafen est très connue en Chine pour ses ateliers de copies de peintures à l'huile qui exportent vers l'Europe, l'Amérique et l'Asie. Cette production a, selon les architectes, longtemps été considérée comme « un étrange mélange d'art, de mauvais goût et de commerce ... ». Leur but a été de réinterpréter cette image dans une approche innovante qui cherche à « hybrider » différents programmes dont des galeries de peintures, des boutiques, des espaces commerciaux et des ateliers. Les passages à travers les espaces publics des immeubles encouragent les interactions entre les habitants. Cette stratégie est en fait assez audacieuse puisqu'ils reconnaissent que ce projet va à l'encontre de l'idée typique que l'on se fait d'un musée : « Les murs d'un musée traditionnel définissent clairement la limite entre le monde de l'art et le monde extérieur. Ce caractère exclusif protège le contenu du musée des réalités de la vie quotidienne telle qu'elle se déroule ailleurs. Mais ici le nom de « musée » définit difficilement le contenu de ce nouveau bâtiment car il contient bien plus que ce qu'un musée classique est désireux ou capable de proposer. L'ironie est que dans un lieu que l'on n'aurait pas imaginé adapté à un musée typique, nous espérons que se tiendront les expositions artistiques les plus avant-gardistes tout en présentant le pop art vernaculaire local. Ce devrait être un ensemble hautement mélangé, un concentré d'hybridité. »

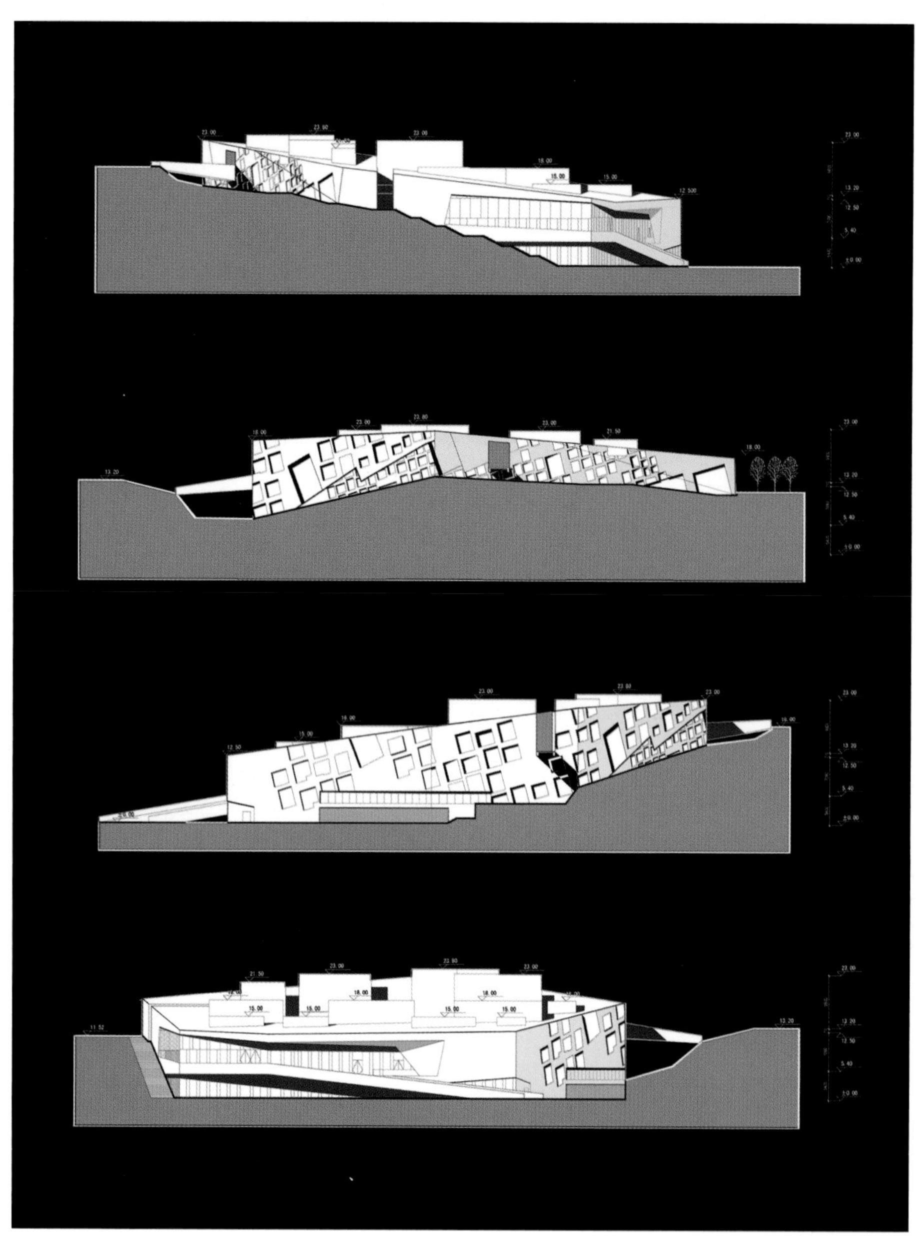

Creating a complex, leaning, undulating form, the architects are fitting themselves into a chaotic urban pattern and in some sense deriving their inspiration from it.

Dank der komplexen, geneigten und gewundenen Form fügt sich die Architektur in eine chaotische urbane Struktur ein, von der sich die Architekten in gewissem Sinn anregen ließen.

En créant cette forme complexe, ondulatoire en plan et en coupe, les architectes s'adaptent à un tissu urbain chaotique d'où, en un certain sens, ils tirent leur inspiration.

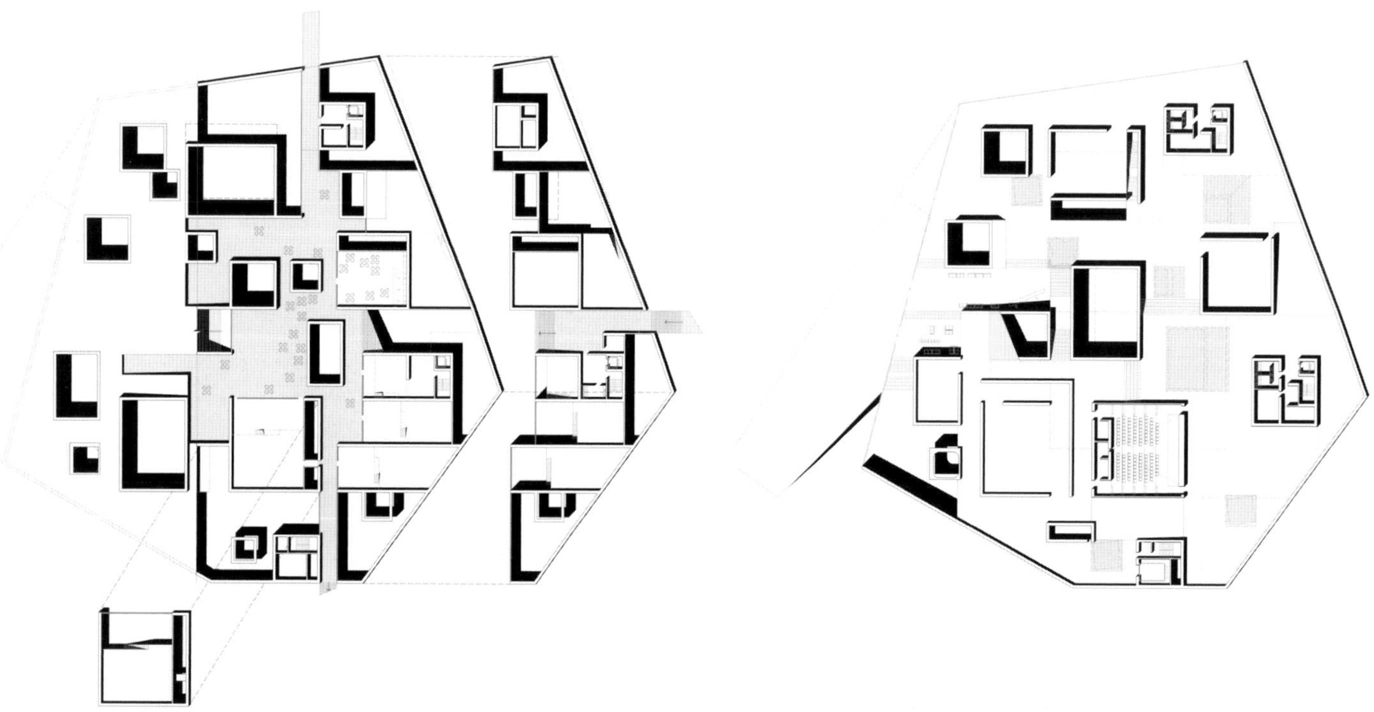

Computer perspectives show the exterior of the museum in its setting and an interior view with a light well.

Computerperspektiven zeigen das Museum von außen in seinem Umfeld und eine Innenansicht mit einem Lichtschacht.

Perspectives en image de synthèse montrant l'extérieur du musée dans son environnement et un puits de lumière intérieur.

Within its apparently monolithic form, the museum is actually constituted of a variety of openings and passages that are intended to bring life back to this neighborhood.

Im Inneren der scheinbar monolithischen Form besteht das Museum aus einer Vielzahl von Öffnungen und Durchgängen, die zur Belebung dieses Viertels beitragen sollen.

Pris dans une forme apparemment monolithique, le musée est en fait constitué de diverses ouvertures et passages qui le relient à l'animation de son voisinage.

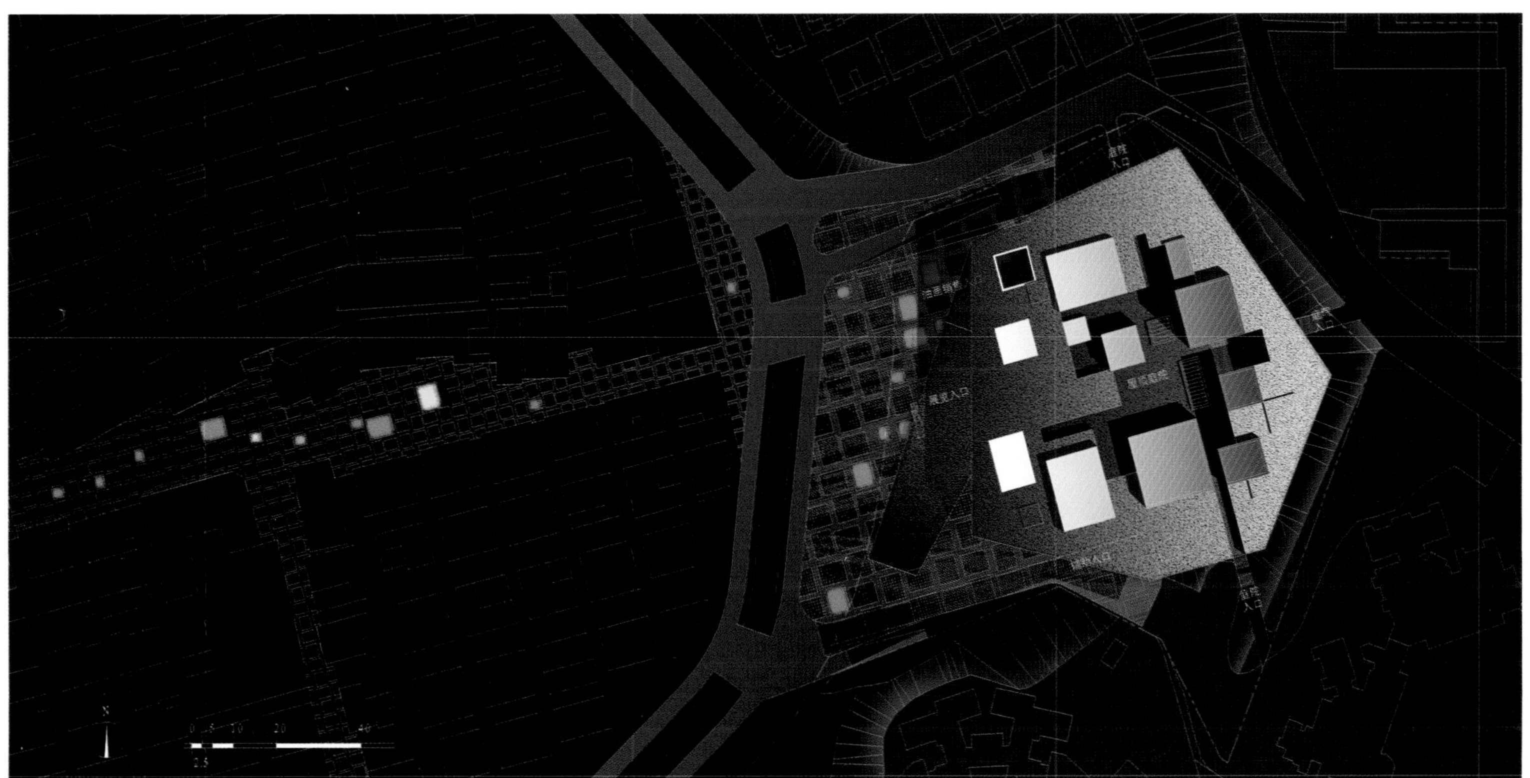

The plan above details the composition of the structure as seen from above and shows how it is meant to fit into its site.

Der Plan oben beschreibt aus der Vogelperspektive genau den Aufbau des Baukörpers und zeigt, wie er sich in das Baugelände einfügen soll.

Le plan (ci-dessus) détaille la composition de la structure, vue de dessus, et montre son adaptation au site.

#17

VARIOUS ARCHITECTS
JINHUA ARCHITECTURE PARK

Working in collaboration with the architects Herzog & de Meuron, the artist-architect Ai Wei Wei was called on by the Jindong District Municipal Government (Jinhua) to help with the design and construction of 17 small structures on the north bank of the Yiwu River. Ai Wei Wei also worked on the south bank of the river opposite this site (see page 60). Seventeen architects from seven countries have proposed pavilions for the site whose average width is 80 meters for a total length of 2200 meters. Cost considerations mandated the use of local materials only.

Der mit den Architekten Herzog & de Meuron kooperierende Künstler und Architekt Ai Wei Wei wurde von der Verwaltung des Stadtbezirks Jindong in Jinhua aufgefordert, bei Entwurf und Bau von 17 kleinen Gebäuden am Nordufer des Flusses Yiwu mitzuwirken. Darüber hinaus war Ai Wei Wei auch am gegenüberliegenden Südufer des Flusses tätig (s. S. 60). 17 Architekten aus sieben Ländern planten Pavillons für dieses Gelände, dessen durchschnittliche Breite 80 m beträgt bei einer Gesamtlänge von 2200 m. Aus Kostengründen beschränkte man sich auf die Verwendung heimischer Materialien.

Travaillant en collaboration avec Herzog & de Meuron, l'artiste-architecte Ai Wei Wei a été appelé par l'Administration du district de Jindong pour participer à la conception et la réalisation de dix-sept petites constructions sur la rive nord du Yivu. Il est également intervenu juste en face, sur la rive sud du fleuve (voir page 60). Dix-sept architectes de dix-sept pays différents ont proposé des pavillons pour ce site mesurant 2200 m de long sur 80 m de large. Pour des raisons financières, seuls des matériaux locaux ont été utilisés.

HERZOG & DE MEURON
Rheinschanze 6
4056 Basel / Switzerland
Tel: + 41 61 385 5757
Fax: + 41 61 385 5758
E-mail: info@herzogdemeuron.com

HHF ARCHITECTS
St. Johanns-Vorstadt 17
4056 Basel / Switzerland
Tel: + 41 61 263 8080
Fax: + 41 61 263 8090
E-mail: info@hhf.ch
Web: www.hhf.ch

MICHAEL MALTZAN ARCHITECTURE, INC.
2801 Hyperion Avenue Studio 107
Los Angeles, CA 90027 / USA
Tel: + 1 323 913 3098
Fax: + 1 323 913 5932
E-mail: info@mmaltzan.com
Web: www.mmaltzan.com

TOSHIKO MORI ARCHITECT
180 Varick Street
Suite 1322
New York, NY 10014 / USA
Tel: + 1 212 337 9644
Fax: + 1 212 337 9647
E-mail: info@tmarch.com
Web: www.tmarch.com

JINHUA STRUCTURE 1—CUBE

JINHUA, ZHEJIANG 2004-06

CLIENT: Jindong New District Construction Headquarters, Jinhua
COST: not disclosed ARCHITECTS: Herzog & de Meuron
PARTNERS: Jacques Herzog, Pierre de Meuron, Ascan Mergenthaler
PROJECT ARCHITECT: Mark Loughnan (associate)
ASSOCIATE ARCHITECTS: Ai Wei Wei / FAKE Design

Herzog & de Meuron were already working on the master plan for the new city center of the Jindong District of Jinhua. As they explain, for the pavilion that Ai Wei Wei asked them to design, "Everything appeared quite simple and logical: our Jinhua Pavilion would merely be a shell consisting of the same geometric pattern we had developed for the buildings in the Jindong district. Like a dominant ordering scheme, the pattern was to cover windows, doors, and all façades as a playful, ornamental element that would contrast with the brick body of the building itself." They compare the result to a "molecular structure or a genetic code." They projected their pattern (an accumulation of intersecting lines) onto an imaginary cube, creating a "virtual spatial grid" with a powerful computer, and generating the "inconceivable and unimaginable forms and spaces of the pavilion." Despite the complexity of the forms thus generated, conventional construction methods and dyed concrete were used in Jinhua. The architects decided to create two other versions of the structure—*Jinhua Structure II—Vertical*, a laminated wood design for the Berower Park at the Fondation Beyeler in Basel, and *Jinhua Structure III—Horizontal*, a temporary structure intended for Genoa that was not actually executed.

Herzog & de Meuron arbeiteten bereits am Gesamtplan für das neue Zentrum des Stadtbezirks Jindong von Jinhua. Zu dem Pavillon, den sie im Auftrag von Ai Wei Wei entwarfen, äußern sie sich wie folgt: »Alles schien ganz einfach und logisch: Unser Jinhua-Pavillon sollte nur ein Gehäuse werden, bestehend aus demselben geometrischen Muster, das wir für die Bauten im Bezirk Jindong entwickelt hatten. Wie ein beherrschendes Ordnungssystem sollte das Muster als spielerisches Schmuckelement Fenster, Türen und sämtliche Fassaden überziehen und sich vom aus Backstein bestehenden Baukörper des eigentlichen Gebäudes abheben.« Sie verglichen das Ergebnis mit einer »Molekularstruktur oder einem genetischen Code«. Sie projizierten ihr Muster (eine Zusammenballung sich überschneidender Linien) auf einen imaginären Kubus und schufen mit einem leistungsstarken Computer ein »virtuelles Raumgitter«, mit dessen Hilfe die »fabelhaften, unvorstellbaren Formen und Räume des Pavillons« entstanden. Ungeachtet der Komplexität der so entstandenen Formen nutzte man in Jinhua herkömmliche Bauverfahren und eingefärbten Beton. Die Architekten entschieden sich darüber hinaus dafür, zwei weitere Fassungen des Gebäudes zu entwerfen, Jinhua-Struktur II – Vertikal, ein Schichtholzentwurf für den Berower Park bei der Fondation Beyeler in Basel, und Jinhua-Struktur III – Horizontal, ein für Genua vorgesehenes, temporäres Bauwerk, das nicht realisiert wurde.

Herzog & de Meuron travaillaient déjà sur le plan directeur du nouveau centre-ville du district de Jindong de Jinhua lorsque Ai Wei leur a demandé de concevoir ce pavillon : « Tout semblait assez simple et logique : notre pavillon de Jinhua serait tout au plus une coquille reprenant les principes de construction géométrique que nous avions mis au point pour les immeubles du district. À la manière d'un schéma ordonnateur, le motif devait recouvrir les fenêtres, les portes et toutes les façades, ornement ludique contrastant avec la structure en brique de la maison elle-même. » Ils comparent le résultat à une « structure moléculaire ou un code génétique ». Ce motif (une accumulation de lignes sécantes) projeté à l'aide d'un puissant ordinateur sur un cube imaginaire a créé une « trame spatiale virtuelle » et généré les « formes et espaces incroyables et inimaginables du pavillon ». Malgré cette complexité formelle, des méthodes traditionnelles de construction et un béton teinté ont pu être utilisés. Les architectes ont décidé d'en créer deux autres versions – Jinhua Structure II Vertical, un projet en bois lamellé pour le Berower Park de la Fondation Beyeler à Bâle, et Jinhua Structure III-Horizontal, construction temporaire destinée à Gênes, mais qui n'a pas été réalisée.

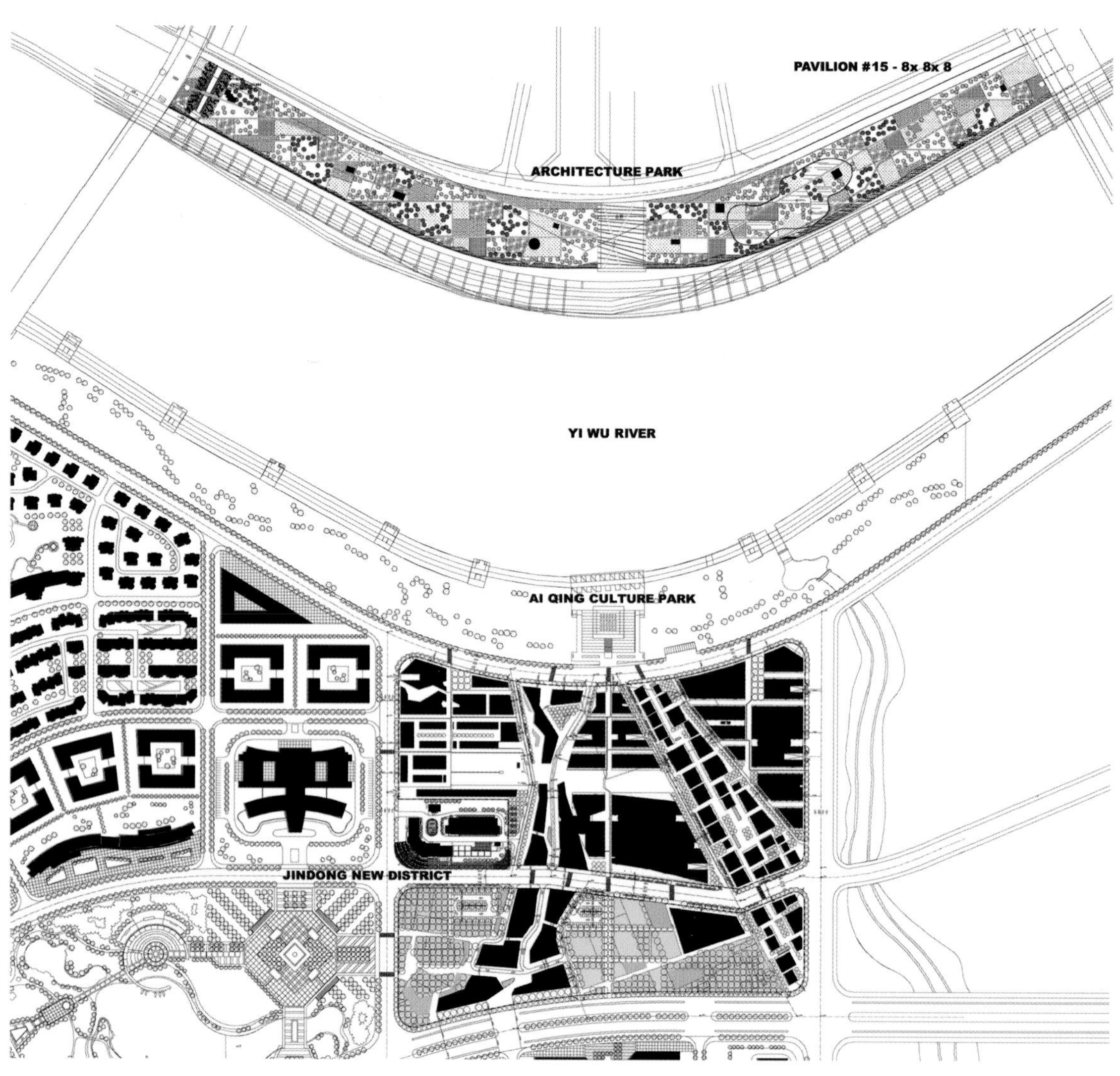

The honeycomb-like structure of the pavilion represents an unusual exploration of space based on a kind of "genetic code" developed by the architects. The plan above shows the overall sculpture park.

Die wabenförmige Struktur des Pavillons stellt eine ungewöhnliche Raumerkundung dar, die auf einer Art, von den Architekten entwickelten »genetischem Code« basiert. Auf dem Plan oben ist der gesamte Skulpturenpark zu sehen.

La structure en nid d'abeille du pavillon offre une exploration inhabituelle de l'espace à partir d'une sorte de « code génétique » mis au point par les architectes. Le plan (ci-dessus) montre l'ensemble du parc de sculpture.

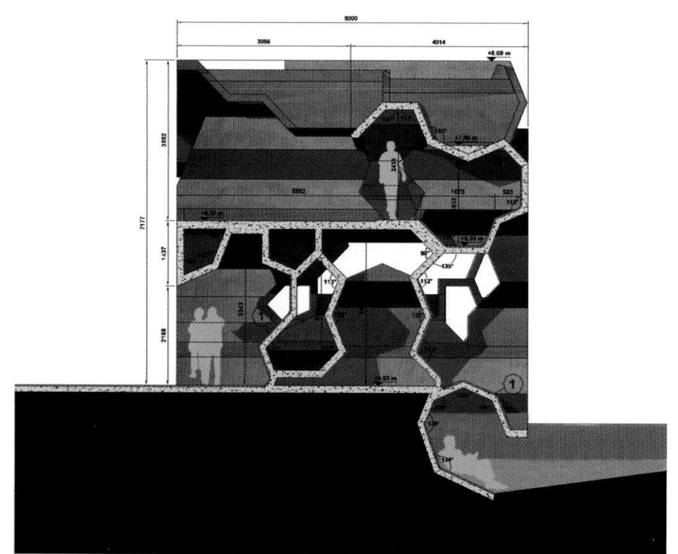

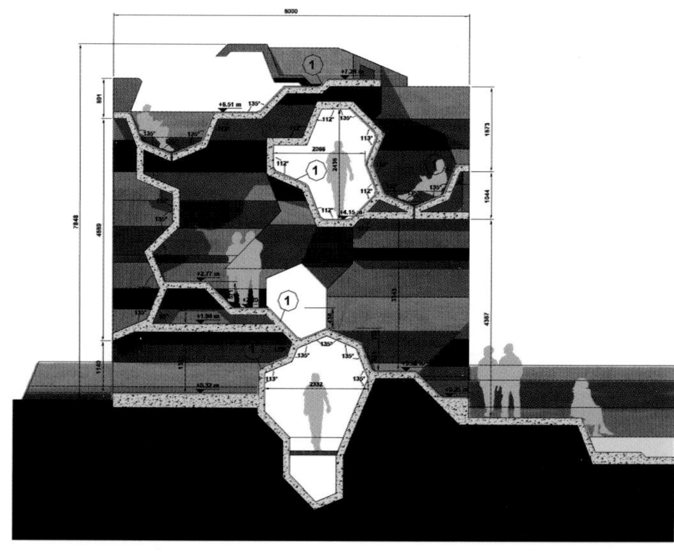

At first glance the unusual surfaces and openings of the pavilion may not be conducive to specific uses aside from the exploration of space and light.

Die ungewöhnlichen Oberflächen und Öffnungen des Pavillons sind, abgesehen von der Erforschung von Raum und Licht, auf den ersten Blick nicht für eine bestimmte Nutzung konzipiert.

Les surfaces et les ouvertures curieuses de ce pavillon ne se prêtent peut-être pas à première vue à des usages spécifiques, mais à une exploration de l'espace et de la lumière.

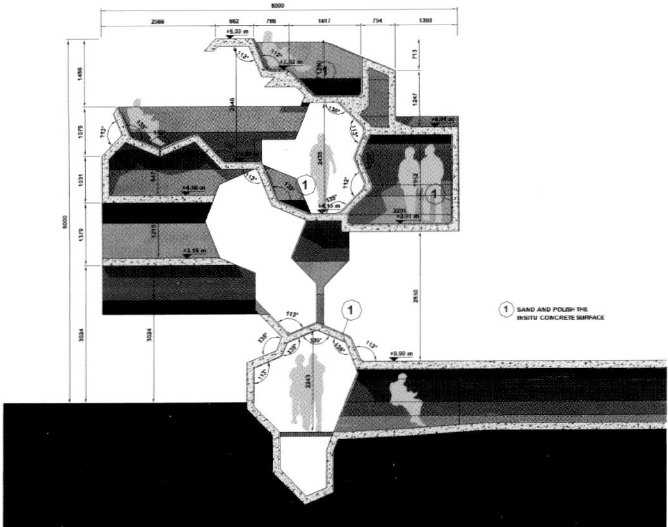

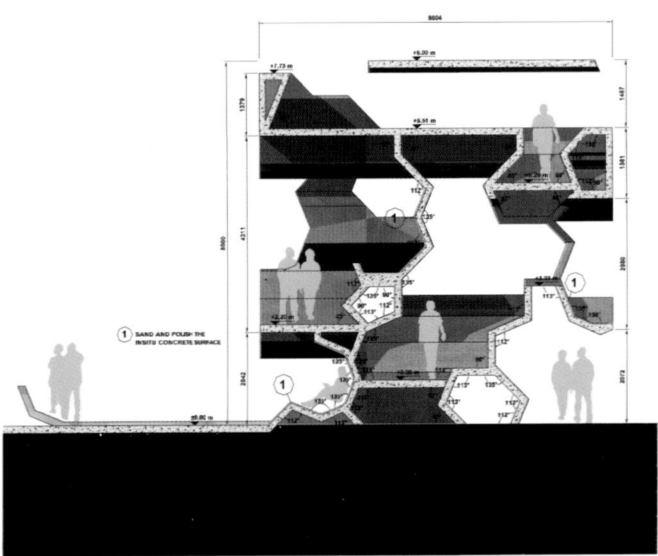

BABY DRAGON
JINHUA, ZHEJIANG 2004–05

LENGTH: 30 m HEIGHT: 4.5 m
MAXIMUM THICKNESS OF WALL: 2.1 m
CLIENT: Jindong New District Construction Headquarters, Jinhua
COST: not disclosed ARCHITECTS: HHF Architects
TEAM: Herlach Hartmann Frommenwiler
with Tom Strub, Nelson Tam, Chris Thüer

The young Swiss architects HHF had never worked in China before, and they chose, as they say, "To design a structure with very few details. Even if the built shape is complex in its geometry, the process of the construction could be described in a very simple way. The result is a mysterious object without a recognizable scale." Built entirely with dyed concrete, the "mini structure for children" allows parents to watch their children or to interact with them in various ways. The floor is partially covered with the same gray clinker used for the pathways of the park. Eleven different shapes were selected for the openings in the concrete wall, allowing an "endless pattern" of combinations." The architects are currently completing another project, the Treehouse, a guesthouse for a golf club in Lijiang, Yunnan, also in collaboration with Ai Wei Wei / FAKE Design.

Die jungen Schweizer Architekten vom Büro HHF hatten nie zuvor in China gearbeitet und entschieden sich dafür, »ein Bauwerk mit sehr wenigen Details zu entwerfen«. Selbst wenn die gebaute Form in ihrer Geometrie komplex erscheint, lässt sich das Bauverfahren sehr einfach erklären. Das Ergebnis ist ein geheimnisvolles Objekt ohne erkennbaren Maßstab. In diesem gänzlich aus eingefärbtem Beton errichteten »Mini-Gebäude für Kinder« können Eltern ihre Kindern beim Spielen beobachten oder auf verschiedene Weise mit ihnen interagieren. Der Boden ist teilweise mit dem gleichen grauen Klinker gepflastert wie die Fußwege im Park. Für die Öffnungen in der Betonwand wurden elf verschiedene Formen gewählt, mit denen »unendliche Kombinationsmuster« möglich sind. Die Architekten sind gegenwärtig, ebenfalls in Zusammenarbeit mit Ai Wei Wei FAKE Design, mit einem weiteren Projekt befasst, dem »Baumhaus«, einem Gästehaus für den Gold Club in Lijang, Yunnan.

Les jeunes architectes suisses de HHF n'avaient encore jamais travaillé en Chine auparavant et ont choisi « de concevoir une structure avec très peu de détails. Même si la forme construite est complexe dans sa géométrie, le processus de construction se décrit de façon très simple. L'objet obtenu est mystérieux et sans échelle identifiable. » Entièrement construite en béton teinté cette « ministructure pour enfants » permet aux parents de surveiller leur progéniture ou d'échanger avec elle de diverses façons. Le sol est en partie recouvert du mâchefer des allées du parc. Onze formes différentes ont été déterminées pour les ouvertures pratiquées dans les murs de béton, permettant un « motif sans fin » de combinaisons. Les architectes achèvent actuellement un autre projet, la « Maison dans l'arbre », maison d'hôtes pour un club de golf à Lijiang dans le Yunnan, également en collaboration avec Ai Wei Wei FAKE Design.

Like the Herzog & de Meuron pavilion, the work of HHF in Jinhua is more an exploration of spatial possibilities than it is a "usable" structure in the more traditional sense of the term. Both would quite obviously be attractive to children to play in for example.

Ähnlich wie der Pavillon von Herzog & de Meuron stellt auch die Arbeit von HHF in Jinhua eher eine Auslotung räumlicher Möglichkeiten dar als ein im üblichen Sinn des Wortes nutzbares Bauwerk. Zweifellos würden sich beide Bauten zum Beispiel bestens als Spielorte für Kinder eignen.

Comme pour le pavillon d'Herzog & de Meuron, l'œuvre des architectes HHF à Jinhua est davantage une exploration de possibilités spatiales que la construction d'une structure « utilisable » au sens plus traditionnel du terme. Tous deux pourraient certainement attirer les jeux d'enfants, par exemple.

The essentially sculptural nature of the project, and the fact that it has neither interior nor exterior in the usual sense, frees the architects to model space and light as they wish.

Der im Grunde skulpturale Charakter des Projekts und die Tatsache, dass es weder Innen- noch Außenbau im herkömmlichen Sinn gibt, erlauben es den Architekten, Raum und Licht nach ihren Wünschen zu gestalten.

La nature essentiellement sculpturale du projet et le fait qu'il ne comporte ni intérieur ni extérieur au sens classique donnent aux architectes la liberté de modeler l'espace et la lumière comme ils le souhaitent.

MINISTRUCTURE NO. 16 / BOOK BAR JINHUA, ZHEJIANG 2005–06

FLOOR AREA: 120 m²
CLIENT: Jindong New District Construction Headquarters, Jinhua
COST: not disclosed DESIGN PRINCIPAL: Michael Maltzan
DESIGN TEAM: David Gwinn, Nadine Quirmbach, Tim Williams

As Michael Maltzan, the Californian architect of the temporary home of New York's Museum of Modern Art (MoMA QNS, Long Island City, 2002), explains, "The project's concept expands on an important confluence between the book and architecture in Chinese history: in the third century B.C., a descendant of the philosopher Confucius concealed several of his texts in a wall when the emperor ordered all Confucian writings burned. The texts, essential relics of Chinese culture, were not discovered until nearly four centuries later. From this historic juncture of books and building, the pavilion's form pulls its central wall outward into two unequal, cantilevered arms, each concealing within a public space for learning. The shorter of the structure's wings contains a bookstore and café, organized into a series of terraces, which rise to a framed view of the park to the west. The pavilion's smaller wing is perforated by an abstract pattern, forming a reading porch open to the park beyond."

Wie Michael Maltzan, der in Kalifornien ansässige Architekt der temporären Heimat des Museum of Modern Art (MoMA QNS, Long Island, 2002) erläutert, »beruft sich das Konzept des Projekts auf eine wichtige Schnittstelle von Buch und Architektur in der chinesischen Geschichte: Als im 3. Jahrhundert v. Chr. der Kaiser befahl, sämtliche konfuzianischen Schriften zu verbrennen, verbarg ein Nachfahre des Philosophen einige von dessen Texten in einer Mauer. Erst nahezu vier Jahrhunderte später wurden die Texte, bei denen es sich um bedeutende Zeugnisse der chinesischen Kultur handelte, wiederentdeckt. Dieses historische Geschehen liegt der Form des Pavillons zugrunde, dessen zentrale Wand sich zu zwei ungleichen, auskragenden Armen erweitert, die beide im Inneren einen öffentlich zugänglichen Studierraum enthalten. Der kürzere der beiden Flügel bietet einer Buchhandlung und einem Café Platz; Letzteres ist in eine Folge von Terrassen gegliedert, die sich zu einem gerahmten Ausblick auf den Park im Westen erheben. Die Wände des kleineren Pavillonflügels sind mit einem abstrakten Muster durchbrochen und bilden eine zum unten liegenden Park hin offene Leseveranda.«

Comme Michael Maltzan, l'architecte californien des installations temporaires du Museum of Modern Art de New York (MoMA QNS, Long Island City, 2002) l'explique : « Le concept du projet se développe autour de l'importante confluence qui existe entre le livre et l'architecture dans l'histoire chinoise : au IIIe siècle av. J.-C., un descendant du philosophe Confucius dissimula plusieurs des textes de celui-ci dans un mur lorsque l'empereur ordonna que tous les écrits du maître soient brûlés. Ces textes, reliques essentielles de la culture chinoise, ne furent découverts que quatre siècles plus tard. S'appuyant sur ce lien historique entre livres et bâti, la forme du pavillon étire son axe central en deux bras inégaux en porte-à-faux, chacun contenant un espace public pour l'enseignement. Le bras le plus court contient une librairie et un café disposé en une suite de terrasses qui s'élèvent jusqu'à une perspective cadrée sur le parc à l'ouest. L'autre est perforé selon un motif abstrait constituant un porche de lecture ouvert sur le parc. »

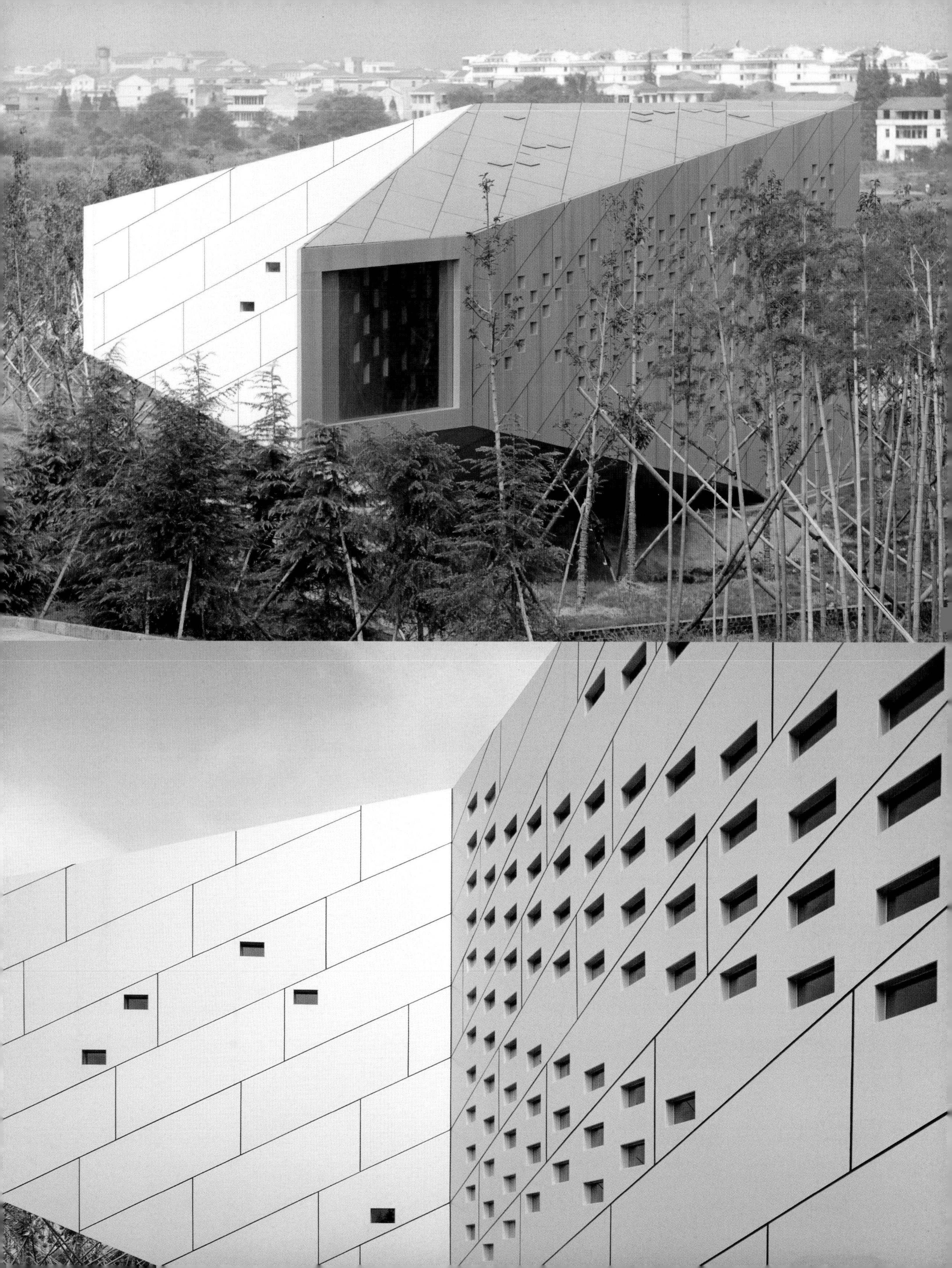

Michael Maltzan's design has a more clearly defined interior than its neighbors in the Jinhua Park, but it also assumes an architectural liberty born of a freedom from functional constraints.

Michael Maltzans Bau verfügt über einen deutlicher bezeichneten Innenraum als die benachbarten Objekte im Jinhua-Park, aber er schwelgt ebenfalls in der aus dem Fehlen funktionaler Zwänge entstandenen architektonischen Freiheit.

Le projet de Michael Malzan présente un volume intérieur plus clairement défini que celui de ses voisins du Jinhua Park, mais prend également ses libertés par rapport aux contraintes fonctionnelles.

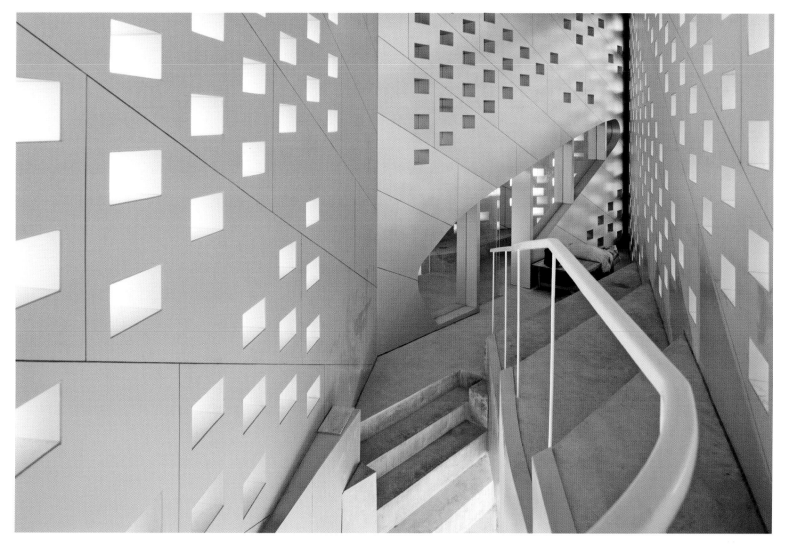

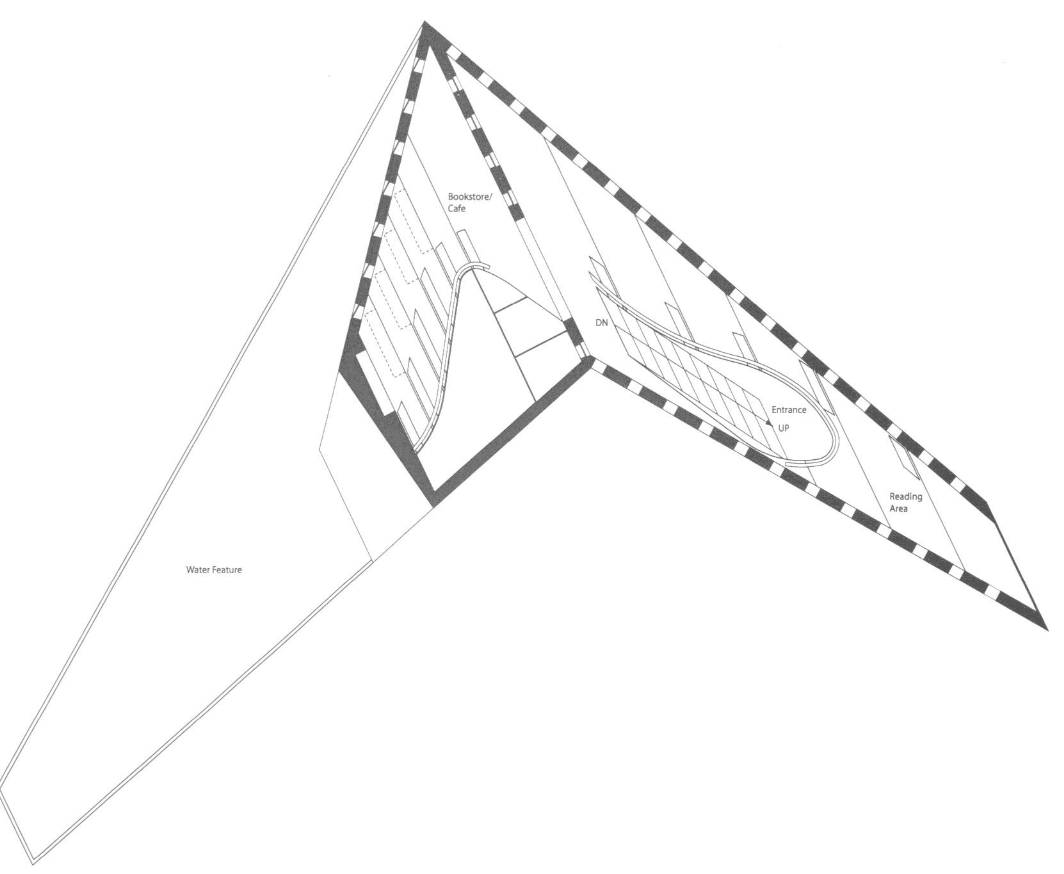

THE NEWSPAPER CAFÉ
JINHUA, ZHEJIANG 2005–06

CLIENT: Jindong New District
Construction Headquarters, Jinhua
COST: not disclosed
ARCHITECT: Toshiko Mori

Toshiko Mori, Chair of the Department of Architecture at the Harvard School of Design, designed her pavilion in the Jinhua Architecture Park as a "narrow folded plane" with two faces. The north face, facing the city, provides steel shelf modules for 1200 standard-size folded Chinese newspapers. She writes, "When the newspapers are incorporated into the façade, they create an atomized and pixilated decorative pattern. Viewed at different distances and angles, the wall reveals or hides its content. At a further distance, the newspapers are no longer individually discernible, thus becoming an abstract texture." As she explains, the south face, "represents a totally different feeling–that of the quiet, more permanent but more abstract quality of nature and the Yiwu River. Its blank white plaster wall looks toward the Museum next to the Newsstand and the Ai Qing Culture Park across the river, in a sense contemplating the relationship between nature and art. While retaining the same shape as the News wall, it is now convex and sheds the color, pattern and textures of the News wall in order to become a neutral surface representing a blank folded page, a *tabula rasa*. This façade that faces the river is a wall of white plaster, left blank and abstract to invite display, inscriptions and projections of art." A viewing platform and reading terrace is located on the roof, while a café and public toilet occupy the space between the two faces of the pavilion.

Toshiko Mori, Professorin am Fachbereich Architektur der Harvard School of Design, konzipierte ihren Pavillon im Architekturpark Jinhua als »schmale, gefaltete Ebene« mit zwei Außenflächen. Die der Stadt zugewandte Nordseite umfasst stählerne Module für 1200 in Standardgröße gefaltete chinesische Zeitungen. Sie schreibt: »Wenn die Zeitungen in die Fassade inkorporiert werden, entsteht ein atomisiertes, bizarres Dekor. Aus verschiedenen Entfernungen und Blickwinkeln gesehen offenbart oder verbirgt die Wand ihren Inhalt. Aus noch größerer Entfernung sind die Zeitungen nicht mehr einzeln erkennbar und werden so zu einer abstrakten Struktur.« Den Erläuterungen der Architektin zufolge »bietet die Südseite eine völlig andere Anmutung – die des ruhigen, dauerhafteren, aber abstrakteren Charakters der Natur und des Flusses Yiwu. Die leere, weiß verputzte Wand ist dem Museum neben dem Zeitungskiosk und dem Ai-Qing-Kulturpark auf dem anderen Flussufer zugewandt, gleichsam als bedenke sie die Beziehung zwischen Natur und Kunst. Diese Wand weist zwar dieselbe Form wie die Zeitungswand auf, ist aber konvex und kommt ohne die Farbe, Musterung und Struktur der Zeitungswand aus. Sie wird zur neutralen Oberfläche, die eine gefaltete, leere Seite, eine Tabula rasa verkörpert. Diese dem Fluss zugewandte Seite ist eine weiß verputzte Mauer, die leer und abstrakt belassen ist, um Ausstellung, Beschriftungen und Projektionen von Kunst herauszufordern.« Auf dem Dach befinden sich eine Aussichtsplattform und eine Leseterrasse, während zwischen den beiden Wänden des Pavillons ein Café und eine öffentliche Toilette untergebracht sind.

Toshiko Mori, présidente du Département d'Architecture de la Harvard School of Design, a conçu ce pavillon du Parc d'architecture de Jinhua comme un « étroit plan plié » à deux faces. La face nord qui regarde directement vers la ville est équipée de modules en acier qui reçoivent 1 200 journaux quotidiens chinois de taille standard pliés. Elle précise : « Les journaux déposés dans la façade créent un motif décoratif atomisé et pixellisé. Selon la distance ou l'angle de vision, le mur révèle ou cache son contenu. De plus loin, les journaux ne sont plus discernables en tant que tels et se transforment en une texture abstraite. ... La face sud donne une impression totalement différente par sa qualité tranquille, plus permanente mais plus abstraite, tournée sur la nature et la rivière Yiwu. Son mur en plâtre blanc aveugle est tourné vers le musée près du kiosque de presse et du Parc de la culture d'Ai Qing de l'autre côté de l'eau, contemplant en un sens la relation entre l'art et la nature. Tout en conservant la même forme que le Mur des quotidiens, est convexe mais dépouillé de la couleur, de la trame et des textures du Mur il des journaux, pour n'être plus qu'une surface neutre, une plage blanche pliée, une tabula rasa. Cette façade est un mur de plâtre blanc, vierge et abstrait qui invite à des présentations, des inscriptions et des projections d'ordre artistique. » Un belvédère et une terrasse pour la lecture ont été aménagés en toiture, tandis qu'un café et des toilettes occupent l'espace entre les deux faces du pavillon.

#18

WANG HUI

WANG HUI / NENO 2529 DESIGN
103 No. 1 Building, 2nd Yard
1st District
San Li He North Street
Xi Cheng Area, Beijing 100823

MIMA DESIGN WORKSHOP
1st Floor, Today Art Museum
32 Baiziwan Road
Chaoyang District
Beijing 100022

WANG HUI was born in Xi'an, in Shaanxi Province, in 1969. He studied architecture at the Northwest Polytechnical University in Xi'an (1988–92) and was an assistant to Professor Zhang Yao Zeng at the NPU (1992–93) before working with the AE Design Workshop in Beijing (1993–97), FCJZ in Beijing (1998–2003), and the MIMA Design Workshop in Beijing (2003–04). He founded his own firm, NENO 2529 Design Group, in March 2005. Despite the very recent creation of NENO, the three very different projects presented here, the Mima Café, Neno Corridor, and Apple Elementary School, demonstrate that this young architect has ideas and the capacity to give them form, even if he has not yet accumulated a number of projects to fill pages on an Internet site. Wang Hui also differs somewhat from a number of the other architects in this book in that his experience is entirely Chinese, without foreign education or work experience.

MIMA CAFÉ
BEIJING 2003

FLOOR AREA: original building 100 m^2; new building 15 m^2
CLIENT: Wang Hui COST: $ 19 500

This unusual project is located close to the East Gate of the Summer Palace near Beijing. The architect and his wife are actually the owners of the café and the instigators of the conversion of a gardener's pavilion. They were given authorization to complete the work, their first independent project, on the condition that they would agree to demolish it if authorities, wary of contemporary architecture, did not approve of the result. They painted the interior of the garden shed white and built a small stainless-steel cube in the garden. The mirrored cube features a glazed roof with a pond containing carp. The new building includes a toilet, a kitchen, and a roof restaurant. The architects explain that "the new construction has been designed as a virtual device to emphasize mainly two elements: one is to embody disappearance to an acceptable degree and the other is to express the feeling of space in a more affirmative way. The stainless steel with a mirror-like surface, creates a feeling of melting into the surroundings. The floor and roof of the toilet use transparent materials to express the suspension of space. Sunshine spreads into the structure through the transparent roof, where fish are swimming, bringing refreshment to the users both inside the structure and in the roof-restaurant."

Dieses ungewöhnliche Projekt befindet sich beim Osttor des Sommerpalastes in der Nähe von Peking. Der Architekt und seine Frau sind die Eigentümer des Cafés und initiierten den Umbau des Gärtnerpavillons. Die beiden erhielten die Genehmigung für ihr erstes selbstständiges Projekt unter der Bedingung, dass sie mit dem Abriss einverstanden wären, falls die Behörden, zeitgenössischer Architektur gegenüber notorisch argwöhnisch, das Ergebnis nicht gutheißen sollten. Der Innenraum des Gartenhäuschens wurde weiß gestrichen; im Garten entstand ein kleiner Edelstahlkubus. Der Spiegelkubus weist ein verglastes Dach mit einem Karpfenteich auf. Zu dem neuen Gebäude gehören eine Toilette, eine Küche und ein Dachrestaurant. Die Architekten führen aus, dass »der Neubau so konzipiert wurde, dass er praktisch als Mittel dient, um vor allem zwei Elemente zu betonen: Zum einen sollte Verschwinden in annehmbarem Maß verkörpert werden, zum anderen sollte Raumgefühl in positiverer Weise ausgedrückt werden. Der Edelstahl mit der spiegelnden Oberfläche erzeugt den Eindruck, er verschmelze mit der Umgebung. Für Boden und Dach der Toilette wurden transparente Materialien verwendet, um der Aufhebung des Raums Ausdruck zu verleihen. Durch das transparente Dach fällt Sonnenlicht in das Gebäude, das im Verein mit den oben schwimmenden Fischen die Besucher sowohl im Inneren des Gebäudes als auch auf der Dachterrasse erheitert.«

Cette curieuse construction se trouve près de la Porte orientale du Palais d'été, aux environs de Pékin. L'architecte et sa femme, les propriétaires de ce café, sont à l'origine de la conversion de ce pavillon de jardinier. Ils reçurent l'autorisation d'achever leur travail – le premier projet réalisé de leur agence – à condition d'accepter qu'il soit démoli si les autorités, inquiètes devant tout projet contemporain, n'appréciaient pas le résultat. Ils ont peint l'intérieur de l'abri de jardin en blanc et construit un petit cube en acier inoxydable dans le jardin. Ce cube à effet de miroir est surmonté d'un toit de verre doté d'un bassin qui contient des carpes. Le nouveau bâtiment comprend une cuisine, un restaurant sur le toit et des toilettes. Les architectes expliquent que « la nouvelle construction est un procédé virtuel pour mettre essentiellement en valeur deux éléments : l'un qui incarne jusqu'à un certain degré la disparition, l'autre qui exprime le sentiment d'espace de façon plus affirmée. L'acier inoxydable à finition miroir donne l'impression d'une fusion avec l'environnement tandis que le sol et le toit des toilettes font appel à des matériaux transparents pour exprimer la suspension dans l'espace. Le soleil inonde la structure grâce à la toiture transparente dans laquelle nagent des poissons, qui créent pour les clients, qu'ils soient à l'intérieur ou sur le toit-terrasse, une atmosphère de détente. »

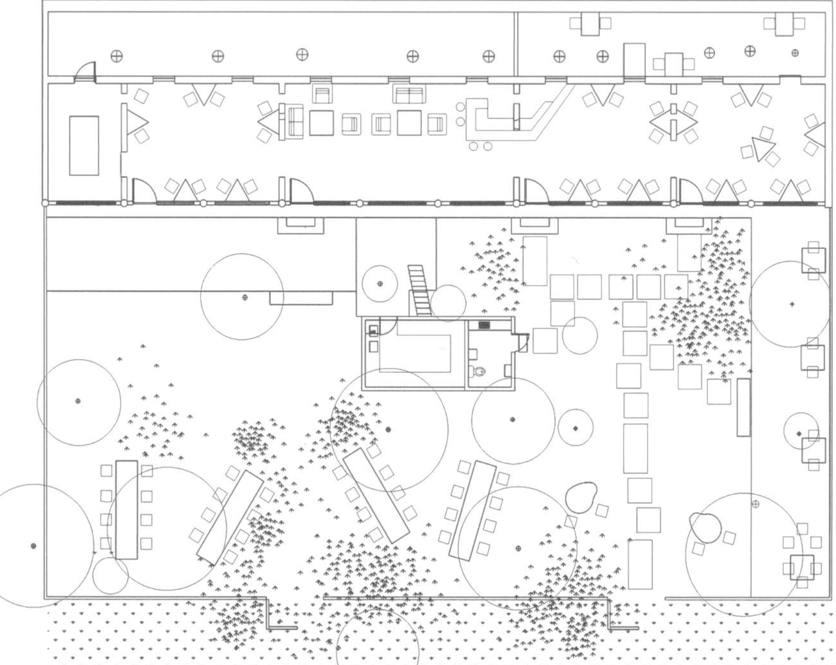

The lightness and simplicity of the space are evident, with such touches as a desk made of books enlivening the interior.

Helligkeit und Einfachheit des Raumes sind augenfällig, Einfälle wie ein aus Büchern bestehender Schreibtisch beleben das Interieur.

La légèreté et la simplicité de l'espace s'imposent par de petits détails comme un bureau construit à partir de livres qui animent l'intérieur.

The use of water, gravel, and goldfish confirm a light-hearted reference to Chinese tradition, with the whole assuming an ephemeral aspect.

Die Verwendung von Wasser, Kies und Goldfischen bekräftigt den unbeschwerten Verweis auf die chinesische Tradition und lässt das Ganze vorläufig erscheinen.

La présence d'eau, de gravier et de poissons rouges fait référence, comme en passant, à la tradition chinoise. L'ensemble présente un aspect éphémère.

NENO CORRIDOR
BEIJING 2004

FLOOR AREA: 210 m²
COST: $ 1500/m²

The idea of a corridor in traditional Chinese gardens inspired the architects in this instance. As they explain, "The corridor connects different parts of a garden, while it also divides the space and draws time into the experience of visitors. The corridor leads people through the space, and thus views change constantly while walking through it." At the end of the corridor there is a pavilion for "reading, tea, and viewing." The corridor, according to Wang Hui, is composed of various doors, walls, interior columns, and furniture (a set of wall cupboards). All of these are made from eight different types of wood, and their natural colors and different textures "enhance the sense of time and space." By giving form to the idea of passage—the physical passage of visitors, but also the element of time—the architects have taken a relatively abstract notion and made it into architecture.

Die Architekten wurden in diesem Fall von der Vorstellung eines Korridors in traditionellen chinesischen Gärten inspiriert. Sie erläutern: »Der Korridor verbindet verschiedene Bereiche des Gartens, während er zugleich den Raum unterteilt und den Faktor Zeit in das Erleben des Besuchers einbringt. Der Korridor führt die Leute durch den Raum, die dabei ständig wechselnde Aussichten erleben.« Am Ende des aus acht verschiedenen Holzarten gefertigten Korridors befindet sich ein Pavillon »zum Lesen, Teetrinken und Schauen«. Wang Hui zufolge setzt sich der Korridor aus verschiedenartigen Türen, Wänden, inneren Stützen und Mobiliar zusammen (einer Abfolge von Wandschränken). Auch diese Elemente bestehen aus acht verschiedenen Holzarten, deren natürliche Färbung und unterschiedliche Beschaffenheit das Empfinden von Zeit und Raum steigert. Indem sie der Vorstellung des Vorübergehens Form geben – das tatsächliche Vorübergehen von Besuchern, aber auch das der Zeit – verwandelten die Architekten einen eher abstrakten Gedanken in Architektur.

L'idée du corridor, élément caractéristique des jardins traditionnels chinois, a inspiré les architectes : « Le corridor réunit différentes parties d'un jardin tout en divisant l'espace et introduisant une notion de chronologie dans la découverte du jardin par les visiteurs. Il les conduit à travers l'espace tandis que les vues changent en permanence au fur et à mesure qu'ils se déplacent. » À l'extrémité du corridor, réalisé en huit variétés de bois différentes, se trouve un pavillon pour « la lecture, le thé, la vue ». Il se compose de murs, de plusieurs portes, de colonnes et de mobilier (un ensemble de placards). La couleur naturelle et les textures des variétés de bois « accroissent le sentiment de temps et d'espace ». En donnant forme à l'idée de passage – celui des visiteurs, qui est physique, mais aussi celui du temps – les architectes ont transformé une notion relativement abstraite en architecture.

Although it is linked to the passageways in Chinese gardens, according to the architect, this corridor made with eight different woods also resembles a work of installation art.

Obwohl dieser aus acht verschiedenen Hölzern gefertigte Korridor im Zusammenhang mit den Verbindungsgängen in chinesischen Gärten zu sehen ist, ähnelt er dem Architekten zufolge auch einer Installation.

Bien que ce corridor s'attache à rappeler les passages couverts des jardins chinois, son habillage, composé de huit variétés de bois, évoque aussi une installation artistique.

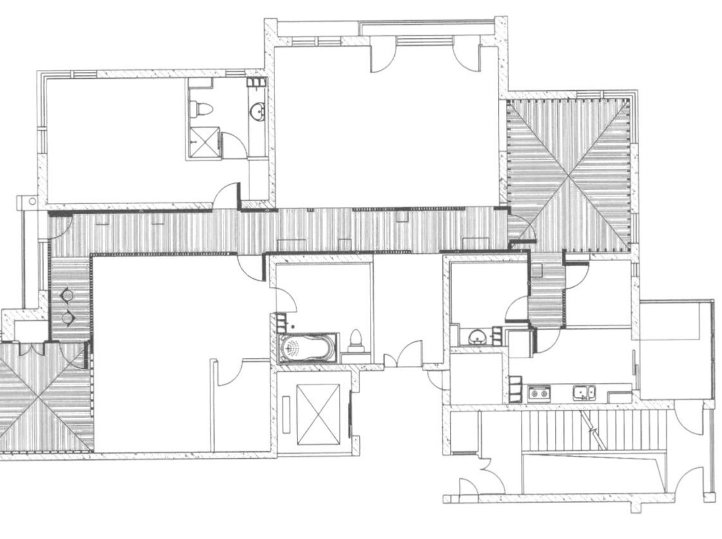

A plan and an axonometric view situate the corridor and its form. The vertical bands of wood give an almost abstract pattern to the surfaces, a pattern that varies as the visitor moves through the space.

Lageplan und axonometrische Ansicht verdeutlichen Lage und Form des Korridors. Die vertikalen Holzlatten erzeugen auf der Oberfläche ein abstraktes Muster, das sich verändert, wenn sich der Besucher durch den Raum bewegt.

Plan et vue axonométrique de la situation du corridor et de sa forme. Les lattes de bois verticales créent un motif presque abstrait qui varie au fur et à mesure que le visiteur se déplace dans l'espace.

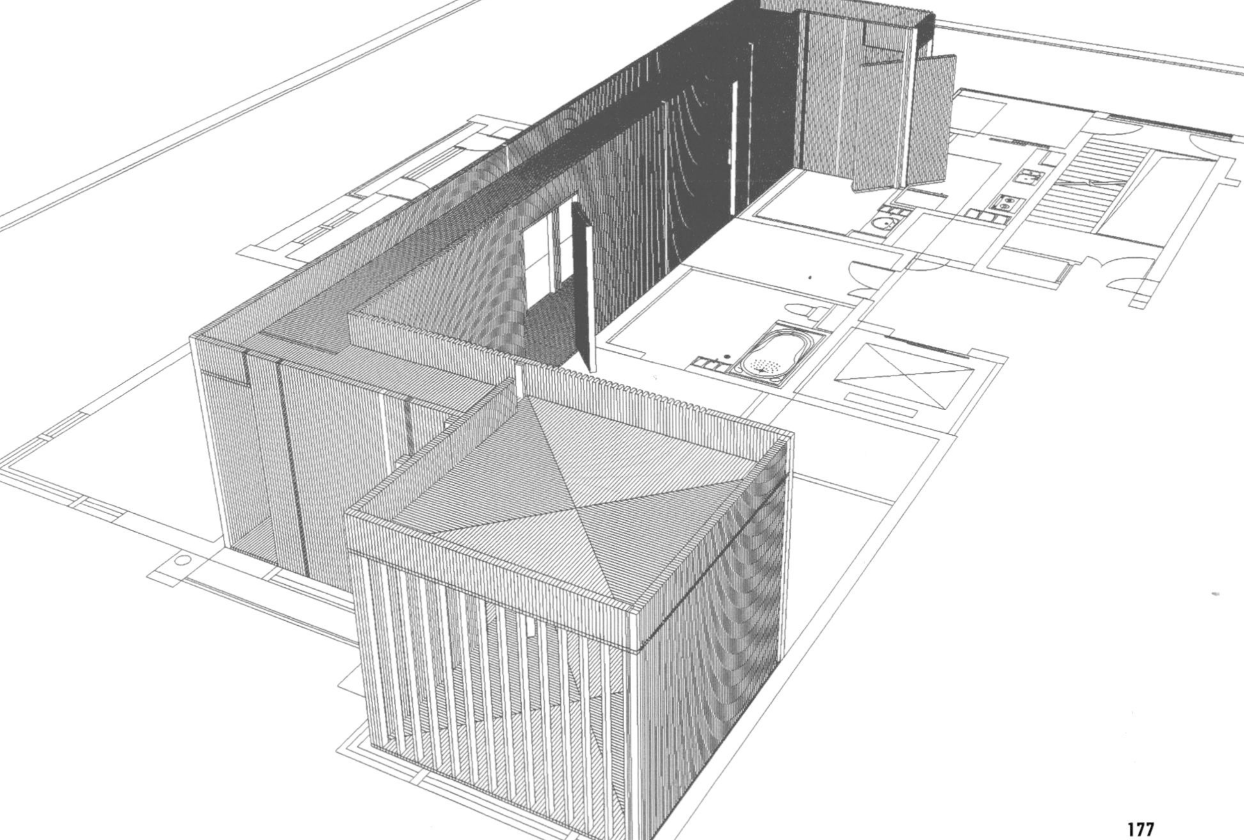

Some fixed elements function as furniture within the corridor. The blurred figure of a man in the image below emphasizes the notion of transit or transition that is implicit in this unusual work of architecture.

Einige fest eingebaute Elemente spielen in dem Korridor die Rolle des Mobiliars. Die unscharfe Figur eines Mannes auf der Abbildung unten betont die in diesem ungewöhnlichen Architekturobjekt implizite Vorstellung vom Durch- oder Übergang.

Certains éléments fixes jouent le rôle de meubles. La figure floue (ci-dessous) illustre l'idée de transit ou de transition implicite dans cette œuvre architecturale curieuse.

Above, the "pavilion for reading, tea, and viewing" located at the end of the corridor, where pure white surfaces replace the complex wooden patterns of the passageway itself.

Der am Ende des Durchgangs befindliche Pavillon (oben) zum »Lesen, Teetrinken und Schauen«, in dem rein weiße Flächen an die Stelle der komplexen Holzmusterung des eigentlichen Korridors treten.

Ci-dessus, le pavillon pour « la lecture, le thé, la vue » situé à l'extrémité du corridor. Les vastes surfaces blanches nues succèdent ici à la complexité de l'habillage de bois du corridor.

APPLE ELEMENTARY SCHOOL

A LI, TIBET 2004–05

FLOOR AREA: 2270 m^2
COST: $ 205 000

The Apple Elementary School is located at an altitude of 4800 meters in Tarqing, Tibet, at the foot of Mount Kailash. This mountain is considered sacred by four religions—Hinduism, Buddhism, Jainism, and the Bön faith. The site, almost four day's travel from Beijing, was particularly challenging—no electricity or water, severe weather, and only scree (broken rock found at the bottom of crags, mountain cliffs, or valleys) as a building material. Funding to create a school for the children of nomads in the area had been provided by an acquaintance of Wang Hui. As the architects say, "The most important source of the design comes from the study of local culture and environment." Solar energy panels were used to obviate the electrical problem and walls made of scree designed to protect the students. The architects paid careful attention to views of Mount Kailash. Blending into the remarkable arid landscape, the school is astonishing both in form and in the accomplishment that it represents.

Die Apfel-Grundschule liegt auf einer Höhe von 4800 m in Tarqing, Tibet, am Fuß des Kailash. Dieser Berg wird von vier Religionen – Hinduismus, Buddhismus, Jainismus und Bön-Glaube – als heilig betrachtet. Das fast vier Reisetage von Peking entfernt gelegene Baugelände erwies sich als eine besondere Herausforderung: keine Elektrizität, kein Wasser, schlechtes Wetter und nur Geröll als Baumaterial. Ein Bekannter von Hui hatte sich um die Beschaffung der Mittel zum Bau der Schule für die Kinder der in der Gegend lebenden Nomaden gekümmert. Der Architekt äußert: »Die wichtigste Quelle für den Entwurf bestand im Studium der lokalen Kultur und Umgebung.« Solarzellen lösten das Problem der fehlenden Elektrizität, und aus Geröll aufgemauerte Wände schützen die Schüler vor der Witterung. Ein besonderes Augenmerk legte der Architekt auf Ausblicke auf den Kailash. Die mit der kargen Landschaft verschmelzende Schule erstaunt sowohl durch ihre formale Gestaltung als auch durch die dahinter stehende Leistung.

L'école élémentaire de la Pomme est située à 4800 m d'altitude à Tarqing, au Tibet, au pied du Mont Kailash, montagne sacrée pour quatre religions, l'hindouisme, le bouddhisme, le jainisme et la tradition Bön. Ce site, qui se trouve à presque quatre jours de voyage de Pékin, était un défi : pas d'électricité, pas d'eau, un temps rigoureux et la pierre d'éboulis pour seul matériau de construction. Le financement de cette école pour enfants de nomades a été fourni par une relation de Wang Hui. Pour l'architecte : « La source d'inspiration la plus importante de ce projet est l'étude de la culture et de l'environnement locaux. » Des panneaux à énergie solaire ont été utilisés et les murs montés en pierres trouvées sur place. Le projet a pris en compte les vues sur le Mont Kailash. Se fondant dans ce paysage aride et remarquable, l'école étonne à la fois par sa forme et par la réussite qu'elle représente.

A plan and model show how the finger-like elements of the design fit into the harsh, linear landscape.

Legeplan und Modell belegen, wie sich die fingerartigen Elemente des Projekts in die karge, lineare Landschaft einfügen.

Le plan et une maquette montrent l'intégration de la conception en « doigts » dans les lignes sévères du paysage.

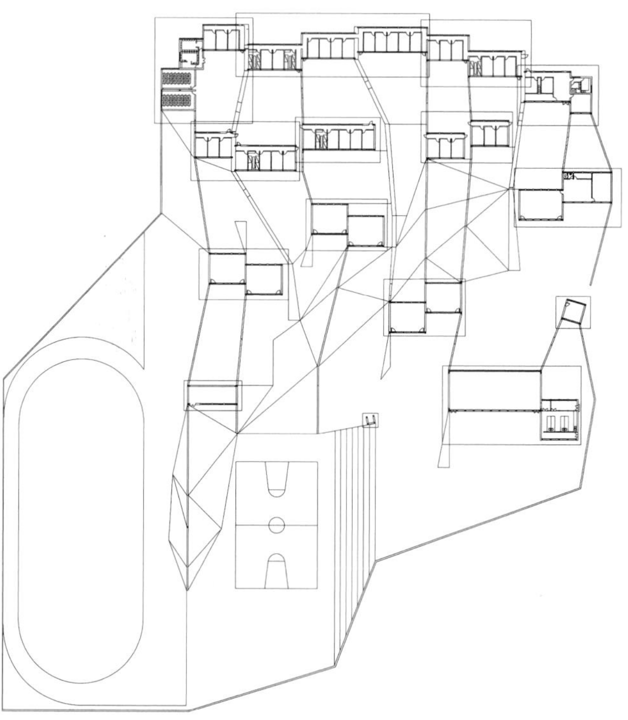

The rough stone-block walls seem to rise quite naturally from the rubble strewn around the school. The interior, too, is austere.

Das Natursteinmauerwerk scheint sich ganz natürlich aus dem um die Schule verteilten Geröll zu erheben. Auch die Innenräume sind nüchtern und asketisch.

Les murs en moellons de pierre équarris semblent s'élever naturellement des déblais qui entourent l'école. L'intérieur est tout aussi austère.

#19

ZHU XIAOFENG/ SCENIC ARCHITECTURE

SCENIC ARCHITECTURE INC
200 Zhen Ning Road
Xin An Building
East Tower, Suite 20B
Shanghai 200040

Tel: +86 21 6279 1313
Fax: +86 21 6289 8381
E-mail: office@scenicarch.com

Born in Shanghai in 1972, ZHU XIAOFENG received his B.Arch degree from the Shenzhen University School of Architecture (1994) and his M.Arch from the Harvard Graduate School of Design (1997). He worked at Kohn Pedersen Fox Associates PC New York (1999–2004), and created his firm, Scenic Architecture Inc., in Shanghai in 2004. His work since leaving KPF includes: the Qingpu New Downtown Xiayang Lake Lot 6—hotel, recreation, office, and retail complex—Shanghai (2004); Renjie Riverfront Club Villa clubhouse, Shanghai (2004); and the Qingpu Bus Station Plaza office, and retail, Shanghai (2004); Jingze Church, Shanghai (2004–05); The Green Pine Garden clubhouse, restaurant, and landscape, published here; Sunrise Plaza office building, Shanghai (2005); Vanke Chunshen Community Center, Shanghai (2005); Lai Zhi Fu Boutique Hotel and restaurant, renovation and extension, Shanghai (2006); and Presidential Hotel, restaurants and cultural facilities, Nanjing (2006). His current projects include the Zhu Jiajiao Watertown Granary Warehouse, renovation and extension of historical industry buildings, in collaboration with other architects, Shanghai, and the Jingze Modern Life Training Center, Lots 2 and 4, Qingpu, Shanghai.

THE GREEN PINE GARDEN

QINGPU, SHANGHAI 2004–05

FLOOR AREA: 1603 m²
CLIENT: Yiluhua Industry Development Co. Ltd
COST: $ 380 000
TEAM: Zhu Xiaofeng, Guo Dan

Located near the highway from Shanghai to Zhujiajiao, this project involved the renovation of two factory buildings and their conversion into a restaurant and bar. Zhu states that "the reorganization of volume and space of the two buildings follows the logic of the originals." Set in an extensively planted 30 000-square-meter green area, the restaurant building is characterized on its eastern side by a folding screen made of local pine battens. This screen provides "privacy for the VIP dining rooms and creates an exterior space for the air conditioning unit." Similar wooden screens are applied in a more removed way on the eastern side of the bar building, while solid brick marks the west façade to limit traffic noise inside. Alternating thick and thin gray bricks typical of construction in southeastern China are applied here in a modern way. Zhu Xiaofeng demonstrates here that local materials and existing buildings can be converted to a new use without recurring to Western models, and without any hint of pastiche.

Bei dem nahe der Schnellstraße von Shanghai nach Zhujiajiao gelegenen Projekt geht es um die Instandsetzung von zwei Fabrikgebäuden und deren Umbau zu einem Restaurant und einer Bar. Zhu erklärt, dass »die Umgestaltung von Baumasse und Raum der beiden Bauten der Logik der ursprünglichen Gebäude folgt«. Das in einer üppig bepflanzten, 30 000 m² großen Grünzone liegende Restaurantgebäude zeichnet sich auf seiner Ostseite durch eine gefaltete Schutzwand aus heimischen Kiefernleisten aus. Die Schutzwand schirmt »die VIP-Speisezimmer ab und schafft Außenraum für die Klimaanlage«. Ähnliche Holzschirme finden sich in größerem Abstand auf der Ostseite der Bar, während an ihrer Westfassade massive Ziegelmauern den Verkehrslärm dämpfen sollen. Die für den Südosten Chinas typische Mauerung aus abwechselnd dickeren und dünneren grauen Ziegeln kommt hier in moderner Ausprägung zur Anwendung. Zhu Xiaofeng zeigt, dass vorhandene Gebäude mit heimischen Materialien für neue Zwecke umgebaut werden können, ohne auf westliche Vorbilder zurückzugreifen oder einen Hauch von Imitation.

Ce projet portait sur la rénovation de deux bâtiments d'usine en bordure de l'autoroute de Shanghai à Zhujiajiao et leur conversion en bar et restaurant. Zhu explique que « la réorganisation du volume et de l'espace des deux bâtiments suit la logique des constructions d'origine ». Dans un espace vert de 30 000 m² abondamment planté, le restaurant se caractérise sur sa façade par un écran repliable en lattes de pin local. Il offre « l'intimité aux salles à manger des VIP et délimite un espace extérieur pour l'installation de climatisation ». Des écrans de bois similaires sont utilisés de façon moins affirmée sur la façade est du bâtiment du bar, tandis que la façade ouest est traitée en brique pleine pour limiter la pollution sonore due à la circulation automobile. L'alternance de briques grises fines et épaisses est un procédé de construction typique du Sud-Est de la Chine, mais appliqué ici de façon moderne. Zhu Xiaofeng prouve ce faisant que les matériaux locaux et les bâtiments existants peuvent être convertis à un nouvel usage sans faire appel aux modèles occidentaux ni à la moindre trace de pastiche.

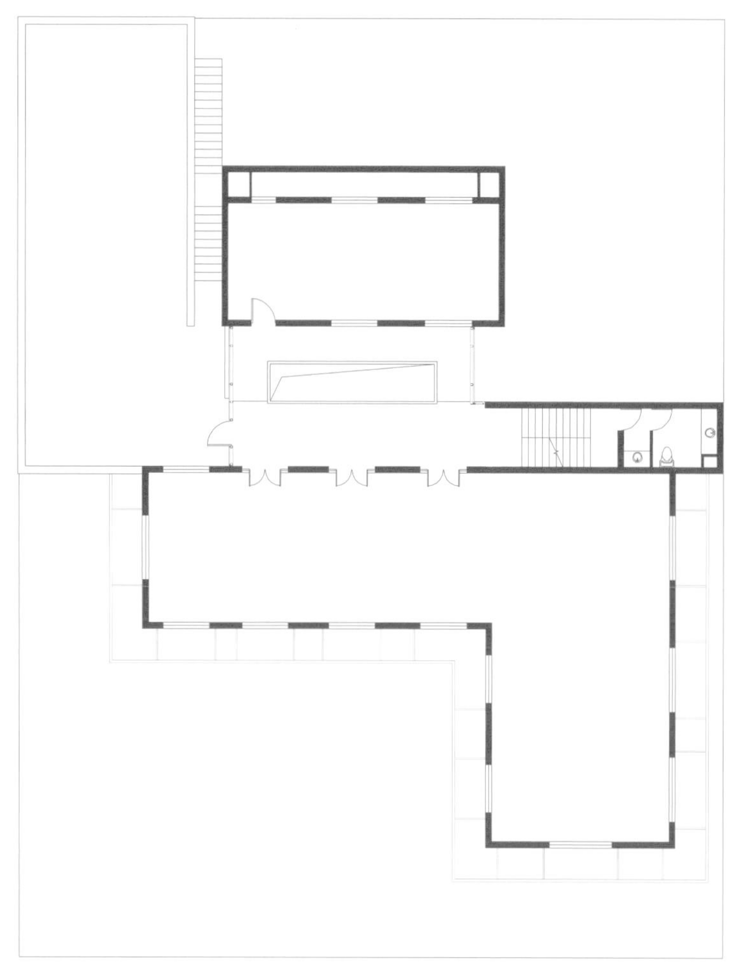

Folding pine screens that certainly evoke the traditions of Chinese architecture are visible in the image to the right, but the architect has created an unusual composition in which cladding and the accumulation of essentially geometric forms speak more of modernity than anything ancient.

Faltwände aus Kiefernholz, die an traditionelle chinesische Architektur erinnern, sind auf dem Bild rechts zu sehen; der Architekt schuf jedoch eine unkonventionelle Anlage, bei der die Verkleidung und die Häufung geometrischer Grundformen stärker an Modernität als an etwas Altertümliches denken lassen.

Les écrans en pin qui évoquent les traditions de l'architecture chinoise sont visibles à droite, mais l'architecte a su créer une composition nouvelle dans laquelle l'habillage et l'accumulation de formes essentiellement géométriques parlent davantage de modernité que de passéisme.

Set in a large site, the buildings are attached, but almost appear to be separate entities when they are photographed.

Die auf einem großen Gelände stehenden Bauten sind miteinander verbunden, wirken jedoch unter einem bestimmten Blickwinkel wie seperate Einheiten.

Implantés sur un vaste terrain, les bâtiments sont reliés entre eux, mais semblent presque séparés selon certains angles de de vue.

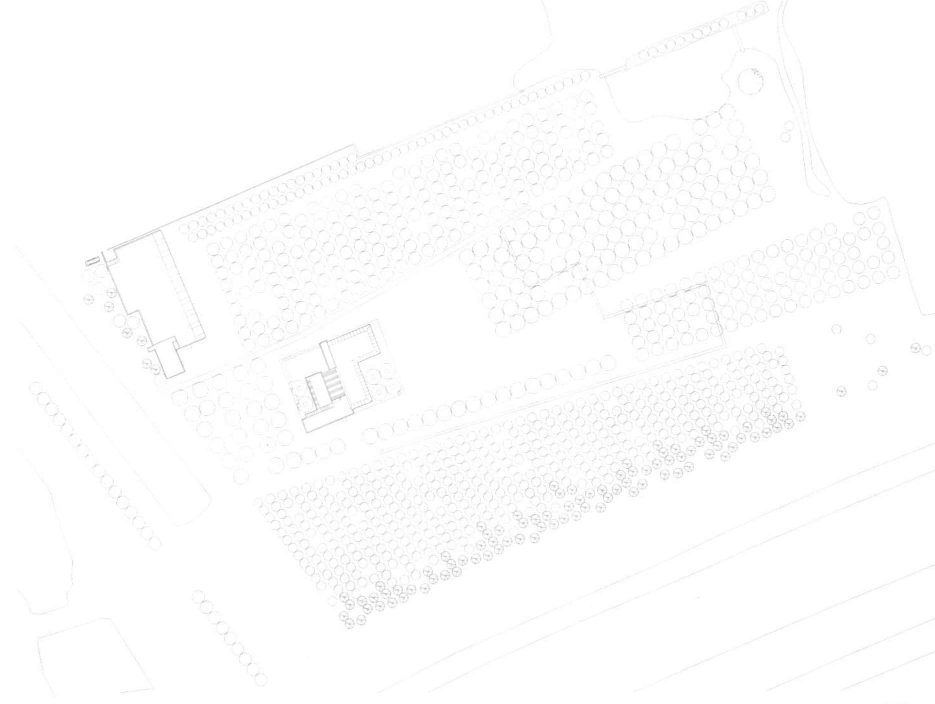

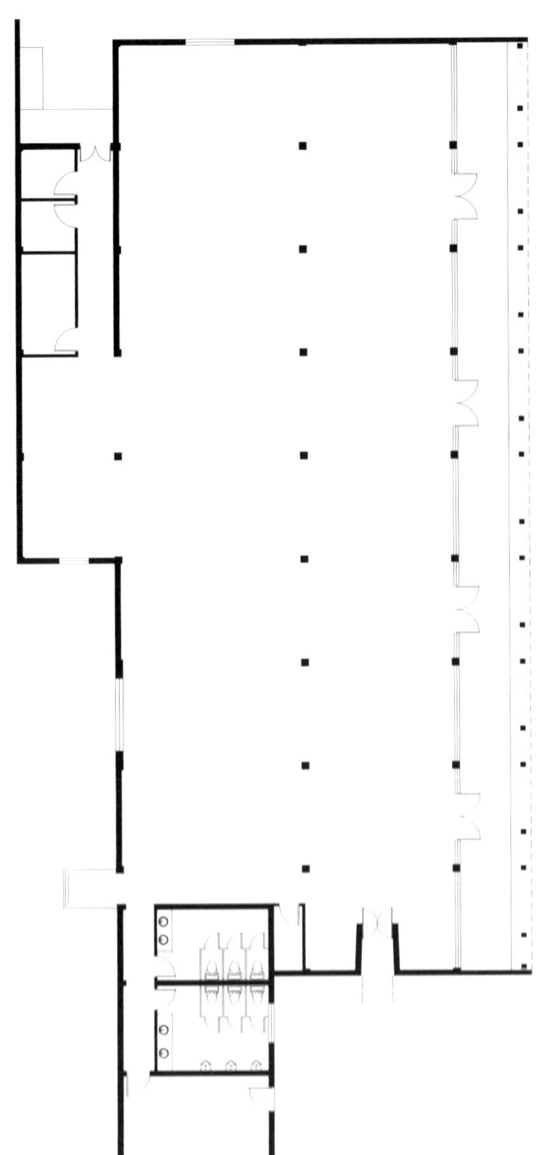

Gray brick and limited openings mark another façade, while the architect uses open pine screens along the eastern front of the bar building (above).

Grauer Backstein und vereinzelte Öffnungen zeichnen die eine Fassade aus, während der Architekt entlang der östlichen Seite der Bar durchlässige Wände aus Kiefernholz verwendet hat (oben).

La brique grise et des ouvertures soigneusement contrôlées caractérisent une des façades, tandis que l'architecte utilise des écrans en pin sur la façade est du bâtiment en barre (ci-dessus).

PHOTO CREDITS
IMPRINT

CREDITS: PHOTOS/PLANS/DRAWINGS/CAD DOCUMENTS

18–21, 22 bottom, 23–27 top and middle © Zhang Si Yi / 22 top, 27 bottom © Atelier Deshaus / 28–31, 32 bottom, 33 top, 34 bottom, 35–37 top, 38–39 top © Shu He / Fu Xing / 32 top, 33 bottom, 34 top, 37 bottom, 39 bottom, 42, 43 bottom © Atelier Feichang Jianzhu (FCJZ) / 41, 43 top © Crystal Digital Technology Co. Ltd. / 44–49 © Atelier Zhanglei / 50–59 © Gary Chang / Howard Chang / 60–65 © FAKE Design / 66–70 top and middle, 71 © Herzog & de Meuron / 70 bottom © Iwan Baan / 72–75, 76 bottom, 77–79 top, 80–81 © H. K. Rihan Int'l Culture Spread Limited / Chen Zhong / 76 top, 79 bottom © Arata Isozaki & Associates Nogizaka Atelier / 82–86 top left, 86 bottom, 87 top, 88 bottom, 89 © Bi Kejian / 86 top right, 87 bottom, 88 top and middle © Jiakun Architects / 90–94, 95 bottom, 96–97 © Mitsumasa Fujitsuka / 95 top, 96 left © Kengo Kuma & Associates / 98–102, 103 bottom © Melvin Tan / 103 top and middle © Li Xiaodong / 104–108 top, 109 © Shu He / 108 bottom © MAD Ltd. / 110–115 top, 116 top, 117–119, 121 © Zhanhui Chen / 115 bottom, 116 bottom, 120 © MADA S.P.A.M. / 122–127 © NODE / 128, 132 bottom, 133 top © OMA/Rem Koolhaas / 131–132 top © Hans Werlemann / 133 bottom © Iwan Baan / 134–138 top, 139 © Yuanjing Inc. / 138 bottom © Studio Pei Zhu / 140–151 © Urbanus Architecture & Design / 152–155, 157 top right, 159–164, 165 bottom, 167 © Iwan Baan / 156, 157 top left and bottom © Herzog & de Meuron / 165 top © Michael Maltzan Architecture, Inc. / 168–183 © Mima Design Workshop / 184–187, 188 bottom, 189 top, 190, 191 top right and bottom © Shen Zhonghai / 188 top, 189 bottom, 191 top left © Scenic Architecture Inc.

To stay informed about upcoming TASCHEN titles, please request our magazine at www.taschen.com/magazine or write to TASCHEN, Hohenzollernring 53, D-50672 Cologne, Germany, contact@taschen.com, Fax: +49-221-254919. We will be happy to send you a free copy of our magazine which is filled with information about all of our books.

Hohenzollernring 53, D-50672 Köln
www.taschen.com

PROJECT MANAGEMENT: Florian Kobler, Cologne
COLLABORATION: Barbara Huttrop and Mischa Gayring, Cologne
PRODUCTION: Thomas Grell, Cologne
DESIGN: Sense/Net, Andy Disl and Birgit Reber, Cologne
GERMAN TRANSLATION: Christiane Court, Frankfurt
FRENCH TRANSLATION: Jacques Bosser, Paris

Printed in Italy
ISBN 978-3-8228-5264-4